IT Service Management based on ITIL® 2011 Edition

Other publications by Van Haren Publishing

Van Haren Publishing (VHP) specializes in titles on Best Practices, methods and standards within four domains:
- IT and IT Management
- Architecture (Enterprise and IT)
- Business Management and
- Project Management

Van Haren Publishing offers a wide collection of whitepapers, templates, free e-books, trainer materials etc. in the **Van Haren Publishing Knowledge Base**: www.vanharen.net for more details.

Van Haren Publishing is also publishing on behalf of leading organizations and companies: ASLBiSL Foundation, CA, Centre Henri Tudor, Gaming Works, IACCM, IAOP, IPMA-NL, ITSqc, NAF, Ngi, PMI-NL, PON, The Open Group, The SOX Institute.

Topics are (per domain):

IT and IT Management	Architecture (Enterprise and IT)	Project, Program and Risk Management
ABC of ICT	ArchiMate®	A4-Projectmanagement
ASL®	GEA®	DSDM/Atern
CATS CM®	Novius Architectuur Methode	ICB / NCB
CMMI®	TOGAF®	ISO 21500
COBIT®		MINCE®
e-CF	**Business Management**	M_o_R®
ISO 20000	BABOK® Guide	MSP™
ISO 27001/27002	BiSL®	P3O®
ISPL	EFQM	PMBOK® Guide
IT Service CMM	eSCM	PRINCE2®
ITIL®	IACCM	
MOF	ISA-95	
MSF	ISO 9000/9001	
SABSA	Novius B&IP	
	OPBOK	
	SAP	
	SixSigma	
	SOX	
	SqEME®	

For the latest information on VHP publications, visit our website: www.vanharen.net.

IT Service Management based on ITIL® 2011 Edition

Colophon

Title:	IT Service Management based on ITIL® 2011 Edition
Author:	Pierre Bernard
Reviewers (Dutch edition):	Bert Boesjes (Sogeti Nederland)
	Dick Pondman (Leaneraz)
	René Visser (Pink Elephant)
Publisher:	Van Haren Publishing, Zaltbommel, www.vanharen.net
Design & layout:	CO2 Premedia, Amersfoort
NUR code:	981 / 123
ISBN Hard copy:	978 94 018 0017 4
ISBN eBook:	978 94 018 0556 8
ISBN ePub:	978 94 018 0557 5
Edition:	First edition, first impression, October 2014
Copyright:	© Van Haren Publishing, 2012, 2014

Foreword

The aim of this book is to provide an easy to read and easy to use introduction to the broad library of ITIL core books and to support the understanding and the further distribution of ITIL as a popular industry framework. The previous editions of this book, based on ITIL V2 and ITIL V3, have gained a worldwide reputation as an easy access training aid, used by many IT professionals as study guidance for the ITIL Foundation and ITIL Intermediate (lifecycle and capability) exams. This book is a certainly a true successor, aiming at the same target groups.

Van Haren Publishing has been publishing supporting material on ITIL since 2002 and have been very fortunate in gaining the expertise and support of many global industry experts in authoring and reviewing the material. Over this period ITIL has developed from a set of simple processes into a framework that reflects the increasing trends for organizations to work within large enterprise environments across national borders. However it is also clear that many of our readers fall into either of the following two broad categories: those starting their careers within IT service management and those involved with the execution of processes. For these readers simple, concise overviews and explanations of the elements of the framework will be the most useful. Introductory books are very useful as reference material. In addition many organizations use multiple frameworks and methods and thus, there is a requirement for colleagues in other disciplines to understand the basics of ITIL and how it might affect and support their own operations.

Looking forward: There is no "one-size-fits-all framework" or "the mother of all methods". Organizations around the world will continue to adopt newer technologies and service offering such as mobile computing and cloud-based services. Therefore it is paramount for the success of the IT organizations that they adopt and adapt the various elements of ITIL and other frameworks and methods to suit their innovative solutions. This title celebrates the 'select and integrate' approach of many around the world by presenting ITIL elements in succinct, discrete packages.

The continued publication of up-to-date material that covers the key elements of the ITIL Lifecycle approach is therefore very welcome. Like previous editions, this title benefits from the wisdom and support of many colleagues within the IT service management industry and we believe that it presents a strong, quality piece of text that will continue to prove extremely useful to students, executives and managers alike.

Acknowledgements: The format of the content of this book is based on the Dutch edition that was edited by René Visser. The role of René for improving the consistency of the text was very important to realize this English language edition.

September 2014,
Pierre Bernard

Contents

X

1 Introduction

Introduction

■ 1.1   BACKGROUND

Since the year 2000, technological developments such as smartphones, tablets, cloud services, near-field-content, Wi-Fi, and especially social media have had a tremendous effect on the world we live in. With the emergence of extremely powerful hardware, highly versatile software and super-fast networks – and their wide-spread acceptance and use – organizations worldwide have been able to develop their information-dependent products and services to a greater extent, and to bring them to the market much faster. These, as well as many other socio-economic and political developments have marked the superimposition of the **information age** upon the industrial age. In this *"information age"*, where everything is connected, the dissemination of data and information has become faster and more dynamic as well as a worldwide phenomenon.

Quoting from one of Bob Dylan's[1] songs titled *"The Times They Are A-Changin"* is quite appropriate here as indeed the traditional view and role of the Information Technology organization (IT) are dramatically altered based on the above. To be successful, organizations will need to be as nimble as possible in order to react to rapidly changing market demands and technologies. First, there is a movement concerning renaming IT to Information Services (IS). Second, cloud computing is becoming a more viable option and a more common solution. This is a result of organizations realizing that technology is not always one of their core competences and that outsourcing provides them with a more accurate and predictable cost structure.

Organizations should also start considering the significant impact of the arrival in the workplace of extremely technology-savvy employees. These new employees have been using technology almost since birth; they are not only the early adopters of mobile technologies but of social media as well. Information is now at their fingertips and they will expect the same in the workplace. In addition to this new generation of employees,

---

1   Bob Dylan – American singer, songwriter, musician (1941 -)

organizations need to consider how they will handle the same demands from their existing and potential customers.

There are numerous books, whitepapers, and articles[2] about the need to break down vertical business silos and shift the business model to more horizontal **processes**, thus *"flattening"* the organization. The authors of these documents are advocating that decision-making powers should be increasingly bestowed on the employees. Again, according to these various sources, an important advantage of process-oriented organizations is that processes can be designed to support a **customer-oriented approach**. This has made the alignment between the IT organization (responsible for supplying information) and the customer (responsible for using these information systems in their business) increasingly significant. This is usually known as **Business-IT Alignment (BITA)**.

It is against this background that the world of IT Service Management (ITSM) has arisen and gained in popularity.

The above authors are not wrong, nor are they lacking vision; on the contrary. As organizations gained more experience with the **process-oriented approach** of ITSM, it became clear that these processes must be managed coherently. Moreover, it became obvious that the introduction of a process-oriented work method meant a major change for organizations that were primarily line and project-oriented. Culture and change management are crucial elements for a successful organizational design. Change management here refers to business change, as well as changes in attitudes, aptitudes, behaviors, the adoption of frameworks and methodologies adapted to suit the organizational needs.

The truth about processes and BITA is that organizations have always used processes and IT has always been part of the organization. However, we must acknowledge that processes are often conducted in isolation by a few individuals or groups. Processes are often neither shared nor documented. One of the causes for the above is that many people believe that *"knowledge is power"*[3], as illustrated in the following two quotes:

Knowledge is power. Information is liberating. Education is the premise of progress, in every society, in every family.

- Kofi Annan

Knowledge is power. Information is power. The secreting or hoarding of knowledge or information may be an act of tyranny camouflaged as humility.

- Robin Morgan

---

2   See Appendix A for some examples
3   Attributed to Sir Frances Bacon (Viscount of Saint Alban, 1561 – 1626)

In the author's opinion, "*knowledge **sharing** is power*".

Another important lesson learned was that the IT organization must not lose itself in a process culture. Just like the one-sided project-oriented organization, a one-sided process-oriented organization was not the optimum type of business. Balance was, as always, the magic word. In addition, it became clear that the customer-oriented approach required that an **end-to-end** and **user-centric** approach must be followed: it was of no help to the user to know that "*the server was still in operation*" if the information system was not available at the user's workplace. IT services must be viewed in a larger context. The need for the recognition of the **Service Lifecycle**, and the management of IT services in light of that lifecycle, became a concern.

Due to the fast growing dependency of business upon information, the quality of information services in companies is being increasingly subjected to stricter **internal and external requirements**. The role of **standards** is becoming more and more important, and **frameworks** of "*best practices*" help with the development of a management system to meet these requirements. Organizations that are not in control of their processes will not be able to realize great results on the level of the Service Lifecycle and the end-to-end-management of those services. Organizations that do not have their internal organization in order will also not achieve great results. For these reasons, all these aspects are handled alongside each other in the course of this book.

■ 1.2   WHY THIS BOOK

This book has been developed for all those responsible for setting up and delivering the information services. Additionally, it contains a lot of useful information for those who are responsible for strategic information issues. This is supported by both the description of the Service Lifecycle, as documented in ITIL and by the description of the processes that are associated with it. The ITIL core books are very extensive: almost 2000 pages. These ITIL core books can be used for a thorough study of contemporary best practices of ITSM. This book provides the reader with an easy-to-read comprehensive introduction to the broad library of ITIL core books. And finally, the contents of this book cover the specifications for the ITIL Foundation exam from AXELOS; this book has proven useful in preparing for this exam.

In 2007 Version 3 of the ITIL framework was published. This version offered a new concept or ITSM. Additional to the processes approach the concept of the lifecycle approach was introduced with ITIL V3. In 2011 a second edition of ITIL V3 was published. This new ITIL 2011 Edition is comprised mostly of cosmetic, grammatical, and syntactic modifications.

ITIL offers a systematic approach to the delivery of quality of IT services. It provides a detailed description of most of the important processes for an IT organization, and includes information about procedures, tasks, roles, and responsibilities. These can be used as a basis for tailoring the framework to the needs of individual organizations.

Over the years, ITIL has become much more than a series of useful books about ITSM. The framework for the "*best practice*" in ITSM is promoted and further developed and influenced by advisors, educators, trainers, and suppliers. These suppliers include a wide variety of technological solutions such as hardware, software, and cloud computing products. Since the 1990s, ITIL has grown from a theoretical framework to the de facto approach and philosophy shared by the people who work with it in practice.

Being an extended framework of best practices for ITSM itself, the advantages and disadvantages of frameworks in general, described in Section 2.6, are also applicable to ITIL. Of course, ITIL was developed because of the advantages mentioned earlier. Many of the pointers from "*best practices*" are intended to avoid potential problems or, if they do occur after all, to solve them.

ITIL examinations

For the new 2011 Edition of ITIL, the syllabuses for all qualifications have been updated. The most significant changes relate to new/modified section numbers as well as improved wording and/or clarification for some learning objectives and section details.

At the publication date of this book, well over 2 million people worldwide have achieved one or more levels of ITIL certification.

There are four qualification levels relating to the ITIL framework. They are:
- Foundation Level
- Intermediate Level (Lifecycle Stream & Capability Stream)
- ITIL Expert
- ITIL Master

For more information about the ITIL V3 Qualification Scheme, please visit http://www.itil-officialsite.com.

■ 1.3   ORGANIZATIONS INVOLVED IN ITIL

Cabinet Office and AXELOS

Initially ITIL was a product of CCTA, a UK government organization. In 2001 CCTA was incorporated by the Office of Government Commerce (OGC) who became the new owner of ITIL. As a result, the UK Government became the owner of the Intellectual

Property Rights (IPR), including the copyrights and trademark rights, of ITIL. Since June 2010 the operational and control tasks were in the hands of the Cabinet Office.

On 1 July 2013 a new organization was created for the further development and exploitation of ITIL and the PPM portfolio (including PRINCE2): AXELOS. This Limited company is a joint venture of the Cabinet Office and Capita PLC. As a result, this joint venture became the new owner of ITIL and the PPM portfolio. The UK government holds 49 percent of the shares of AXELOS while Capita PLC holds the remaining 51 percent.

itSMF

The target group for this publication is anyone who is involved or interested in ITSM. A professional organization, working on the development of the ITSM field, has been created especially for this target group.

In 1991 the Information Technology Service Management Forum (itSMF), originally known as the Information Technology Infrastructure Management Forum (ITIMF), was set up as a UK association. In 1994, a sister-association was established in the Netherlands, following the UK example. Since then, independent itSMF organizations have been set up in nearly fifty countries, spread across the globe, and the number of "chapters" continues to grow. All itSMF organizations operate under the umbrella organization, itSMF International (itSMF-I).

The itSMF is aimed at the entire professional area of ITSM. It promotes the exchange of information and experiences that IT organizations can use to improve their service provision. The itSMF is also involved in the use and quality of the various standards and methods that are important in the field. One of these is ITIL. The itSMF-I contributes to the promotion of the role of ITIL.

Certification, examination, and accreditation

AXELOS is responsible for managing the ITIL copyrights, the certification of the ITIL examinations and the accreditation of examination institutes. AXELOS is also responsible for the publication of the ITIL certification system and for the official ITIL publications (manuals).

In 2014 AXELOS has accredited seven Exam Institutes (EIs) for the distribution around the globe of the ITIL exams:
- BCS-ISEB CERT-IT,
- CSME, DANSK IT,
- DF Certifiering AB,
- EXIN,
- LCS (Loyalist Certification Services),

- PEOPLECERT Group,
- TÜV SÜD Akademie.

For more information, see www.itil-officialsite.com.

1.4   DIFFERENCES FROM PREVIOUS EDITIONS

Previous editions of this book have played a key role in the distribution of ideas on ITSM and ITIL for many years. The title has been translated into thirteen languages and is recognized as the most practical introduction to the leading *"best practices"* in this field. Earlier editions of this book focused on the content of three books from the ITIL series (Version 2): Service Support, Service Delivery, and Security Management, and placed them in a broader context of quality management.

The main difference between ITIL Version 2 and 3 lies in the Service Lifecycle, introduced in Version 3. Where the scope of Version 2 focused on single practices, clustered in Delivery, Support, and Security Management, the scope in Version 3 takes the entire Service Lifecycle into account.

1.5   STRUCTURE OF THIS BOOK

This book starts with an introduction on the backgrounds and general principles of ITSM and the context for ITIL (**Chapter 1**). It describes the parties involved in the development of best practices and standards for ITSM, and the basic premises and standards that are used.

The body of the book is set up in two large parts: **Part 1** deals with the Service Lifecycle and the four functions in ITIL, **Part 2** deals with the individual processes that are described in ITIL.

Part 1, consisting of **Chapters 2 and 3**, introduces the Service Lifecycle, in the context of ITSM and IT Governance. It discusses principles of organizational maturity, and the benefits and risks of following a service management framework. The section introduces and discusses the functions involved in service management good practices. This enables the reader to better relate the processes in Part 2, and their related concepts and activities, back to the *"people aspect"* of ITSM.

In **Part 2**, consisting of **Chapters 4 to 8**, each of the phases in the Service Lifecycle are discussed in detail, following the structure of the ITIL core books: Service Strategy, Service Design, Service Transition, Service Operation, and Continual Service Improvement.

These chapters provide a detailed view on the characteristics of the Service Lifecycle, its structure and its elements. The main points of each phase are presented in a consistent way to aid readability and clarity.

Each of these processes is described in an identical manner, in terms of:
1. Introduction (containing: Goal, Objectives, Scope, Value for the business)
2. Activities, methods and techniques
3. Management information
4. Interfaces
5. Triggers
6. Inputs
7. Outputs
8. Critical Success Factors
9. Metrics
10. Challenges
11. Risks

The **Appendices** provide useful sources for the reader. Appendix A is a reference list of the sources used in this book is provided. Appendix B offers an overview of the most important differences between ITIL V3 (2007) and ITIL 2011 Edition.

■ 1.6 HOW TO USE THIS BOOK

Readers who are primarily interested in the Service Lifecycle can focus on Part 1 of the book, and pick whatever they need on functions and processes from Part 2.

Readers who are primarily interested in the functions and processes and are not ready for a lifecycle approach yet, or who prefer a process approach, can read the introductory chapters, and then focus on the functions and processes of their interest.

Readers who want a thorough introduction to ITIL, exploring its scope and main characteristics, can read Part 1 on the Lifecycle, and add as many of the processes from Part 2 as required.

This book aims to provide support to a variety of approaches to ITSM based on ITIL.

This book covers all exams specs for the ITIL Foundation exam and is therefore a useful tool when preparing for this exam. However, this book covers more subjects than the exam specs. If a reader intends to study only the subject of the exam specs, he should best rely on the Preparation Guide (ITIL Foundation Syllabus), available through:

http://www.itil-officialsite.com/Qualifications/ITILQualificationLevels/
ITILFoundation.aspx.

Additionally this book offers a useful support when preparing for the ITIL Intermediate examination (lifecycle and capability exams).

The official ITIL Glossary, the official list of all ITIL terminology, is available via the product page for this book on www.vanharen.net.

PART

1

THE ITIL SERVICE LIFECYCLE

2 Introduction to Service Management and the Service Lifecycle

■ 2.1 BASIC CONCEPTS

The information provision role and system have grown and changed since the launch of ITIL Version 2 (in 2000/02). IT supports and is part of an increasing number of goods and services. In the business world, the information provision role has changed as well: the role of the IT organization role is no longer just supporting, but has become the baseline for the creation of business value.

ITIL intends to include and provide insight into the new role of IT in all its complexity and dynamics. To that end, a new service management approach has been chosen that does not center on processes, but focuses on the Service Lifecycle.

Before describing the Service Lifecycle, we first need to explain some basic concepts.

2.1.1 Best practice
ITIL is presented as a best practice. This is an approach or method that has proven itself in practice. These good practices can be a solid backing for organizations that want to improve their IT services. In such cases, the best thing to do is to select a generic standard or method that is accessible to everyone – ITIL®, COBIT®, CMMI®, PRINCE2®, and ISO/IEC 20000®, for example. One of the benefits of these freely accessible generic standards is that they can be applied to a number of real-life environments and situations.

2.1.2 Service
A service is about creating value for the customer. ITIL defines a service as follows:

A **service** is a means of delivering value to customers by facilitating outcomes the customers want to achieve without the ownership of specific costs or risks.

The above definition is not very useful when trying to provide additional details. Table 2.1 provides further explanation about the above definition.

Table 2.1 Definition of key terms in the "service" definition

Mean:	The actual "*physical*" product the customer can actually see, touch, or use.
Value:	The customer defines value based on the desired business outcomes by the customer, their preferences, and their perceptions.
Outcome:	The business activity or result to be used by the business or delivered to the external customer.
Specific costs:	The customer does not want to worry about all costs relating to the end-to-end provision of the service. The customer prefers to consider IT as a utility, which is a more predictable expense.
Specific risks:	The IT organization takes on most of the risks on behalf of the customer, allowing the latter to focus on their core business competences.

Outcomes are possible from the performance of tasks, and they are limited by a number of constraints. Services enhance performance and reduce the pressure of constraints.

IT service

IT services are offered by IT service providers. ITIL's definition of an IT service is:

An **IT service** is a combination of people, processes, and technology. A customer oriented IT service offers a direct support to the business processes of one or more customers; the service level targets involved have to be specified in a service level agreement. Other IT services, also known as supporting services, will not be used directly by the business, but are services that are required for the service provider in order to be able to offer customer oriented services. The service provider purchases supporting services from internal or external suppliers.

Three groups of services

ITIL makes a distinction between three groups of client oriented services: core, enabling and enhancing (see Table 2.2).

A service provider may decide to offer a custom (unique) service to a small group of customers. The cost price for this will be very high because of the development costs and specific resources required. The market for these services will therefore be very limited. Therefore many service providers follow the strategy that enables them to deliver the more generic service to a large group of customers. Bundling these services into one group will result in an economy of scale. In this way the service providers are able to offer a variety of service packages to their customers. A service package is a collection of two or more services that have been combined to help deliver specific business outcomes. It is also possible that a service or service package is offered in different levels of utility (fitness for purpose) and warranty (fitness for use). For example as bronze, silver or gold service level packages.

Table 2.2 Three types of customer related services

Core services	Delivers the basic outcomes desired by one or more customers. E.g.: the service *"Document processing"* would enable clients to create, read, change, and store documents.
Enabling services	Services required for the successful delivery of a core service. E.g.: downloading and automatic installation of updates.
Enhancing services	Services added to a core service to make it more appealing or enticing to the customer. E.g.: the printing of documents on a professional color printer for high quality brochures.

Utility and warranty of a service

From the customer's point of view, value is subjective. Although, at its core, value consists of achieving business objectives, it is influenced by the customer's perceptions and preferences. From a service provider point of view, the value of a service is created by combining two primary elements: utility (fitness for purpose) and warranty (fitness for use). These two elements work together to achieve the desired outcomes upon which the customer and the business base their perceptions of a service.

Utility is the functionality offered by a product or service to meet a particular need. Utility can be summarized as *"what the service does"*, or *"fit for purpose"*. Utility refers to those aspects of a service that contribute to tasks associated with achieving outcomes: the removal of constraints and an increase in performance.

Warranty is an assurance that a product or service will meet its agreed requirements. Warranty refers to the ability of a service to be available when needed, to provide the required capacity, and to provide the required reliability in terms of continuity and security. Warranty can be summarized as *"how the service is delivered"* or *"fit for use"*.

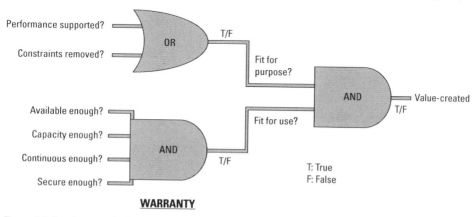

WARRANTY

Figure 2.1 Services are designed, built, and delivered with both utility and warranty

(source: AXELOS)

2.1.3 Service management

In order to offer and provide services, the service provider must effectively and efficiently manage the entire lifecycle of the services. Transforming the service provider's capabilities and resources into valuable services is the core of service management. Service management is also a professional practice supported by an extensive body of knowledge, experience, and skills.

ITIL defines service management as:

Service management is a set of specialized organizational capabilities for providing value to customers in the form of services.

2.1.4 ITSM

An IT organization is, by definition, a service provider. It uses the principles of service management to ensure the successful delivery of the outcomes desired by the customers.

Table 2.3 ITSM and IT service providers

ITSM	ITSM is performed by IT service providers through an appropriate mix of people, process, and information technology.
IT service provider	A service provider that provides IT services to internal or external customers

The IT service provider must utilize ITSM effectively and efficiently. By managing IT from the business perspective (as opposed to simply being a technology broker) the service provider will generate higher organizational performance and create greater value.

2.1.5 Service providers

There are three main types of service provider. Although almost all aspects of service management apply equally to all types of service provider, there are certain aspects that take on different meanings depending on the type of provider. These aspects include terms such as customers, contracts, competition, market spaces, revenue, and strategy.

Table 2.4 Service provider types

Type I Internal service provider	An internal service provider that is embedded within a business unit.
Type II Shared services unit	An internal service provider that provides shared IT services to more than one business unit
Type III External service provider	A service provider that provides IT services to external customers

2.1.6 Stakeholders in service management

A stakeholder is an individual or a group that has a vested interest in an organization, project, service, etc. Of interest to the stakeholders are such service management deliverables as activities, targets, resources, etc.

Table 2.5 Stakeholders

Customers	Those who buy goods or services.
Users	Those who use the service on a day-to-day basis.
Suppliers	Third parties responsible for supplying goods or services that are required to deliver IT services
Internal customers	These are customers who work for the same organization as the IT service provider.
External customers	These are customers who work for a different organization from the IT service provider.

2.1.7 Assets, resources, and capabilities

The use of assets forms the basis for the relationship between service providers and their customers. Each relationship involves an interaction between the assets of each party.

Table 2.6 Assets

Asset	Any resource or capability. Assets of a service provider include anything that could contribute to the delivery of a service. Assets can be one of the following types: management, organization, process, knowledge, people, information, applications, infrastructure, and financial capital.
Customer asset	Any resource or capability used by a customer to achieve a business outcome
Service asset	Any resource or capability used by a service provider to deliver services to a customer.

Resources and capabilities are two types of asset used by both service providers and customers. Resources are direct inputs for production; they are *"consumed"* or *"modified"*. According to ITIL the most important resources are: financial capital, applications, infrastructure, information, and people. Capabilities represent an organization's ability to coordinate, control, and deploy the resources. According to ITIL the capabilities of an organization are found in people, knowledge, processes, organization, and management.

■ 2.2   FUNCTIONS AND PROCESSES

2.2.1 Functions

ITIL defines service management as a set of specialized organizational capabilities that have been developed by an organization. Using these capabilities a IT service provider is able to provide value to customers in the form of services. These capabilities are taking shape as functions and processes. Well implemented functions and processes enable an IT service provider to manage services throughout their entire lifecycle.

It is of the utmost importance for anyone in an organization, especially in the IT organization, to understand the difference between a function and a process.

A **function** is a subdivision of an organization that is specialized in fulfilling a specified type of work, and is responsible for specific end results. Functions are semi-autonomous groupings with capabilities and resources that are required for their performance and results. They have their own set of tasks, roles, and area of responsibilities as well as their own body of knowledge.

A poor coordination between functions combined with an inward focus leads to the rise of "*silos*". This does not benefit the success of the organization. Processes run through the hierarchical structure of functions; functions often share many processes. This is how processes contribute to an ever improved coordination between functions.

Table 2.7 Organizational structure breakdown

Group	A group is a number of people who are similar in some way
Team	A team is a more formal type of group. These are people who work together to achieve a common objective, but not necessarily in the same organizational structure
Department	Departments are formal hierarchical, organizational-reporting structures which exist to perform a specific set of defined activities on an on-going basis
Division	A division refers to a number of departments that have been grouped together, often by geography or product line

According to ITIL four important functions are required in the design, testing, deployment and improvement of IT services:
1. Service Desk
2. IT Operations Management
3. Technical Management and
4. Application Management

These functions will be described in Chapter 3. Additional to these four functions ITIL contains 26 processes. These processes will be described in Chapter 4 to 8.

Table 2.8 The four functions in ITIL

Service Desk	This function acts as the single point of contact and communication to the users and a point of coordination for IT groups and processes
IT Operations Management	This function executes the daily operational activities needed to manage IT services and the supporting IT infrastructure. Consists of two sub-functions; IT operations control and facilities management.
Technical Management	This function provides detailed technical skills and resources needed to support the on-going operation of IT services and the management of the IT infrastructure.
Application Management	Is responsible for managing applications throughout their lifecycle. The Application Management function supports and maintains operational applications.

2.2.2 Processes

Processes comprise groups of activities executed for a specific goal. ITIL's definition of a process is:

> A process is a structured set of activities designed to accomplish a specific objective. Processes result in a goal-oriented change, and utilize feedback for self-enhancing and self-corrective actions. Processes simply group together related activities to simplify and unify their execution and accomplishment.

The characteristics of these processes are described in Table 2.9.

People and tools execute the activities of processes. Employees, related to a specific function, will execute the day to day activities within various processes. Service Desk personnel may be involved in processes such as Incident Management, Problem Management, Request Fulfilment, and Change Management.

Table 2.9 The four characteristics of processes

Measurability	Processes are designed for a specific target. They are measurable because it is possible to set specific targets related to the process performance and measure against them: i.e.: they are performance-oriented.
Specific results	The reason a process exists is to deliver a specific result. This result must be delivered at the right moment and at the right quality level.
Customers and/or stakeholders	Every process delivers its primary results to a customer or stakeholder.
Responsiveness to specific triggers	They respond to an identified trigger. A process is indeed continual and iterative, but it is always originating from a certain identified trigger.

For some people, it may be difficult to differentiate between a function and a process. The difficulty arises when an organization already has a group of people called by the name of a process. This group is usually dedicated primarily to the execution of what appears to be a single process. However, every group of people is involved in the execution of process activities.

In themselves, processes do nothing. People (and tools) execute the activities of various processes. Based on the above definitions, a function (group of people) performs the activities of various processes. A good example of a function is the Service Desk; a good example of a process is Change Management.

A poor coordination between functions combined with an inward focus leads to the rise of "silos". This does not benefit the success of the organization. Processes run through the hierarchical structure of functions; functions often share many processes. This is how processes contribute to an ever-improved coordination between functions.

When arranging activities into processes, we look at the **objective** of the process and the **relationships** with other processes. A process is a series of activities carried out to convert input into an output, and ultimately into an outcome. The **input** is concerned with the resources being used in the process. The (reported) **output** describes the immediate results of the process, while the **outcome** indicates the long-term results of the process (in terms of meaningful effect). Through **control** activities, we can associate the input and output of each of the processes with **policies and standards** to provide information about the results to be obtained by the process. Control regulates the input and the **throughput** in case the throughput or output parameters are not compliant with these standards and policies. This produces chains of processes that show the input that goes into the organization and what the result is, and it also monitors points in the chains in order to check the quality of the products and services provided by the organization on specific points in the chains.

The standards for the output of each process have to be defined, in such a way that the complete chain of processes in the process model meets the corporate objective. If the output of a process meets the defined requirements, then the process is **effective** in transforming its input into its output. To be really effective, the outcome should be taken into consideration rather than merely focusing on the output. If the activities in the process are also carried out with the minimum required effort and cost, then the process is **efficient**. It is the task of process management to use **planning and control** to ensure that processes are executed in an effective and efficient way.

When a person performs an activity within a certain process, he/she does this as part of a specific role. Roles are often confused with job titles. However, they are not the same. Each organization must define appropriate job titles and job descriptions to suit their needs. Individuals holding these job titles can perform one or more of the required roles.

> **Role:** A role is a set of responsibilities, activities, and authorities granted to a person or team. A role is defined in a process or function. One person or team may have multiple roles.

2.2.3 Roles and responsibilities

Highly performing organizations are able to take the right decisions fast and accurately and execute them successfully. To achieve this, it is crucial that the roles and responsibilities of the process are clearly defined.

The RACI model is one of many useful model in achieving this. RACI is an acronym for the four most important roles:
- **Responsible** – the person who is responsible for completing the task
- **Accountable** – the only person who is accountable for each task
- **Consulted** – people who give advice
- **Informed** – people who must be kept in the loop regarding the progress of the project

In establishing a RACI system, the following steps are necessary:
- Identify activities and processes
- Identify and define functional roles
- Conduct meetings and delegate the RACI-codes
- Identify gaps and potential overlaps
- Distribute the RACI chart and build in feedback
- Ensure that the allocations are followed

Role or Employee / Process activities	Process owner	Service owner	Service desk	Support team #2	Support team #3	External support	End user	Customer
Activity #1	A	R	R	R	R	R	R	R
Activity #2	A	C	R					C
Activity #3	A	C	R					C/I
Activity #4	A		R					C/I
Activity #5	A	C	R	R	R	R	R	C
Activity #6	A	C	R	R	R	R	R	C/I
Activity #7	A		R	C/I	C/I	C/I	C/I	C/I

Figure 2.2 Sample of filled out RACI model

In establishing a RACI system, the following steps are necessary:
- Identify activities and processes
- Identify and define functional roles
- Conduct meetings and delegate the RACI codes
- Identify gaps and potential overlaps
- Distribute the RACI chart and build in feedback
- Ensure that the allocations are followed

ITIL distinguishes three generic process roles: process owner, process manager, and process practitioner.

The **process owner** is responsible for defining the process goals, the strategy related to the process, the guidelines for the process output, the performance indicators, availability of the required resources and the process results.

The **process manager** is responsible for the realization and structure of the process, and reports to the process owner. He/she is responsible for the operational management of the process. The responsibilities of a process manager are: planning and coordination of all activities that have to be achieved, and the monitoring and reporting of the process.

The **process practitioners** are responsible for correctly completing specific activities within the process.

The management of the organization can provide control based on the process quality of the process as demonstrated by data from the results of each process. In most cases, the relevant **performance indicators** and standards will already be agreed upon. In this case the process manager can do the day-to-day control of the process. The process owner will assess the results based on a **report** of performance indicators and checks whether the results meet the agreed standard. Without clear indicators, it would be difficult for a process owner to determine whether the process is under control, and if planned improvements are being implemented.

Processes are often described using **procedures** and **work instructions**.

A **procedure** is a specified way to carry out an activity or a process. It describes the "*how*", and can also describe "*who*" carries the activities out. A procedure may include stages from different processes. A procedure can vary depending on the organization.

A set of **work instructions** defines how one or more activities in a procedure should be carried out in detail, using technology or other resources.

A process is defined as a logically related series of activities executed to meet the goals of a defined objective. Processes are composed of two kinds of activities: the activities to realize the goal (operational activities concerned with the throughput), and the activities to manage these (control activities). The control activities make sure the operational activities (the workflow) are performed in time, in the right order, etc. (For example, in the processing of changes it is always ensured that a test is performed *before* a release is taken into production and not *afterwards*.)

Processes and departments
Most businesses are hierarchically organized. There are departments that are responsible for the activities of a group of employees. There are various ways of structuring departments, such as by customer, product, region, or discipline. IT services generally depend on several departments, customers, or disciplines. For example, if there is an IT service to provide users with access to an accounting program on a central computer, this will involve several disciplines. The computer center has to make the program and database accessible, the data and telecommunications department has to make

the computer center accessible, and the PC support team has to provide users with an interface to access the application.

Processes should span several departments (teams) in order to adequately measure the end-to-end quality of a service by monitoring the utility and warranty aspects of the service. These aspects include the removal of constraints on the enhancement of performance, availability, capacity, continuity, security, as well as costs and stability. A service organization will try to match these quality aspects with the customer's demands. The structure of such processes can ensure that good information is available about the provision of services, so that the planning and control of services can be improved.

Processes, projects, programs and portfolios

Activities can be managed from a process perspective, from an organizational hierarchy (line) perspective, from a project perspective, or from any combination of these three. Organizations that tend to apply just one of these management systems often miss the benefits of the others. The practical choice often depends upon history, culture, available skills and competences, and personal preferences.

There are no "*hard and fast laws*" for the way an organization should combine processes, projects, and programs. However, it is recommended that a common understanding of processes, projects, programs, and even portfolios is created. The following definitions may be used:

Process	A process is a structured set of activities designed to accomplish a defined objective.
Project	A project is a temporary organization, with people and other assets required to achieve an objective.
Program	A program consists of a number of projects and activities that are planned and managed together to achieve an overall set of related objectives.
Portfolio	A portfolio is a set of projects and/or programs, which are not necessarily related, brought together for the sake of control, coordination, and optimization of the portfolio in its totality.

The most elementary difference between a process and a project is the one-off character of a project, versus the continuous character of the process. If a project has achieved its objectives, it means the end of the project. Processes can be run many times, both in parallel and in sequence. The nature of a process is aimed at its repeatable character: processes are defined only in case of a repeatable string of activities that are important enough to be standardized and optimized.

Projects are aimed at changing a situation A into a situation B. This can involve a simple string of activities, but it can also be a very complex series of activities. Other elements of importance for projects include money, time, quality, organization, and information.

2.2.4 Organizational culture and behavior

Organizational culture is the set of shared values and norms that control the interactions between a service provider and all stakeholders, including customers, users, suppliers, internal personnel etc. An organization's values are desired modes of behavior that affect its culture. Examples of organizational values include high standards, customer care, respecting tradition and authority, acting cautiously and conservatively, and being frugal.

Constraints such as governance, standards, values, capabilities, resources, and ethics play a significant role in shaping and/or influencing the culture and behavior of an organization. The management structure and styles may impact positively, or negatively, the organizational culture. Organizational structures and management styles are also contributing factors to the behavior of people, process, products, and partners.

Adopting service management practices and adapting them to suit the organization will affect the culture and it is important to prepare people with effective communication plans, policies, procedures, education, training, coaching, and mentoring to achieve the desired the new attitudes and behaviors.

While improving the quality of their services, organizations will eventually be confronted with their current organizational culture. The organization will have to identify and address any changes to this culture as a consequence of the overall improvement initiative. The organizational culture, or corporate culture, refers to the way in which people deal with each other in the organization; the way in which decisions are made and implemented; and the attitude of employees to their work, customers, service providers, superiors, and colleagues.

Culture, which depends on the standards and values of the people in the organization, cannot be controlled, but it can be influenced. Influencing the culture of an organization requires leadership in the form of a clear and consistent policy, as well as a supportive personnel policy.

■ 2.3   GOVERNANCE AND MANAGEMENT SYSTEMS

2.3.1 Governance

With the growing role of information, information services, and ITSM, so do the management requirements for the IT organization grow. These requirements focus on two aspects. The first is compliance with internal and external policies, laws, and regulations. The second is the provision of benefits (value-add proposition) for the stakeholders of the organization. A definition for IT governance receiving much support is the one by Wim van Grembergen:

IT governance consists of a comprehensive framework of structures, processes, and relational mechanisms. Structures involve the existence of responsible functions such as IT executives and accounts, and a diversity of IT committees. Processes refer to strategic IT decision-making and monitoring. Relational mechanisms include business/IT participation and partnerships, strategic dialogue and shared learning.

IT governance works to apply a consistent, managed approach at all levels of the organization. This starts by setting a clear strategy that defines the policies whereby the strategy will be achieved. The policies define boundaries: what is in or out of scope of organizational operations.

The International Organization for Standardization (ISO®) introduced in 2008 a standard for IT governance: ISO/IEC 38500:2008.

2.3.2 Management systems

The ITIL definition for a system is:

A system is a group of, interrelating, or interdependent components that form a unified ensemble, operating together for a common purpose.

Systems should be self-regulating for agility and timeliness. In order to accomplish this, the relationships of all components within the system must influence one another for the sake of the whole. Key components of the system are the structure and processes that work together.

Feedback and learning are two key aspects in the performance of systems; they turn processes, functions, and organizations into dynamic systems. Feedback can lead to learning and growth, not only within a process, but also within an organization in its entirety.

Within a process, for instance, the feedback about the performance of one cycle is, in its turn, input for the next process cycle. Within organizations, there can be feedback between processes, functions, and lifecycle phases. Behind this feedback is the common goal: the customer's objectives.

A service provider can deliver many benefits by understanding the structure, the relationships between components and the effects of changes over time.
Examples of these benefits:
- Adaptability to the ever-fluctuating needs of customers and markets
- Sustainable performance
- Defined approach to managing services, risks, costs, and value
- Effective and efficient service management
- Reduced conflict between processes and personnel
- Reduced duplication and bureaucracy

A well-organized management system is a prerequisite to realizing these benefits.

Management system (ISO 9001): the framework of policy, processes, functions, standards, guidelines, and tools that ensures an organization or part of an organization can achieve its objectives. An organization may use multiple management system standards, such as in Table 2.10.

Table 2.10 ISO Management systems aligned with ITSM

ISO 9001	Quality management system
ISO 14000	Environmental management system
ISO/IEC 20000	Service management system
ISO/IEC 27001	Information security management system
ISO/IEC 19770	Management system for software asset management
ISO/IEC 31000	Risk management
ISO/IEC 38500	Corporate governance of information technology

Developing and maintaining a quality system which complies with the requirements of the ISO 9000 (ISO 9000: 2000®) series can be considered a tool for the organization to reach and maintain the system-focused (or *"managed"* in IT Service CMM) level of maturity. These ISO standards emphasize the definition, description, and design of processes. For ITSM organizations, a specific ISO standard was produced: the ISO/IEC 20000 (see Figure 2.3).

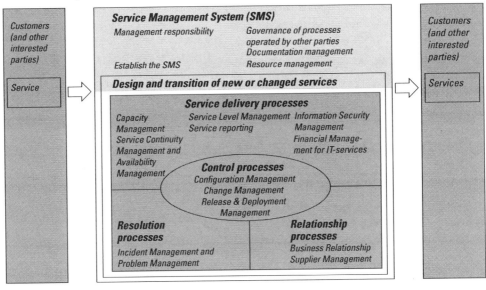

Figure 2.3 Overview of the ISO/IEC: 20000 service management system

■ 2.4 ORGANIZATIONAL MATURITY

From the moment Richard Nolan introduced his *"staged model"* for the application of IT in organizations in 1973 many people have used stepwise improvement models. These models were quickly recognized as suitable instruments for quality improvement programs, thereby helping organizations to climb up the maturity ladder.

Dozens of variations on the theme can easily be found, ranging from trades such as software development, acquisition, systems engineering, software testing, website development, data warehousing and security engineering, to service desks and knowledge management. Obviously the *Kaizen* principle (improvement works best in smaller steps) was one that appealed to many people.

After Nolan's staged model in 1973, the most appealing application of this modeling was found when the Software Engineering Institute (SEI) of Carnegie Mellon University, USA, published its Software Capability Maturity Model (SW-CMM®). The CMM® was copied and applied in most of the cases mentioned above, making CMM something of a standard in maturity modeling. The CMM was later followed by newer editions, including CMMI® (CMM Integration).

2.4.1 Maturity model: CMMI

In the IT industry the most common approach for measuring and improving the process maturity is the **Capability Maturity Model Integration (CMMI)**.

The **CMMI staged representation** model defines five maturity levels, each a layer in the base for the next phase in the on-going process improvement, designated by the numbers 1 through 5 (Table 2.11).

Table 2.11 CMMI Capability levels

1. Initial	Processes are ad hoc and chaotic
2. Managed	The projects of the organization have ensured that processes are planned and executed in accordance with policy
3. Defined	Processes are well characterized and understood, and are described in standards, procedures, tools and methods
4. Quantitatively managed	The organization and projects establish quantitative objectives for quality and process performance, and use them as criteria in managing processes
5. Optimizing	Focuses on continually improving process performance through incremental and innovative process and technological improvements

■ 2.5   BENEFITS AND RISKS OF ITSM FRAMEWORKS

Benefits to the customer/user:
■ The provision of IT services becomes more customer-focused and agreements about service quality improve the relationship.
■ The services are described better, in customer language, and in more detail.
■ Managing service quality, availability, and reliability and service costs is improved.
■ Communication with the IT organization is improved by agreeing contact points.

Benefits to the IT organization:
■ The IT organization develops a clearer structure, becomes more efficient, and is more focused on the corporate objectives.
■ The IT organization is more in control of the infrastructure and services it has responsibility for, and changes become easier to manage.
■ An effective process structure provides a framework for the effective outsourcing of elements of the IT services.
■ Following best practices encourages a cultural change towards providing services, and supports the introduction of quality management systems based on the ISO 9000 series or on ISO/IEC 20000.
■ Frameworks can provide coherent frames of reference for internal communication and communication with suppliers, and for the standardization and identification of procedures.

Potential problems/mistakes:
■ The introduction of ITSM can take a long time and require significant effort, and may require a change of culture in the organization; an overambitious introduction can lead to frustration because the objectives are never met.
■ If process structures become an objective in themselves, the service quality may be adversely affected; in this scenario, unnecessary or over-engineered procedures are seen as bureaucratic obstacles, which are to be avoided where possible.
■ There is no improvement in IT services due to a fundamental lack of understanding about what the relevant processes should provide, what the appropriate performance indicators are, and how processes can be controlled.
■ Improvements in the provision of services and cost reductions are insufficiently visible, because no baseline data was available for comparison and/or the wrong targets were identified.
■ A successful implementation requires the involvement and commitment of personnel at all levels in the organization.
■ If there is insufficient investment in appropriate training and support tools, justice will not be done to the processes and the service will not be improved.

■ 2.6   THE SERVICE LIFECYCLE

ITIL approaches service management from the lifecycle of a service. The Service Lifecycle is an organization model providing insight into:
- ■ The way service management is structured
- ■ The way the various lifecycle components are linked to each other
- ■ The impact that changes in one component will have on other components and on the entire lifecycle system

The Service Lifecycle consists of five phases: Service Strategy, Service Design, Service Transition, Service Operation, and Continual Service Improvement. See Table 2.12.

Table 2.12 The five stages of the Service Lifecycle

Service Strategy	The phase of defining the guidelines for creating business value and achieving and maintaining a strategic advantage
Service Design	The phase of designing and developing appropriate IT services, including architecture, processes, policy and documents, in order to meet current and future business requirements
Service Transition	The phase of planning and managing the realization of new and modified services according to customer specifications
Service Operation	The phase of managing and fulfilling all activities required to provide and support services, in order to ensure value for the customer and the service provider
Continual Service Improvement	The phase of continual improvement of the effectiveness and efficiency of IT services against business requirements

Service Strategy is the axis of the Service Lifecycle (Figure 2.4) that *"binds"* all other phases. This phase defines perspective, position, plans, patterns, and policies. The phases Service Design, Service Transition, and Service Operation transform the strategy into reality; their continual theme is adjustment and change. The Continual Service Improvement phase stands for learning and improving, and embraces all phases. This phase analyses and initiates improvement programs and projects, and prioritizes them based on the strategic objectives of the organization.

The dominant theoretical pattern in the Service Lifecycle is the succession of Service Strategy to Service Design, to Service Transition and to Service Operation, and then, through Continual Service Improvement, back to Service Strategy, and so on. In practice, all phases occur iteratively for the management of a particular service. Moreover, the cycle encompasses many concurrent patterns as organizations already have services in stages. All organizations have services at the concept/idea stage; some are being designed (either new or modified), some are in transition, some are in operation and some are being investigated for improvement opportunities.

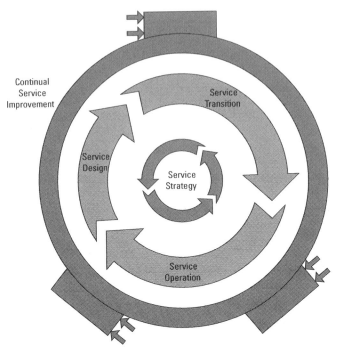

Figure 2.4 The ITIL Service Lifecycle

(source: AXELOS)

All four functions and the 26 processes are located in one of the five phases of the lifecycle. However we need to make two comments:

1. A number of processes support all or more than one phase in the lifecycle. An example is the Change Management process that supports all phases, but it has been located in the Service Transition phase because of the crucial role it plays in the transition of services to deployment.
2. The four functions have been located in the Service Operation phase, but they have an important role in all lifecycle phases.

Figure 2.5 gives a complete overview of all lifecycle phases with the 26 processes and the four functions.

ITIL Library
The IT Infrastructure Library[4] (ITIL) encompasses the following components:

Core Library – the five Service Lifecycle publications
- Service Strategy
- Service Design

---

4   The use of the complete definition for the ITIL acronym has been discontinued.

Processes in the ITIL lifecycle

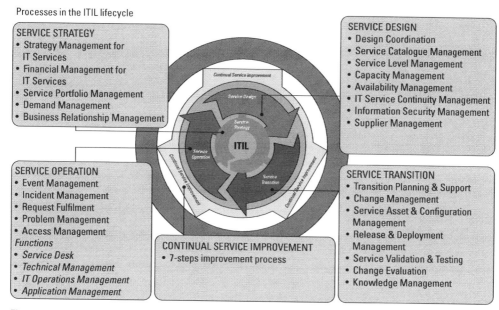

Figure 2.5 The 26 processes and 4 functions in ITIL, related to the ITIL lifecycle

- Service Transition
- Service Operation
- Continual Service Improvement

Complementary portfolio

Official complementary material published by TSO

- *ITIL Foundation Handbook – pocket book published by TSO*
- *ITIL Guide to Software Asset Management*
- *ITIL Lite, a road map to full or partial implementation*
- *Designing and transforming IT organizations*
- *Delivering IT Services using ITIL, PRINCE2 and DSDM*
- *Building an ITIL-based Service Management Department*
- *Agile Project and Service Management – Delivering IT Services using PRINCE2, ITIL and DSDM*
- *Secrets of Service Level Management – A process owner's guide*

3 Functions

The four functions in ITIL are, see Figure 3.1:

1. IT Operations Management
2. Service Desk
3. Technical Management
4. Application Management

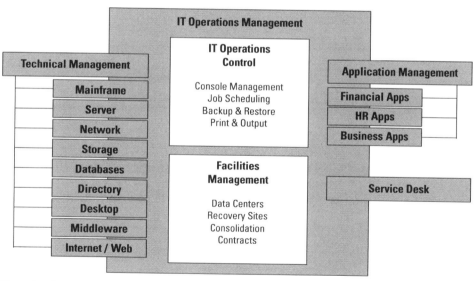

Figure 3.1 Overview of the four functions in ITIL

■ 3.1 IT OPERATIONS MANAGEMENT

3.1.1 Introduction

IT Operations Management is the **function** that is responsible for performing the day-to-day operational activities. They ensure that the agreed level of IT service is provided to the business.

IT Operations Management plays a dual role:

■ It is responsible for implementation of activities and performance standards that have been defined during Service Design and have been tested during Service Transition. In this sense, the role of IT operations focuses on maintaining the status quo, whereby stability of the IT infrastructure and consistency of IT services are the most important tasks of IT operations.

■ Simultaneously, IT operations are part of the process that adds value to the business and supports the value network (see Chapter 4 on Service Strategy). IT operations must be capable of continual adaptation to business requirements and demands.

3.1.2 IT Operations Management objectives

■ Maintaining the existing situation to achieve stability in the processes and activities of the organization

■ Continual research and improvement to achieve better service at lower costs while maintaining stability

■ Rapid application of operational skills to analyze operational failures and to resolve them

3.1.3 IT Operations Management metrics

IT Operations Management measures both the effective implementation of defined activities and procedures, as well as execution of process activities. Examples include:

■ Successful completion of planned tasks

■ The number of exceptions to planned activities and tasks

■ Process metrics, e.g.: response time to events, resolving time for incidents, the number of unauthorized changes that has been identified, etc.

■ Metrics of maintenance activities. Possible examples are the number of instances that the time for maintenance has been exceeded, the percentage of maintenance work that has been executed according to schedule, etc.

■ Metrics related to facility management. Possible examples are: costs versus budget related to maintenance and security of a building, metrics regarding energy consumption, the number of security incidents, the way these incidents have been solved, etc.

3.1.4 IT Operations Management documentation

IT Operations Management generates and uses a number of documents, including:

■ **Standard Operating Procedures (SOP)** – A series of documents providing detailed instructions and activity schedules for each IT Operations Management team, department, or group.

■ **Operations logs** – Each activity that is performed as part of IT operations must be registered for a variety of reasons, in order to:
  • Confirm successful completion of specific tasks or activities
  • Confirm that an IT service was provided as agreed

- Provide a basis for Problem Management to research the underlying cause of incidents
- Provide a basis for reports about performance of IT operations teams and departments

■ **Shift schedules and reports** – Documents that display the exact activities that must be performed during a shift; there is also a list showing all dependencies and the sequence of activities. There may be more than one operational schedule because each team may be provided with a version for its own systems.

3.1.5 Roles within IT operations management
■ IT operations manager
■ Team leaders
■ IT operations analysts
■ Console operators
■ Input/output operators
■ Facility managers
■ Facility practitioners

3.1.6 IT Operations Management organization
IT Operations Management is described as a separate function, but often technical and application management personnel contribute to this function. The IT Operations Management function is divided into two sub-functions: **IT Operations activities and Facility Management.**

1. IT Operations activities
IT Operations activities oversee the execution and monitoring of operational activities and events within the IT infrastructure. These activities are executed from a so-called *"operations bridge"*. The Operations Bridge is a physical location where IT services and IT infrastructure are monitored and managed.

An operations bridge gathers all the crucial observation points in the IT infrastructure, so that they can be monitored and controlled from a central location with minimum effort.

The operations bridge combines many activities such as console management, event handling, first-line network management, job scheduling, and support after regular office hours. In some organizations, the service desk is part of the operations bridge.

In addition to standard routines, such as queries or reports that technical and application management teams have handed over as part of the service or of routine daily maintenance tasks, IT Operations executes these specific tasks:
■ **Console management** – executing event management, monitoring and control activities, based on information from consoles

■ **Backup and restore** – activities initiated by the technical and application management or by the users. Some organizations – such as financial service providers and listed companies – are required by law and industry regulations to implement and monitor a formal backup and restore strategy.

The precise requirements vary per country and industry. An organization must protect its data, which includes backup and storage of data in secure locations where it is protected.

A **restore** can be initiated from several sources, varying from an event indicating data corruption to a *service request* from a user or customer. A restore may be necessary in case of:
■ Corrupt data
■ Lost data
■ A catastrophe plan / IT service continuity situation
■ Historical data required for forensic investigation

■ **Print and output** – many services provide their information in print or electronic form (output). The service provider must ensure that the information ends up in the right places, correctly and in the right form. Information security often plays a part in this respect.
■ **Job planning** – managing batch jobs or scripts.
■ **Maintenance and performance** related activities commissioned by the technical management or the application management.

2. Facility management
Facility management refers to management of the physical environment of IT operations, usually located in data centers or computer rooms. The two main tasks of Facility management are:
1. Managing the physical infrastructure of the IT (physical entry, buildings maintenance, lighting, air humidity, supply of electricity etc.).
2. Coordinating large scale consolidation projects: data center consolidation or server consolidation projects.

■ 3.2 SERVICE DESK

A service desk is a **functional unit** with a number of personnel members who deal with a variety of service events. Requests may come in through phone calls, the internet or as automatically reported infrastructure events.

The Service Desk is a very important part of the organization's IT department. It should be the prime contact point for IT users, and it processes all incidents and service requests. Often the personnel use software tools to record and manage events.

3.2.1 Justification and the role of a service desk

Many organizations consider a service desk as the best resource for first-line of IT problems. A service desk provides the following advantages:

- Improved customer service, improved customer perception of the service and increased customer satisfaction
- Increased accessibility due to a single point of contact, communication and information
- Customer and user requests are resolved better and faster
- Improved cooperation and communication
- An improved focus on service and a proactive service approach
- Reduced negative business impact
- Improved infrastructure management and control
- Improved use of resources for IT support, and increased business personnel productivity
- More meaningful management information for decision support
- It is a good career entry position for IT personnel

3.2.2 Service Desk objectives

The principal goal of the Service Desk is to restore the "*normal service*" for users as soon as possible. This could entail resolving a technical error, fulfilling a service request or answering a question.

3.2.3 Organizational structure of a service desk

There are all sorts of ways to structure a service desk. The solution will vary for each organization. The most important options are:

- Local service desk
- Centralized service desk
- Virtual service desk
- "*Follow the sun*" – "*24/7*" service
- Specialized service desk groups

These options are elaborated further below. In practice, an organization will implement a structure that combines a number of these options in order to satisfy the needs of the business.

The **local service desk** (Figure 3.2) is located at or physically close to the users it is supporting. Because of this, communications are often much smoother and the visible presence is attractive for some users. However, a local service desk is expensive and may be inefficient if the amount of service events does not really justify a service desk.

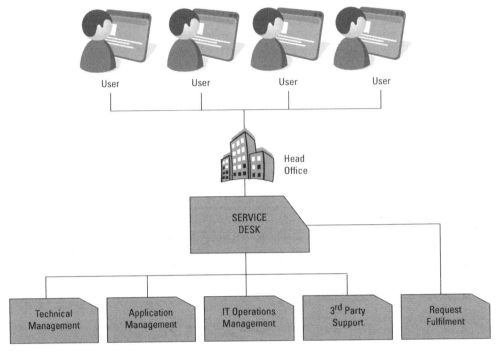

Figure 3.2 An example of a local service desk

(source: AXELOS)

There may be a few sound reasons for maintaining a local service desk:
- Linguistic, cultural, and political differences
- Different time zones
- Specialized groups of users
- Existence of adjusted or special services for which specialized knowledge is required
- Status of the users

The number of service desks can be reduced by installing them at one single location (or by reducing the number of local service desks). In that case, the associates are assigned to one or more **centralized service desk** structures. This may be less expensive and more efficient, because fewer associates can deal with the service events (calls), while the level of knowledge of the service desk is bound to increase.

By using technology, specifically the internet, and the use of support tools, it is possible to create the impression of a centralized service desk, whereas the associates are in fact spread out over a number of geographic or structural locations: this is the **virtual service desk** (Figure 3.3).

Some international organizations like to combine two or more geographically spread out service desks in order to offer a **24/7 service**. In this way, a service desk in Asia, for example, can deal with incoming service events during standard office hours, whereby

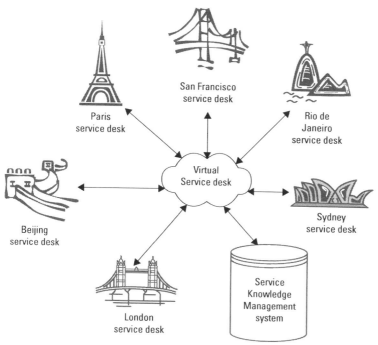

Figure 3.3 An example of a virtual service desk

(source: AXELOS)

at the end of that period, a service desk in Europe takes care of any outstanding events. That desk deals with those service events together with its own events. At the end of the working day, responsibility is transferred to a service desk in America, which then returns responsibility to the Asian service desk, thus completing the cycle.

It may be attractive for some organizations to create specialized **service desk groups**, so that incidents relating to a specific IT service are routed straight to the specialized group. In this way, incidents can be resolved more promptly.

The **environment** of the service desk must be carefully selected, preferably a location where workstations have adequate space with natural light. A quiet environment with good acoustics is equally important, because the associates should not be bothered by each other's telephone conversations. Ergonomic office furniture is also important.

3.2.4 Service desk personnel

It is important to ensure the availability of the correct **number of personnel members**, so that the service desk can meet the business demands at any time. It is important to consider all activities executed by the service desk personnel. This includes call handling, monitoring, and updating records, creating documentation, attending meetings, escalation, and reporting. The number of calls can fluctuate significantly each day and from hour to hour. When scheduling, a successful organization takes both the patterns of business activities (PBA) and business schedules into account.

The necessary levels and skills required for service desk personnel are also important. The agreed target resolution times should be balanced against the complexity of the supported systems and what the business is willing to pay to determine the required **skill level**. Most of the time the optimal and most cost-effective approach is first-line support through the service desk and IT Operations. In order to increase the effectiveness and efficiency of first-line support, third-line support should *"offload"* as much as possible of their mundane tasks onto second-line support through documenting, educating, and training, mentoring, and coaching. In turn, the second-line support *"offloads"* their mundane tasks to first-line support by doing the same as per above. The use of knowledge management is a key success factor for this to be successful.

Care should be taken that a sufficient **number of associates** are available, so that the service desk can meet the business demand at any time. The number of service events can, of course, strongly fluctuate from day to day and hour to hour. An organization will take peak hours and quiet periods into account.

A decision should be made as to which skill levels are necessary for the service desk personnel. To determine the required **skill level**, weigh the arranged resolution times against the complexity of the **supported systems**, and the outlay the business is willing to pay. The optimal and most efficient approach is generally a first line support via the service desk, which records the service event and transmits escalations promptly to more expert second-level and third-level support groups.

If the skill levels have been established, the service desk must be directed in a way that the associates receive and maintain the necessary skills. During all work hours, there has to be a good mix of skills present.

It is essential that all service desk associates receive sufficient **training**. All new associates must follow a formal introduction program. The precise content of it will vary with each new associate, subject to the existing expertise and experience.

In order to keep the service desk associates up-to-date, a program is necessary so that they can be kept informed of new developments, services, and techniques. The timing of these types of activities is essential, because they should not affect the normal tasks. Many service desks organize short training sessions during quiet periods when the associates are handling fewer service events.

It is very important that all IT associates realize the importance of the service desk and the people working there. A considerable attrition of associates has a disturbing effect and can lead to an incoherent service. Thus the managers have to engage in efforts **to retain the associates**.

Many organizations find it meaningful to appoint a number of so-called **super users** in the user community. They function as contact persons with the IT organization in general and the service desk in particular.

3.2.5 Service desk roles

■ Service desk manager
   • Manages service desk activities
   • Acts as escalation point for supervisors
   • Takes on wider customer service role
   • Reports to senior managers about any issue that could significantly impact the business
   • Attends Change Advisory Board meetings
   • Overall responsibility for processing incidents and service requests
■ Service desk supervisor
   • Ensures that personnel and skill levels are maintained
   • Is responsible for production of management reports
   • Acts as escalation point for difficult calls
■ Service desk analysts
   • Deliver first line support by accepting calls and processing the resulting incidents or service requests, using Incident Management and Request Fulfilment processes
■ Super users
   • Business users who act as liaison points between business and IT

3.2.6 Metrics

In order to evaluate the performance of the service desk at regular time intervals, **metrics** must be established. In this way, the maturity, efficiency, effectiveness, and potentials can be established and the service desk actions improved. Metrics for the performance of a service desk must be selected carefully and realistically.

In order to determine this, further analysis and more detailed metrics are necessary which are researched for a certain period of time. Besides the statistics mentioned earlier regarding the handling of service events, the metrics consist, among others, of:

■ First line handling time: the percentage of service events, which are resolved by the first level, without the necessity to escalate to other support groups
■ Average time to resolve an incident (or other type of service call) (if it is resolved by the first level)
■ Average time to escalate an incident (if a first line solution is not possible)
■ Average handling costs of an incident

■ Percentage of client and user updates which are executed within the target values, as set forth in the SLA objectives
■ Average time to evaluate and close out a resolved incident

Besides following "*hard*" metrics in the performance of the service desk, it is also important to use "*soft*" metrics: **the customer and user satisfaction surveys** (e.g.: Do customers and users find that their phone calls are properly answered? Was the service desk associate friendly and professional?). User or customer can best complete this type of metrics, but specific questions about the service desk itself may also be asked.

■ 3.3   TECHNICAL MANAGEMENT

Technical Management refers to the **groups, departments, or teams** who offer technical expertise and general management of the IT infrastructure.

3.3.1 The role of Technical Management
Technical Management has a dual role:
■ It is the custodian of technical knowledge and expertise in relation to managing the IT infrastructure. In this role, Technical Management helps ensure that the knowledge required for designing, testing, managing and improving IT services is established, developed, and refined.
■ It takes care of the actual resources that are needed to support the ITSM lifecycle. In this role, Technical Management helps ensure that the resources are trained and implemented effectively, so that it can design, build, transfer, process, and improve the required technology that is needed to provide and support IT services.

By fulfilling these two roles, Technical Management helps ensure that the organization is able to access the correct type and level of human resources to manage the technology, and consequently, meet the business goals.

Technical Management also drives IT operations while managing the technology operations and providing guidance to IT operations.

3.3.2 Objectives of Technical Management
Technical Management assists in the planning, implementation and maintenance of a stable technical infrastructure to support the organization's business processes. This is done by:
■ Well-designed and cost-effective technical topology
■ Using the appropriate technical skills to maintain the technical infrastructure in an optimal condition
■ Using technical skills effectively, to diagnose and resolve technical failures quickly

3.3.3 General Technical Management activities

Technical Management is involved in several general activities, such as:

- Starting training programs
- Designing and carrying out training for users, the service desk, and other groups
- Researching and developing resolutions that may help to expand the service portfolio, or may be used to simplify or automate IT operations
- Releases that are often implemented with the assistance of Technical Management personnel

3.3.4 Specific activities of Technical Management

Mainframe management

Mainframes form the central part of many services, and their performance forms a baseline for service performance and user and customer expectations.

Server management and support

Most organizations use servers to offer flexible and accessible services for hosting applications or databases, fulfilling client/server services, storage, print and file management.

The server team or department must fulfil the following procedures and activities:

- Supporting the operating system
- License management for all configuration items
- Third-line support
- Procurement advice
- System security
- Definition and management of virtual servers
- Capacity and performance

Network management

Since most IT services are dependent on connectivity, network management is crucial to service provision. Service Operation personnel access important service components, via network management.

Network management is responsible for all Local Area Networks (LANs), Metropolitan Area Networks (MANs), and Wide Area Networks (WANs) within an organization.

Storage and archiving

Many services require that data must be stored for a specific time. Often, such data must be made available as an offline archive when it is no longer required on a daily basis. This is not only for compliance with external regulations and legislation, but also because data may be invaluable internally to an organization for a variety of other reasons.

Storage and archiving does not only demand infrastructure component management, but also policy that prescribes where data must be stored, for how long, in which form, and who can access the data.

Database administration

Database administration must work closely together with key application management teams or departments. In some organizations the functions can be combined or can be brought under one management structure.

Database administration must ensure optimal database performance, security, and functionality. Database administrators have, among others, the following responsibilities:
- Designing and maintaining database standards and policies
- Database design, creation, and testing

Directory services management

A directory service is a specialized software application that manages information about the available resources on a network, and to which users it is accessible. It is the basis for providing access to those resources, and for detecting and preventing unauthorized access.

Directory services look at every resource as an object of the directory server, and name them. Every name will be linked to a resource network address, so that users do not have to remember confusing and complex addresses.

Desktop support

Many users have access to IT services through a desktop or laptop. Desktop support is responsible for all desktop and laptop hardware, software and peripheral equipment in an organization. Specific responsibilities include:

Table 3.1 Specific desktop responsibilities

Desktop policy and procedures	For example, license policy, personal use of laptops and desktops, etc.
Desktop maintenance	Such as release implementation, upgrades, patches and hot fixes
Support of connectivity problems	For home-workers and field personnel

Middleware management

Middleware connects software components, or integrates them with distributed or unlike applications and systems. Middleware enables effective data transfer between applications. For this reason middleware is important for services that depend on multiple applications or data resources. This is especially relevant in the context of service-orientated software/architecture (SOA).

Internet/web management

Many organizations use the internet for their business operations, and are therefore heavily dependent upon the availability and performance of their websites. In such cases, a separate internet/web support team is required. This team has, among others, the following tasks:

■ Designing internet and web services architecture
■ The specification of standards for the development and management of web based applications, content, websites, and web pages; this is usually addressed during Service Design
■ Maintaining all web development and management applications
■ Supporting interfaces with back-end and legacy systems
■ Monitoring and managing web based performance, such as user experience simulation, benchmarking, and virtualization

3.3.5 The Technical Management organization

IT Operations Management consists of a number of technological areas. Each area requires a specific set of skills to manage and operate it. Some skills are related to each other, and can be performed by generalists, while others apply specifically to a component, system, or platform.

Technical Management consists of specialized technical architects, designers, maintenance specialists and support personnel.

3.3.6 Technical Management roles

■ Technical managers/team leaders
  • Responsible for leadership, control and decision-making
■ Technical analysts/architects
  • Defining and maintaining knowledge on how systems are related and ensuring that dependencies are understood
■ Technical operators
  • Performing day-to-day operational tasks

3.3.7 Metrics for Technical Management

Specific metrics for Technical Management depend largely on which technology is being managed. Some general metrics include:

■ Measuring the agreed output
■ Process values
■ Technological performance
■ Mean time between failures (MTBF) of specific equipment
■ Maintenance activity measurement
■ Training and skill development

3.3.8 Technical Management documentation

Among others, Technical Management documentation consists of:

- Technical documentation (manuals, management and administration manuals, user manuals for configuration items – CI)
- Maintenance schedules
- An inventory of skills

■ 3.4 APPLICATION MANAGEMENT

Application Management is responsible for the management of applications during their lifecycle. The Application Management **function** is executed by a department, group, or team that is involved with management and support of operational applications. Application Management also plays an important role in designing, testing and improving applications that are part of IT services.

3.4.1 Application Management role

Application Management is for applications what Technical Management is for IT infrastructure. It plays a role in all applications, whether they are purchased or have been internally developed. One of the most important decisions to which they contribute is whether to purchase an application or to develop it internally (discussed in detail in Service Design). When this decision has been made, Application Management plays a dual role:

- It is the custodian of technical knowledge and expertise for the management of applications
- It provides actual resources for the support of the ITSM lifecycle

Two other roles filled by Application Management:

- It provides advice to IT operations about the best way to carry out the ongoing operational management of applications
- It integrates the Application Management lifecycle with the ITSM lifecycle

3.4.2 Application Management objectives

The objectives of Application Management are to support the business processes of the organization by determining functional and management requirements for applications. Another objective is to assist in design and implementation of the applications and to support and improve them.

3.4.3 Application Management principles

One of the most important decisions in Application Management is whether to **develop or purchase** an application that supports the requested functionality. The Chief Technical Officer (CTO), or the IT steering group/committee, makes the ultimate decision, but in doing so both depend on a number of information sources. If the decision maker wants to have the application developed, they will also have to decide whether to have it developed by personnel or to outsource the development. This is further discussed in detail in Service Design.

3.4.4 Application Management lifecycle

The lifecycle that is followed to develop and manage the application goes by many names, such as the Software Lifecycle (SLC) and the Software Development Lifecycle (SDLC). These are mostly used by application development teams and their project managers to define their involvement in designing, developing, testing, implementing, and supporting applications. Examples of this approach include Structured Systems Analysis and Design Methodology (SSADM) and Dynamic Systems Development Method (DSDM).

> **Relation between Application Management lifecycle and service management lifecycle**
>
> The Application Management lifecycle is not an alternative for the service management lifecycle. Applications are part of services and must be managed as such. Nevertheless, applications are a unique mix of technology and functionality and this requires a special focus during each phase of the service management lifecycle.
>
> Each phase of the Application Management lifecycle has its own specific objectives, activities, deliverables, and dedicated teams. Each phase also has a clear responsibility to ensure that its output corresponds with the specific objectives of the service management lifecycle.

1. During the first phase, the requirements for a new application are collected, based on the business needs of the organization. There are six requirement types for an application, whether it is developed in-house, outsourced, or purchased. See Table 3.2.

Table 3.2 Sample requirements

Functional requirements	What is necessary to support a certain business function?
Management requirements	Concentrate on the need for responsive, available, and secure service, and involve things like deployment, system management, and security
Usability requirements	What are the needs of the user, and how can they be satisfied?
Architecture requirements	Especially if a change in the existing architecture standards is required
Interface requirements	Where dependencies occur between existing applications or tools and the new application
Service level requirements	Specify how the service is to be delivered, what the quality of the output has to be and other qualitative aspects that are measured by the user or client

2. The **design phase** will translate the requirements into specifications. Design of the application and the environment or the operational model in which the application

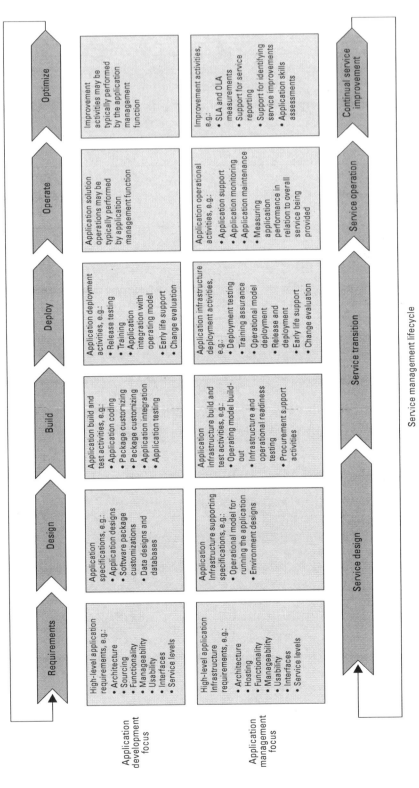

Figure 3.4 Sample of Application Management lifecycle

is run will also take place during the Design Phase. Architectural considerations for design and operation are the most important aspect of this phase, because they can affect the structure and content of both the application and the operational model.

3. The **build phase** gets the application and the operational model ready for deployment. Application components are coded and purchased, integrated and tested. Testing is not a separate phase in the lifecycle although it is a separate activity. Testing forms an integral part of the development and roll-out phase, as validation of the activity and output of those phases.

4. The **deployment phase** deploys the operational model and the application. The existing IT environment absorbs the operational model and the application is installed on top of the operational model. This involves the processes of RDM that are described under Service Transition.

5. During the **operate phase** the service organization uses the application as part of providing services requested by the business. The performance of the application in relation to the total service is measured continually in relation to the service levels and the most important business drivers.

6. The **optimize phase** reviews and analyzes the results of the service level performance metrics. Possible improvements are discussed and the necessary developments are initiated. The two main strategies involve maintaining and iteratively improving service levels at lower costs. This can lead to a change in the lifecycle of an application or to its retirement. Good communication with users is important during this phase.

3.4.5 Generic Application Management activities

Although most Application Management teams and departments are dedicated to specific applications, they share a number of activities. These include:

- Identifying the knowledge needed to manage and operate applications in the Service Operation phase
- Initiating training programs to develop and refine skills in the appropriate Application Management resources and to maintain training reports for these resources
- Defining standards for designing new architectures and determining application architectures during Service Strategy processes
- Testing, designing and executing the functionality, performance and controllability of IT services
- Defining event management standards
- Defining, managing, and maintaining attributes and relations of application CI in the configuration management system

3.4.6 Application Management organization

Although Application Management departments, groups and teams all perform similar functions, each application has its own set of management and operational requirements. Differences may include:

■ The purpose of the application
■ The functionality of the application
■ The platform on which the application is run
■ The type or the brand of technology used

Application Management teams and departments are mostly organized based on the categories of the applications that they support. Examples of typical Application Management organization include:

■ Financial applications
■ HR applications
■ Manufacturing support
■ Sales support
■ Call center and marketing applications
■ Business specific applications
■ IT applications
■ Web portals

Traditionally, application development and management teams/departments have operated as autonomous units. Each team manages its own environment in its own way and they all have a separate interface to the business.

3.4.7 Application Management roles and responsibilities

Application Management has two roles:

■ **The application manager** – supervises and has overall responsibility for management and the decisions that are made
■ **The application analyst/architect** – is responsible for requirements that meet the application specifications

Application Management metrics

The Application Management metrics mainly depend on the way in which the applications are managed, but general metrics include:

■ Measuring agreed-upon outputs
■ Process metrics
■ Performance of the application
■ Measuring maintenance activities
■ Application Management teams cooperate closely with application development teams and the correct metrics must be used to measure this
■ Training and skill development

PART
2

PROCESSES IN THE LIFECYCLE PHASES

4 Service Strategy Phase

■ 4.1   INTRODUCTION TO SERVICE STRATEGY

This chapter sets out the processes and activities on which effective Service Strategy depends. These comprise both lifecycle processes and those almost wholly contained within Service Strategy. Each is described in detail, setting out the key elements of that process or activity.

The processes specifically addressed in this chapter are:
- Strategy Management for IT Services
- Service Portfolio Management
- Financial Management for IT Services
- Demand Management
- Business Relationship Management

Processes in the ITIL lifecycle

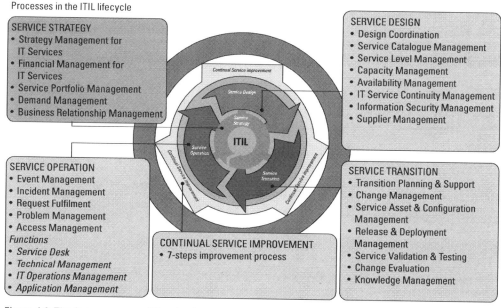

SERVICE STRATEGY
- Strategy Management for IT Services
- Financial Management for IT Services
- Service Portfolio Management
- Demand Management
- Business Relationship Management

SERVICE DESIGN
- Design Coordination
- Service Catalogue Management
- Service Level Management
- Capacity Management
- Availability Management
- IT Service Continuity Management
- Information Security Management
- Supplier Management

SERVICE OPERATION
- Event Management
- Incident Management
- Request Fulfilment
- Problem Management
- Access Management

Functions
- *Service Desk*
- *Technical Management*
- *IT Operations Management*
- *Application Management*

CONTINUAL SERVICE IMPROVEMENT
- 7-steps improvement process

SERVICE TRANSITION
- Transition Planning & Support
- Change Management
- Service Asset & Configuration Management
- Release & Deployment Management
- Service Validation & Testing
- Change Evaluation
- Knowledge Management

Figure 4.0 The five processes of Service Strategy in relation to the ITIL lifecycle

Most of these processes are used throughout the Service Lifecycle, but are addressed in *ITIL Service Strategy* since they are central to effective Service Strategy.

4.1.1 Goal and objectives

The **goal** of Service Strategy is to develop the ability to achieve and maintain a strategic advantage, by defining the:

- perspective
- position
- plans
- patterns

…with regard to its services and the management of those services that will enable an organization to achieve its business outcomes.

By implementing the Service Strategy phase an organization is able to realize the following **objectives**:

- To answer the question: *"what is our strategy"*
- To establish which services to be delivered to who
- To be different from the competition
- To create value for customers
- To define the quality of a service
- To decide how these services will be delivered
- To arrange the required processes

4.1.2 Scope

Service Strategy is aimed at internal and external IT service providers. There are two main topics within Service Strategy:

- Defining a strategy that enables a IT service provider to deliver services that enable customers to achieve their business outcomes (Service Strategy)
- Defining a strategy how these services need to be managed (service management strategy).

■ 4.2 STRATEGY MANAGEMENT FOR IT SERVICES

4.2.1 Introduction

Strategy Management for IT Services is the process of defining and maintaining an organization's perspective, position, plans, and patterns with regard to its services and the management of those services.

The **purpose** of a Service Strategy is to articulate how a service provider will enable an organization to achieve its business outcomes; it establishes the criteria and mechanisms to decide which services will be best suited to meet the business outcomes and the most effective and efficient way to manage these services.

The **objectives** of Strategy Management for IT Services are to:

- Analyze the internal and external environments of the service provider, to identify opportunities benefiting the organization
- Identify (potential) constraints preventing the achievement of business outcomes, the delivery or the management of services; to identify how to remove or reduce effects of the constraints
- Agree the service provider's perspective and review regularly for continued relevance. This will clarify the service provider's vision and mission statements
- Establish the position of the service provider relative to its customers and other service providers. This includes mapping services to market spaces, and maintaining a competitive advantage
- Produce and maintain strategy planning documents ensuring all stakeholders have up-to-date documents. These documents include the strategy for IT, service management, and for each service
- Ensure that strategic plans have been translated into tactical and operational plans for each organizational unit involved with delivering the strategy
- Manage changes to the strategies and related documents to keep pace with changes to the internal and external environments

Scope

Strategy management is the responsibility of the executives of an organization. It enables them to set the objectives of the organization, to specify how the organization will meet those objectives and to prioritize investments required to meet them. An organization's strategy is not limited to a single document or department. The overall strategy of an organization will be broken down into a strategy for each unit of the business.

Key message
A Service Strategy is a subset of the overall strategy for the organization. In the case of an IT organization, the IT strategy will encompass the IT service strategy.

Note on strategy for services
Strategy Management for IT Services is intended for managing the strategy of a service provider. It will include a specification of the type of services it will deliver, the customers of those services and the overall business outcomes to be achieved when the service provider executes the strategy.

The strategy of an individual service is defined during the Service Portfolio Management process and documented in the service portfolio. This will include a description of the specific business outcomes that the service will support, and also define how the service will be delivered.

It is important to note, furthermore, that a service strategy is not the same as an ITSM strategy, which is really a tactical plan. The difference can be summed up as follows:

- **Service strategy** – The strategy that a service provider will follow to define and execute services that meet a customer's business objectives. For an IT service provider the service strategy is a subset of the IT strategy
- **ITSM strategy** – The plan for identifying, implementing, and executing the processes used to manage services identified in a service strategy. In an IT service provider, the ITSM strategy will be a subset of the service strategy.

Value to the business
The strategy of an organization articulates its objectives, and defines how it will meet those objectives and how it will know it has met those objectives. A well-defined and managed strategy ensures that the resources and capabilities of the organization are aligned to achieving its business outcomes, and that investments match the organization's intended development and growth.

Strategy Management for IT Services ensures that all stakeholders are represented in deciding the appropriate direction for the organization and that they all agree on its objectives and the means whereby resources, capabilities, and investment are prioritized. Strategy Management for IT Services also ensures that the resources, capabilities, and investments are appropriately managed to achieve the strategy.

Strategy Management for IT Services further encourages appropriate levels of investment, which will result in one or more of the following:

- Cost savings, since investments and expenditure are matched to achievement of validated business objectives, rather than unsubstantiated demands
- Increased levels of investment for key projects or service improvements
- Shifting investment priorities.

The service provider will be able to de-focus attention from one service, and re-focus on another, ensuring that their efforts and budget are spent on the areas with the highest level of business impact.

4.2.2 Process activities, methods, and techniques
The process for strategy management is illustrated in Figure 4.1.

In Strategic Management for IT services there are three main activities: strategic assessment, strategy generation, and strategy execution.

1. Strategic assessment
The strategic assessment analyzes both the internal environment (the service provider's own organization) and the external environment (the world with which the service provider's organization interacts), and then arrives at a set of objectives which will be used to define the actual strategy.

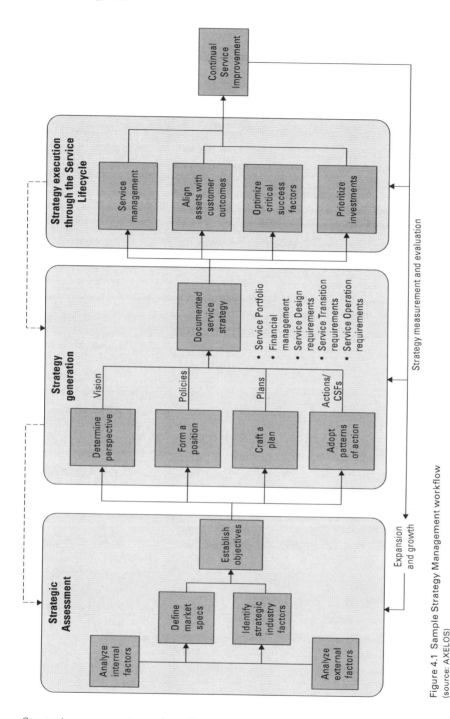

Figure 4.1 Sample Strategy Management workflow
(source: AXELOS)

Strategic assessment: Analyze the internal environment

- Existing services
- Financial analysis
- Human resources
- Operations

- Relationship with the business units
- Resources and capabilities
- Existing projects

Strategic assessment: Analyze the external environment
- Industry and market analysis
- Customers
- Suppliers
- Partners
- Competitors
- Legislation and regulation
- Political
- Socio-economic
- Technology

Strategic assessment: Define market spaces
In summary, market spaces define opportunities where a service provider can deliver value to its customer(s). They identify opportunities by matching service archetypes with customer assets.

Strategic assessment: Identify strategic industry factors
For every market space there are critical factors that determine the success or failure of a Service Strategy. In business literature these factors are called strategic industry factors (Amit and Schoemaker, 1993). These are influenced by customer needs, business trends, competition, regulatory environment, suppliers, standards, industry best practices, and technologies.

Strategic industry factors have the following general characteristics:
- They are defined in terms of capabilities and resources
- They are proven to be key determinants of success by industry leaders
- They are defined by market space levels, not peculiar to any one firm
- They are the basis for competition among rivals
- They change over time, so they are dynamic not static
- They usually require significant investments and time to develop

Critical success factors by themselves are altered or influenced by one or more of the following factors: *Customers; Competitors; Partners; Suppliers; and Regulators.*

Strategic assessment: Establish objectives
The objectives defined as an output of the strategic assessment are the results the service provider expects to achieve by pursuing a strategy. Once the objectives have been defined, the service provider will need to define how it will achieve the anticipated results. This is the strategy (or strategies).

Table 4.1 Questions to assess existing services as differentiators

Which of our services or service varieties are the most distinctive? Are there services that the business or customer cannot easily substitute?	*Are there barriers preventing other service providers from offering the same services?* Barriers to entry could be the service provider's knowledge of the customer's business or the broadness of service offerings. *How expensive would it be to switch to another service provider?* The service provider might have lower cost structures because of specialization or service sourcing. *Do we offer a unique and particular attribute?* These could include product knowledge, regulatory compliance, technical capabilities, or global presence.
Which of our services are the most profitable?	The value could be defined as higher profits or lower expenses, or socially related. *For non-profit organizations, are there services that allow the organization to perform its mission better?* Substitute "*profit*" with "*benefits realized*".
Which of our customers and stakeholders are the most satisfied?	The answer will center on services demonstrating high quality, low cost, unique to a specific customer's requirements *It may be a combination of the three.*
Which customers, channels, or purchase occasions are the most profitable?	The value could be defined as higher profits or lower expenses, or socially related.
Which of our activities in our value chain or value network are the most different and effective?	Activities perceived by the business as a core competency, and therefore will ensure that the service provider is seen as strategic.

A set of guidelines that is frequently used to ensure definition of meaningful objectives is contained in the "*SMART*" acronym. This stands for *Specific; Measurable; Achievable; Realistic; and Time-bounded*.

2. Strategy generation: Evaluation and selection
Once the assessment has been completed and the service provider has defined the objectives of the strategy, it is possible to generate the actual strategy in terms of the "*four Ps*"; *perspective, position, plans and patterns*.

Determine perspective
The perspective of a service provider defines its overall direction, values, beliefs and purpose; and, at a high level, how it intends to achieve this. The most common form of perspective statements is vision and mission statements. The vision statement articulates what it is the service provider aims to achieve.

Form a position
The strategic position defines how the service provider will be differentiated from other service providers in the industry.

Craft a plan
A strategic plan identifies how the organization will achieve its objectives, vision, and position. The plan is a deliberate course of action towards strategic objectives and describes how the organization will move from one point to another within a specific scenario.

Adopt patterns of action
A pattern of action is how an organization works. Formal hierarchies show one view of the organization, but the interactions between these hierarchies, the exchange of information, the handover of units of work, and the exchange of money all contribute to a network of activity that gets things done.

3. Strategy execution
Tactical plans describe what approaches and methods will be used to achieve the strategy. If a strategy answers the question *"where are we going?"* then tactics answer the question *"how will we get there?"*

Other service management processes
For a service provider, no strategy can be executed without being able to manage the services that they will be providing. Service management processes enable the service provider to achieve alignment between the services and the desired outcomes on an ongoing basis.

Align assets with customer outcomes
Strategy execution relies on the ability of the service provider to know what service assets they have, where they are located, and how they are deployed.

Optimize critical success factors
The term *"critical success factor"* refers to any aspect of a strategy, process, project, or initiative that needs to be present in order for it to succeed. Critical success factors could be specific skills, tools, circumstances, finances, executive support or the completion of another activity or project.

Prioritize investments
Each new service or project will require funding. Prioritize strategic investments based on customer needs.

Measurement and evaluation
This stage of strategy management is performed by a number of different areas, including:
- Customers and users
- Service management processes
- Continual Service Improvement
- The organization's executives

Service providers should be aware that in many cases they will not be able to measure something that is important to the customer. In these cases what is important is that the customer takes responsibility for performing the measurement, and the service provider will agree to an appropriate response to any exceptions.

Measurement and evaluation: Continual Service Improvement
CSI activities measure and evaluate the achievement of strategy over time. Firstly, CSI activities identify areas that are not performing to expectation, and therefore threaten the achievement of the strategy. Secondly, CSI activities set the baseline for the next round of strategy assessments. Since the organization exists in (and is itself) a continuously changing environment, the strategy needs to be continually assessed and revised.

Measurement and evaluation: Expansion and growth
As the organization achieves its existing strategy, it gets better at being able to deliver services to its existing market spaces.

4.2.3 Strategy management for internal IT service providers
Internal IT organizations often make the mistake of thinking that they do not play a strategic role in the organization, and that they should confine their activities to tactical planning and execution. However, IT is a strategic part of most businesses, and it is important that the IT organization strategy is closely aligned and measured with the business strategy.

Strategic assessment for internal service providers
Strategic assessment is similar to the strategy management process described above but it defines its environment more specifically. The purpose of the strategic assessment is to determine the IT organization's current situation.

The internal environment that should be assessed by IT organizations includes:
- The organization's business strategy
- Existing services
- Existing technologies
- ITSM
- Human resources
- Relationship with the business units

The external environment that should be assessed by IT organizations specifically includes:
- Other organizations
- Industry IT spending rates
- Vendor strategies and product roadmaps
- Partners
- Technology trends

- Customers
- Standards or regulatory requirements for IT
- Operations
- The relationship between application development and operations

4.2.4 Information management
- Provides data and analysis of information about the current state of services to various audiences
- Results of assessments of the internal environment
- Information about customer needs and satisfaction levels, current service capabilities and performance levels
- Strategy Management for IT Services documentation
- The service portfolio
- Financial Management
- Business Relationship Management
- Demand Management
- Continual Service Improvement

4.2.5 Interfaces
- Provides the guidelines and framework within which the service portfolio will be defined and managed
- Provides input to financial management to indicate types of returns required and to priorities investments
- Identifies any policies that must be taken into account when designing services
- Enables Service Transition to prioritize and evaluate the services that are built to ensure that they meet the original intent and strategic requirements of the services
- Knowledge management strategic planners need to understand the existing environment, its history and its dynamics, and to make informed decisions about the future
- Operational tools and processes must ensure that they have been aligned to the strategic objectives and desired business outcomes
- Continual Service Improvement will help to evaluate whether the strategy has been executed effectively, and whether it has met its objectives

4.2.6 Triggers
- Annual planning cycles
- New business opportunity
- Changes to internal or external environments
- Mergers or acquisitions

4.2.7 Inputs
- Existing plans
- Research on aspects of the environment by specialized research organizations

- Vendor strategies and product roadmaps
- Customer interviews and strategic plans
- Service portfolio to indicate the current and planned future service commitments
- Service reporting to indicate the effectiveness of the strategy
- Audit reports indicating compliance with (or deviation from) the organization's strategy

4.2.8 Outputs

- Strategic plans
- Tactical plans that identify how the strategy will be executed
- Strategy review schedules and documentation
- Mission and vision statements
- Policies regarding how the plans should be executed, services designed, transitioned, operated, and improved
- Strategic requirements for new services

4.2.9 Critical success factors

- Access to structured information about the internal and external environments
- Identification and elimination of constraints for the service provider to meet business outcomes, deliver, and manage services
- A clear understanding of their perspective, positions, patterns and plans
- The ability to produce, store, maintain and communicate strategy planning documents
- The ability to translate strategic plans into tactical and operational plans

4.2.10 Metrics

- Documented evidence exists for every market space
- Every finding or recommendation is based on validated information
- Forecasts and findings from external research are validated
- Number of corrective actions taken to remove constraints, and the result of those actions on the achievement of strategic objectives
- Vision and mission statements have been defined and communicated to all personnel
- Each service in the service portfolio has a statement about which business outcomes it meets, and is measured in terms of these outcomes
- Stakeholders can provide an overview of the content of the strategy documents relevant to their business unit
- All documents are under document control and changes to the documents have been made through the appropriate change control measures
- Deviations from activities and patterns are identified in the strategy

4.2.11 Challenges

- Strategy Management for IT Services is conducted at the wrong level in the organization
- Lack of accurate information about the external environment

- Lack of support by stakeholders
- Lack of the appropriate tools or understanding of how to use the tools and techniques
- Lack of the appropriate document control mechanisms and procedures
- Operational targets need to be matched to the strategic objectives

4.2.12 Risks

- A flawed governance model
- Short-term priorities override the directives of the strategy
- Making strategic decisions when there is missing and/or un-validated information about the internal or external environments
- Choosing the wrong strategy
- Strategies are seen as an exercise that happens once a year and that has no bearing on what happens for the rest of the year

■ 4.3 SERVICE PORTFOLIO MANAGEMENT

4.3.1 Introduction

A service portfolio describes a provider's services in terms of business value. It articulates business needs and the provider's response to those needs. By definition, business value terms correspond to marketing terms, providing a means for comparing service competitiveness across alternative providers. A service portfolio either clarifies or helps to clarify the following strategic questions:

- Why should a customer buy these services?
- Why should they buy these services from us?
- What are the pricing or chargeback models?
- What are our strengths and weaknesses, priorities and risks?
- How should our resources and capabilities be allocated?

The service portfolio is the complete set of services that is managed by a service provider. The service portfolio is used to manage the entire lifecycle of all services. It includes three categories of service: service pipeline (proposed or in development), service catalogue (live or available for deployment) and retired services. The service portfolio represents the investment made in an organization's services, and also articulates the value that services help it to realize.

Service Portfolio Management is responsible for managing the service portfolio. It is therefore also the process that is responsible for defining which services will be entered into the service portfolio and how those services are tracked and progressed through their lifecycle. In other words, Service Portfolio Management acts as a gatekeeper for the service provider, ensuring that they only provide services that contribute to strategic objectives and meet the agreed business outcomes.

The **purpose** of Service Portfolio Management is to ensure that the service provider has the right mix of services to balance the investment in IT with the ability to meet business outcomes. It tracks the investment in services throughout their lifecycle. It ensures that services are clearly defined and linked to the achievement of business outcomes.

The **objectives** of Service Portfolio Management are to:

- Provide a process and mechanisms to enable an organization to investigate and decide on which services to provide
- Maintain the definitive portfolio of services provided
- Provide a mechanism for the organization to evaluate how services enable them to achieve their strategy
- Control which services are offered, under what conditions and at what level of investment
- Track the investment in services throughout their lifecycle
- Analyze which services are no longer viable and when they should be retired

Scope
The scope of Service Portfolio Management is all services a service provider plans to deliver, those currently delivered and those that have been withdrawn from service. The primary concern of Service Portfolio Management is whether the service provider is able to generate value from the services.

Value to the business
Service Portfolio Management enables the business to make sound decisions about investments. Customers are able to make decisions about whether the service is a good or bad investment, and evaluate potential additional opportunities. It is a tool for innovation for the organization. The service provider is viewed as a steward of service assets that are the key to the customer's success.

4.3.2 Policies, principles, and basic concepts
The service portfolio is the complete set of services that is managed by a service provider. The service portfolio also identifies those services in a conceptual stage, namely all services the organization would provide if it had unlimited resources, capabilities and funding.

The service portfolio represents all the resources presently engaged or being released in various stages of the Service Lifecycle. Each stage requires resources for completion of projects, initiatives, and contracts. This is a very important governance aspect of Service Portfolio Management (SPM).

Service pipeline
The service pipeline is a database or structured document listing all services that are under consideration or development, but are not yet available to customers. It also

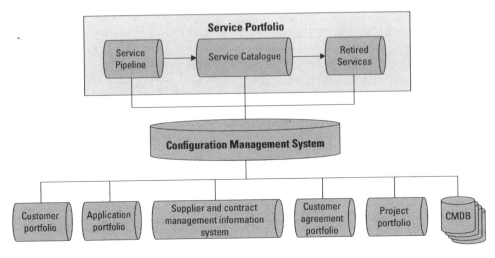

Figure 4.2 The service portfolio relations

(source: AXELOS)

includes any major investment opportunities. The service pipeline provides a business view of possible future services and is part of the service portfolio that is not normally published to customers.

Service catalogue
The service catalogue is a database or structured document with information about all live IT services, including those available for deployment. The service catalogue is the only part of the service portfolio published to customers, and is used to support the sale and delivery of IT services. The service catalogue includes information about deliverables, prices, contact points, ordering and request processes.

Items can enter the service catalogue only after due diligence has been performed on related costs and risks. Only operational services can be found in the service catalogue and resources are engaged to fully support active services.

In addition, the service catalogue serves as a service order and demand channeling mechanism. It defines and communicates the policies, guidelines, and accountability required for the service provider to deliver and support services to its customers.

Figure 4.3 illustrates the linkages between the following:
- The boxes on the left are service assets used by the service provider to provide services. These could be servers, databases, applications, network devices etc.
- Services in the service catalogue. There are two layers of services shown in Figure 4.3. The layer on the left shows supporting services, which are usually not seen by the customer directly (contained in a view of the service catalogue called the technical or supporting service catalogue). The second layer of services is customer-facing services.

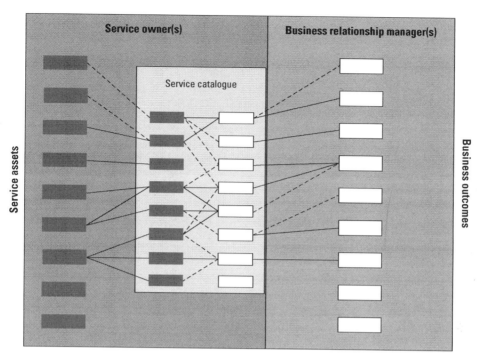

Figure 4.3 The service catalogue and linkages between services and outcomes

(source: AXELOS)

■ The boxes on the right are business outcomes, which the business achieves when it uses these services.

Retired services

Some services in the service portfolio are phased out or retired. There is a decision to be made by each organization, following a service review, on when to move a service from catalogue to retired. This is necessary because such services may cost a lot more to support and may disrupt economies of scale and scope.

Service Portfolio Management will define a policy for the length of time that a service will remain in the service portfolio. This could be expressed in time, or how many alternatives are available in the service catalogue. Retiring services is managed through Service Transition.

Configuration management system (CMS)

The CMS is a set of tools and databases that are used to manage an IT service provider's configuration data. The CMS system also includes information about incidents, problems, known errors, changes and releases, and may contain data about employees, suppliers, locations, business units, customers and users. The CMS includes tools for collecting, storing, managing, updating, and presenting data about all configuration items and their relationships.

Application portfolio

The application portfolio is a database or structured document used to manage applications throughout their lifecycle. The application portfolio contains key attributes of all applications.

Customer portfolio

The customer portfolio is a database or structured document used to record all customers of the IT service provider. The customer portfolio is the business relationship manager's view of the customers who receive services from the IT service provider.

Customer agreement portfolio

The customer agreement portfolio is a database or structured document used to manage service contracts or agreements between an IT service provider and its customers. Each IT service delivered to a customer should have a contract or other agreement that is listed in the customer agreement portfolio.

Project portfolio

The project portfolio is a database or structured document used to manage projects that have been chartered. The project portfolio is used to coordinate projects; ensuring objectives are met within time and cost and to specification, that projects are not duplicated, that they stay within the agreed scope, and that resources are available for each project. The project portfolio is the tool used to manage single projects as well as large-scale programs, consisting of multiple projects.

Charter: A document authorizing the project and stating its scope, terms and references

Service models

Service Portfolio Management uses service models to analyze the impact of new services or changes to existing services. If a service model does not exist for a service in the pipeline, Service Portfolio Management will ensure that one is defined.

Market spaces and service growth

Market spaces are helpful to Service Portfolio Management to evaluate the impact of a proposed new service or change to an existing service, since they clarify the opportunity that is being served.

Aligning service assets, services and business outcomes

Service Portfolio Management plays an important role in achieving this since the service portfolio and configuration management system (CMS) documents the relationship between business outcomes, services, and service assets.

4.3.3 Service Portfolio Management through the Service Lifecycle

Service Strategy

Although SPM is a process within Service Strategy, it also plays an important part in every stage in the Service Lifecycle.

Service Design

In Service Design SPM ensures that design work is prioritized according to business needs, and that there is a clear understanding of how the service will be measured by the business.

Service Transition

Service Transition builds and tests the services that will be placed into the service catalogue. The service portfolio provides guidance to Service Transition in building, testing and evaluating the service. Change Management authorization is necessary to move a service into the service catalogue.

Service Operation

Service Operation delivers the service in the service catalogue part of the service portfolio. SPM provides them with an understanding of the services and how and why they need to be delivered.

Continual Service Improvement (CSI)

CSI evaluates whether the services in the portfolio met the stated objectives, and if not identifies ways in which the situation can be rectified. CSI also evaluates the business cases and objectives to ensure that they are still valid, and therefore that SPM continues to prioritize services appropriately.

4.3.4 Process activities, methods, and techniques

SPM consists of four main phases of activity, illustrated in Figure 4.4: *define; analyze; approve; and charter.*

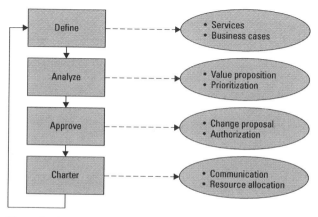

Figure 4.4 Phases of Service Portfolio Management

Process initiation

New services and changes to existing services can be initiated from a number of sources, and in a number of different forms. Changes to plans or the identification of a service improvement plan will often trigger this activity

There are four sub-activities within the process initiation activity.
1. Strategy Management for IT services
2. Business Relationship Management
3. Continual Service Improvement
4. Other service management processes

Process activities

There are four activities within this process:

1. Define

This activity is about defining desired business outcomes, opportunities, utility and warranty requirements and the services themselves.

2. Analyze

The analysis of new or modified services moving between phases of the lifecycle is performed by linking the service to the Service Strategy.

3. Approve: change proposal

The change proposal will allow Change Management to coordinate the activities of all resources required to investigate the customer and infrastructure requirements; and also ensure that these activities are prioritized in relation to other authorized changes already being built, tested, and implemented by the same resources.

4. Service charter

The service charter ensures that all stakeholders, development, testing, and deployment personnel have a common understanding of the cost, timelines, deliverables, and who is involved. The implication of using the term *"charter"* is that the changes will be managed using a project management approach.

4.3.5 Information management

- The service portfolio, service pipeline, service catalogue and retired services
- The project portfolio
- The application portfolio
- The customer portfolio
- The customer agreement portfolio
- Service models
- The service strategy
- The CMS

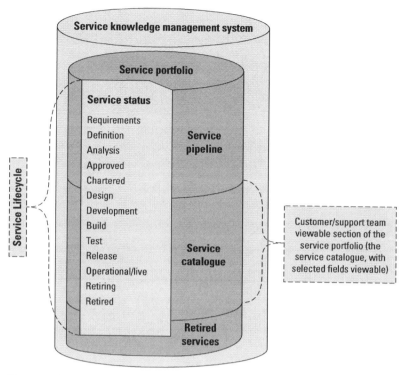

Figure 4.5 Sample contents of the service portfolio

(source: AXELOS)

4.3.6 Interfaces

- Determines which services will be placed into the service catalogue, while Service Catalogue Management performs all the activities required for this to be done.
- **Strategy Management for IT Services** – To define the overall strategy of services, and the objectives for investments.
- **Financial Management for IT Services** – To provide information and tools to enable Service Portfolio Management to perform return on investment (ROI) calculations.
- **Demand Management** – To provide information about the patterns of business activity.
- **BRM** initiates requests and obtains business information and requirements.
- **SLM** – To ensure that services are able to achieve the levels of performance defined.
- **Capacity Management and Availability Management** – To ensure that the capacity and availability requirements of chartered services are designed and built.
- **ITSCM** – To identify the business impact of risks associated with delivering the service, and designs counter-measures and recovery plans.
- **Information Security Management** – To ensure that the confidentiality, integrity, and availability objectives are met.
- **The Supplier Management** process – To indicate that a suppler will no longer be able to supply services or that a supplier relationship is at risk.

- **Change Management** – To evaluates the resources required to introduce new services or changes to existing services.
- **SACM** – To provide the tools, information, and data upon which the service portfolio is based.
- **SVT** – To ensure that the anticipated functionality and returns of each service can be achieved.
- **Knowledge Management** – To enable IT managers and architects to make informed decisions about the best service options.
- **Continual Service Improvement** – To provide feedback about the actual use and return on investment of services against their anticipated use and return on investment.

4.3.7 Triggers
- A new strategy has been devised, or an existing strategy is being changed
- BRM receives a request for a new service or a change to an existing service
- Service improvement opportunities from CSI
- Feedback from design, build and transition teams
- Service Level Management reviews
- Financial Management for IT Services indicates that a service costs significantly more or less than anticipated

4.3.8 Inputs
- Strategy plans
- Service improvement opportunities
- Financial reports
- Requests, suggestions or complaints from the business
- Project updates for services in the charter stage of the process

4.3.9 Outputs
- An up-to-date service portfolio
- Service charters
- Reports on the status of new or changed services
- Reports on the investment made in services in the service portfolio, and the returns on that investment
- Change proposals
- Identified strategic risks and RFC

4.3.10 Critical success factors
- The existence of a formal process to investigate and decide which services to provide
- A model to analyze the potential return on investment and acceptable level of risk for new services or changes to existing services

- The ability to document each service provided, together with the business need it meets and the business outcome it supports
- A formal process to review if services enable the organization to achieve its strategy
- The ability to change services in response to changes in the internal and external environments – where appropriate
- Tools that enable the service provider to track the investment in services throughout their lifecycle
- A formal process exists to evaluate the viability of services, and to retire them when they are no longer viable

4.3.11 Metrics

- The SPM process is audited and reviewed annually and meets its objectives
- Every service has a documented statement of the initial investment made in the service
- Accounting records are produced periodically showing the ongoing investment in each service. The return on investment is calculated
- Customer surveys indicate a high level of satisfaction with the value they are receiving
- Each service has documented risks associated with it. Mitigation or counter-measures have been taken, and where is risk is acceptable
- A service portfolio is used for deciding which services to offer. All services are documented in the service portfolio
- Services are linked to at least one business outcome
- Regular and structured feedback shows the performance of each service and its ability to meet stated business outcomes
- Every change to an environment has a corresponding entry to Service Portfolio Management
- All changed business objectives and outcomes continue to be met by the services in the service portfolio
- Customer surveys show continued high levels of satisfaction
- The investment in each service is quantified in the service portfolio
- Investment in each service is periodically reported from the initial investment

4.3.12 Challenges

- Lack of...
  - access to customer business information
  - a formal project management approach
  - a project portfolio
  - a customer portfolio
  - a customer agreement portfolio
- A service portfolio that only focuses on the service provider aspects of services
- A Change Management process focusing only at the tactical and operational phases

4.3.13 Risks

- Making a decision to offer services without validated or complete information
- Offering services without defining how they will be measured

■ 4.4   FINANCIAL MANAGEMENT FOR IT SERVICES

4.4.1 Introduction

Financial management is a complex process that all organizations use as a basis for conducting business. It is usually owned by a senior executive and managed by a financial management function. Financial management enables the organization to manage its resources, and to ensure that these resources are being used to achieve the organization's objectives.

The IT organization, along with all other departments in the organization, is involved in the organization's financial management process. They apply the organization's financial management procedures and practices to ensure that they are aligned with the organization's objectives and financial policies. In doing so, these departments often create their own financial management processes

In this section, the text will therefore use the term *financial management* as follows:
- **Financial management** – This refers to the generic use of the term
- **Enterprise financial management** – This refers specifically to the process as it is used by the "*corporate*" financial department
- **Financial Management for IT Services** – This refers to the way in which the IT service provider has applied the process

Financial Management for IT Services is the ITIL process responsible for managing an IT service provider's budgeting, accounting and charging requirements. It is also the process that is used to quantify the value that IT services contribute to the business.

More than any other process, financial management enables an IT service provider to play a strategic role in the business. It helps to quantify the value of IT and contributions, and quantifies the business opportunities that IT services enable.

The **purpose** of Financial Management for IT Services is to secure the appropriate level of funding to design, develop, and deliver services that meet the strategy of the organization. Financial Management for IT Services identifies the balance between the cost and quality of service and maintains the balance of supply and demand between the service provider and their customers.

The **objectives** of Financial Management for IT Services include:

- Defining and maintaining a framework to identify, manage and communicate the cost of providing services
- Evaluating the financial impact of new or changed strategies on the service provider
- Securing funding to manage the provision of services
- Facilitating good stewardship of service and customer assets
- Understanding the relationship between expenses and income
- Managing and reporting expenditure on service provision
- Executing the financial policies and practices in the provision of services
- Accounting for money spent on the creation, delivery and support of services
- Forecasting the financial requirements for the organization
- Where appropriate, defining a framework to recover the costs of service provision

Scope

Financial management is normally a well-established and well-understood part of any organization. Professional accountants manage dedicated finance departments, which set financial policies, budgeting procedures, financial reporting standards, accounting practices and revenue generation or cost recovery rules.

Financial management consists of three main processes:

- **Budgeting** – This is the process of predicting and controlling the income and expenditure of money within the organization. Budgeting consists of a periodic negotiation cycle to set budgets and the monthly monitoring of the current budgets
- **Accounting** – This is the process that enables the IT organization to account fully for the way its money is spent. It usually involves accounting systems, including ledgers, charts of accounts, journals etc.
- **Charging** – This is the process required to bill customers for the services supplied to them. This requires sound IT accounting practices and systems

Table 4.2 shows there are two distinct cycles associated with accounting, budgeting and charging:

- A planning cycle (annual), where cost projections and workload forecasting form a basis for cost calculations and price setting
- An operational cycle (monthly or quarterly) where costs are monitored and checked against budgets, bills are issued and revenue collected

Table 4.2 Budgeting, IT accounting and charging cycles

	Budgeting	**IT accounting**	**Charging**
Planning (annual)	Agree overall expenditures	Establish standard unit costs for each IT resource	Establish pricing policy and publish price list
Operational (monthly)	Take actions to manage budget exceptions or changed costs	Monitor expenditure by cost center	Compile and issue bills

Value to the business
Much like their business counterparts, IT organizations are increasingly using financial management to assist in the pursuit of:
- Enhanced decision-making
- Speed of change
- Service Portfolio Management
- Financial compliance and control
- Operational control
- Value capture and creation

Specific benefits to the business include:
- The ability to conduct business in a financially responsible manner and to comply with regulatory and legislative requirements and generally accepted accounting principles
- Accurate planning and forecasting of the budget needed to cover the cost of services
- An understanding of the cost of IT to each business unit
- Better matching of IT services to business outcomes
- The ability to make sound business decisions regarding the use of and investment in IT

4.4.2 Policies, principles, and basic concepts
Enterprise financial management policies
The enterprise financial management policies provide a framework within which IT must work to manage all financial aspects of its services and organization.

Funding
Funding is the sourcing and allocation of money for a specific purpose or project. Funding comes from two sources, external and internal.

Compliance
Compliance relates to the ability to demonstrate that proper and consistent accounting methods and/or practices are being employed. It is important that enterprise financial management policies clearly outline what legislative and other regulatory requirements apply to the service provider and customer's organization.

4.4.3 Process activities, methods, and techniques
There are three main activities within the financial management process: accounting, budgeting and charging.

1. Accounting
Accounting is the process responsible for identifying the actual costs of delivering IT services, comparing these with budgeted costs, and managing variance from the budget. Accounting is also responsible for tracking any income earned by services.

Cost model

A cost model is a framework which allows the service provider to determine the costs of providing services and ensure that they are allocated correctly. Cost models enable the service provider to understand, for example, the impact of proposed changes to the current service. An organization may use any of the following examples of cost models:

- Cost by IT organization
- Cost by service
- Cost by customer
- Cost by location
- Hybrid cost models

Cost centers & cost units

- In the context of cost models and accounting systems, a cost center is anything to which a cost can be allocated.
- A cost unit is the lowest level category to which costs will be allocated. They are (usually) easily measured and communicated in customer terms.

Cost types & cost elements

Cost types are the highest level of category to which costs are assigned in budgeting and accounting – for example, hardware, software, people, consulting services and facilities.

Cost elements are the sub-categories to which costs are assigned in budgeting and accounting. Cost elements are sub-categories of cost types. For example, a cost type of "*people*" could have cost elements of payroll, staff benefits, expenses, training, overtime etc. In general, cost elements are the same as budget line items where the purpose of the model is simple recovery of costs.

Cost classification

There are six major classifications, grouped in three pairs of options. A special type of cost classification (depreciation) is also discussed.

- Capital or operational
- Direct or indirect
- Fixed or variable
- Depreciation

Chart of accounts

The chart of accounts is a list of all the accounts that are used to record income and expenses.

Analysis & reporting

Amongst many other objectives, the analysis and reporting activity is used to generate an organization-wide understanding of the income, expenses, and investments of the service provider. This activity, through the reporting aspects, communicates the cost of services to all stakeholders.

Action plans

Action plans, normally short term, aim at restoring the organization to its planned path within a specified period, usually a month or a quarter. Action plans may assist stakeholders in agreeing to change the original plans and its targets.

2. Budgeting

Budgeting is the activity of predicting and controlling the spending of money. Budgeting consists of a periodic negotiation cycle to set future budgets (usually annual) and the routine monitoring and adjusting of current budgets.

There are five sub-activities within the budgeting activity:
1. Analysis of previous budget
2. Assessment of plans
3. Specification of changes to funding and spending
4. Cost and income estimation
5. Creating the budget(s)

3. Charging

Charging is the activity whereby payment is required for services delivered. For internal service providers charging is optional, and many organizations choose to treat their IT service provider as a cost center. In this situation charging is often referred to as "*chargeback*" since the costs of the service provider are simply re-allocated back to other business units by the central financial function, using an internal charging method.

Unless the IT service organization has the support of the whole organization in introducing charging, it will fail. It has to be simple, fair, and realistic.

There are three sub-activities within the charging activity.
1. Charging policies
   There are two possible charging policies in determining how charging will work and both are defined by enterprise financial management.
   * The first policy decision is whether or not to charge
   * The second policy decision is the level of cost recovery that needs to be achieved
2. Decide chargeable items
   A chargeable item assists the customer in understanding exactly what they are charged. It also helps to set and then manage expectations about the level of service that will be received

3. Pricing

The decision regarding how much to charge depends on two things:
- The chargeable item itself
- The expected value of the service sale and trends of consumption

Billing

Billing is a sub-process of charging. There are three main options for billing:
1. No billing
2. Informational billing (notional charging)
3. Billing and collection (real charging)

4.4.4 Information management
- Financial management systems, such as accounting, budgeting and charging systems
- Financial management policies, legislation and regulations
- Financial reporting structures, templates, reports, and spread sheets
- The organization's chart of accounts
- The service knowledge management system

4.4.5 Interfaces
- **All service management processes** – To use financial management to determine the costs and benefits of the process itself
- **Strategy Management for IT Services** – To work with enterprise financial management to determine the financial objectives for the organization
- **SPM** – To provide the service structure which will be used to define cost models, accounting and budgeting systems and the basis for charging
- **BRM** – To provide information about the way in which the business measures the value of services and what they are prepared to pay for services
- **Capacity Management and Availability Management** – To provide valuable information about the various options of technology and service performance
- **Change Management** – To use financial information in determining the financial impact or requirements of changes
- **SACM** – To document financial data about assets and configuration items
- **CSI** – To determine whether the return of a proposed improvement is worth the investment required to make the improvement

4.4.6 Triggers
1. Monthly, quarterly and annual financial reporting cycles
2. Audit reports
3. Requests for financial information from other service management processes
4. Investigation into a new service opportunity
5. The introduction of charging for IT services
6. A request for change

4.4.7 Inputs

- Policies, standards and practices defined by legislation, regulators and enterprise financial managers
- Generally Accepted Accounting Practices (GAAP) and local variations
- All data sources where financial information is stored
- The service portfolio
- Each service management process delivers financial information about spending money, the services involved
- Service, contract, customer, application and project portfolios
- The knowledge management system of the service provider.

4.4.8 Outputs

- Service valuation
- Service investment analysis
- Compliance
- Cost optimization
- Business impact analysis (BIA)
- Planning confidence

4.4.9 Critical success factors

- There is an enterprise-wide framework to identify, manage, and communicate financial information, costs, and associated returns
- Financial Management for IT Services is a key component of evaluating strategies
- Funding is available to support the provision of services
- Good SACM enables stewardship of service- and customer-assets
- The service provider understands the relationship between expenses and income
- Financial reporting to the organization's stakeholders enables them to make sound decisions
- Must be able to account for the money spent on the creation, delivery, and support of services
- Reporting on, and accurately forecasting, the financial requirements

4.4.10 Metrics

- Enterprise financial management has established standards, policies and charts of accounts
- The Financial Management for IT Services framework specifies how services will be accounted for
- Timely and accurate submission of financial reports
- All strategies have a comprehensive analysis of investment and returns
- Review of strategies indicates financial forecasts were accurate to within acceptable margins
- Timely and accurate provision of financial information for service analysis during SPM

- Internal service providers receive the funding required to provide the agreed services
- External service providers are able to sell services at the required levels of profitability
- Funding exists for research and development of new services or improvements initiatives
- Customer and service assets are recorded in the configuration management system
- Regular reports are provided on the costs of services in design, transition, and operation

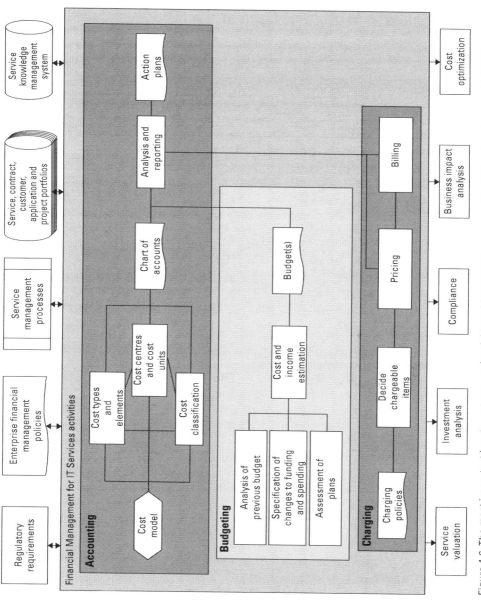

Figure 4.6 The most important inputs, outputs, and activities of Financial Management for IT Services (source: AXELOS)

4.4.11 Challenges

- Financial reporting and cost models focused on infrastructure and applications cost rather than the cost of services
- Complying with enterprise standards and policies
- Focusing on cost saving rather than cost optimization
- In the beginning, it may be difficult to find where financial data is located and how it is controlled
- Internal service providers may find it difficult to introduce charging
- External service providers will need to balance the cost of services with the perceived value of those services to ensure the correct pricing models
- There is funding for research and development into new services or initiatives for improvement
- Customer and service assets are documented in the configuration management system
- On a regular basis reports on the costs of services in the lifecycle phases Service Design, Service Transition and Service Operation.

4.4.12 Risks

- Introducing dedicated financial management processes may be viewed as unnecessary and a waste of money and time
- Not having adequate financial management processes for IT services may expose the organization to penalties for non-compliance with legislative or regulatory compliance
- Lack of available personnel who understand both the world of the service provider and that of cost accounting

■ 4.5 DEMAND MANAGEMENT

4.5.1 Introduction

Demand Management is the process that seeks to understand, anticipate, and influence customer demand for services and the provision of capacity to meet these demands.

Demand Management is a critical aspect of service management. Poorly managed demand is a source of risk for service providers because of uncertainty in demand. Excess capacity generates cost without creating value that provides a basis for cost recovery. Customers are reluctant to pay for idle capacity unless it has value for them.

The **purpose** of Demand Management is to understand, anticipate, and influence customer demand for services and to work with Capacity Management to ensure the service provider has capacity to meet this demand. Demand Management works at every stage of the lifecycle to ensure that services are designed, tested, and delivered to support the achievement of business outcomes at the appropriate levels of activity.

The **objectives** of Demand Management are to:
- Identify and analyze patterns of business activity
- Define and analyze user profiles
- Ensure that services are designed to meet the patterns of business activity
- Work with Capacity Management to ensure that sufficient resources are available at the right time and place
- Anticipate, prevent, or manage situations where demand for a service exceeds the capacity to deliver it
- Balance the utilization of resources to meet the fluctuating levels of demand for those services

Scope

The scope of the Demand Management process is to identify and analyze the patterns of business activity that initiate demand for services, and to identify and analyze how different types of user influence the demand for services.

Demand Management activities should include:
- Identifying and analyzing patterns of business activity associated with services
- Identifying user profiles and analyzing their service usage patterns
- Identifying, agreeing and implementing measures to influence demand

Table 4.3 Comparison of Demand Management and Capacity Management

	Demand Management	Capacity Management
Purpose	Identify, analyze and influence customer demand for services and the capacity to meet this demand	Ensure that current and future capacity requirements of services are provided cost-effectively, and that services are performing at the agreed level
Focus	Anticipating the demand for services based on user profiles and patterns of business activity, and identifying the means to influence that demand to achieve an optimal balance between investment and business outcome achievement	Understanding the current and future requirements for resources and capabilities and ensuring that these are designed, tested and managed to meet the demand on services
Major activities	Identifying patterns of business activity, user profiles, and the resulting demand on services. Anticipating increases or decreases in demand, Influencing demand through incentives, penalties or differential charging	Producing a capacity plan to ensure the investment in the appropriate levels of capacity. Evaluating the impact of new or changed resources and capabilities on existing performance levels

Value to the business

The main value of Demand Management is to achieve a balance between the cost of a service and the value of the business outcomes it supports. Demand Management refines the understanding of how, when and to what level business outcomes, services, resources and capabilities interact.

4.5.2 Policies, principles, and basic concepts

Supply and demand

From a strategic perspective Demand Management is about matching supply to demand. Consumption produces demand and production consumes demand in a highly synchronized pattern. Unlike goods, services cannot be manufactured in advance and stocked in a finished goods inventory.

Gearing service assets

The balance of supply and demand is achieved by gearing the service assets to meet the dynamic patterns of demand on services.

- Identifying the services through the service portfolio
- Quantifying the patterns of business activity
- Specifying the appropriate architecture to deal with the type and quantity of demand
- Working with capacity and availability planning to ensure the right service assets are available at the right time and perform at the right levels
- Performance management and tuning of service assets to deal with variations in demand

4.5.3 Demand Management through the lifecycle

To be fully effective, Demand Management needs to be active throughout the Service Lifecycle. The activities of Demand Management in each stage of the lifecycle will include:

- **Service Strategy** – To identify the services and outcomes, and the patterns of business activity that are generated by achieving these outcomes
- **Service Design** – To confirm customer requirements regarding availability and performance, and validate that the service assets are designed to meet those requirements
- **Service Transition** – Since Demand Management is involved in testing and validating services for forecast utilization and patterns of business activity
- **Service Operation** – Since technical, application, and IT Operations Management functions will monitor service assets and service utilization levels
- **CSI** – Since Demand Management will work to identify trends in patterns of business activity and to initiate improvements to service or customer-assets or to influence customer behaviors

4.5.4 Process activities, methods, and techniques

The most important activities within this process are:

1. Identify sources of demand forecasting

Potential sources of information assisting Demand Management to forecast demand:

- Business plans
- Marketing plans and forecasts
- Production plans

- Sales forecasts
- New product launch plans

Patterns of business activity

Once a pattern of business activity (PBA) has been identified, a PBA profile should be drawn up and details about the PBA documented.

User profiles

User profiles (UP) are based on roles and responsibilities within organizations. Pattern matching using PBA and UP ensure a systematic approach to understanding and managing demand from customers.

Activity-based Demand Management

Business processes are the primary source of demand for services. PBA influence the demand patterns seen by the service providers.

2. Develop differentiated offerings

The analysis of the PBA may reveal that different levels of utility and warranty are needed at different times. Demand Management will work with Service Portfolio Management to define the appropriate service packages.

3. Management of operational demand

This activity works at managing or influencing the demand where live/operational services or resources are being over-utilized.

4.5.5 Information management

- The service portfolio
- The customer portfolio
- The project portfolio
- Minutes of meetings between BRM and customers
- SLA
- The CMS

4.5.6 Interfaces

- **Strategy Management for IT Services** – To identify the key business outcomes and business activities
- **SPM** – To create and evaluate service models, establish and forecast utilization requirements
- **Financial Management for IT Services** – To forecast the cost of providing the demand based on forecast patterns of business activity
- **BRM** – As the primary source of information about the business activities of the customer

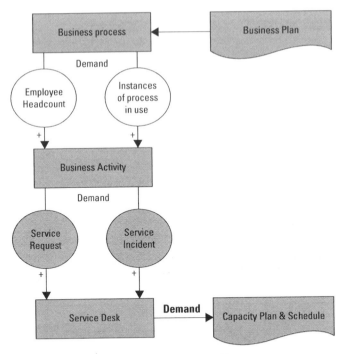

Figure 4.7 Example of activity-based Demand Management

(source: AXELOS)

- **SLM** – To formalize agreements in which the customer commits to levels of utilization, and the service provider commits to levels of performance
- **Capacity Management** – To define exactly how to match supply and demand in the design and operation of the service
- **Availability Management** – To utilize the information about patterns of business activity in determining when service availability is most important
- **ITSCM** – To perform the business impact analysis and determine PBA and UP required during a major outage, crisis, or disaster
- **Change Management** – To assess the impact of changes on how the business uses services
- **SACM** – To identify the relationship between the demand placed on services and the demand placed on systems and devices
- **SVT** – To ensure that the service has correctly dealt with patterns of demand, and that measures taken to prevent over-utilization are effective
- **Event Management** – To provide information about actual patterns of service utilization and validate the anticipated patterns of business activity for a service

4.5.7 Triggers
- A request from a customer for a new service, or change to an existing service
- A new service is being created to meet a strategic initiative
- A service model needs to be defined

- Utilization rates are causing potential performance issues
- An exception has occurred

4.5.8 Inputs
- Initiative to create a new service, or to change an existing service
- Service models
- Patterns of business activity
- The customer portfolio, service portfolio and customer agreement portfolio
- Charging models
- Chargeable items
- Service improvement opportunities and plans

4.5.9 Outputs
- User profiles
- Patterns of business activity
- Policies for management of demand
- Policies for addressing higher or lower, real or anticipated service utilization
- Documentation of options for differentiated offerings

4.5.10 Critical success factors
- Understand levels of demand by identifying and analyzing patterns of business activity
- Understand typical profiles of demand by identifying and analyzing different user profiles
- Services are designed to meet both patterns of business activity and business outcomes
- Working with Capacity Management to ensure that sufficient resources are available at the right place and right time to meet demand

4.5.11 Metrics
- Patterns of business activity
- Each documented user profile that exists contains a demand profile for the services used by that type of user
- Capacity plans include details of patterns of business activity and corresponding workloads
- Utilization monitoring shows balanced workloads
- Capacity plans and service level agreements contain techniques to manage demand

4.5.12 Challenges
- The availability of information about business activities
- Customers might find it difficult to break down individual activities that make sense to the service provider
- Lack of a formal Service Portfolio Management process or service portfolio

4.5.13 Risks
- Lack of, or inaccurate, configuration management information
- Not being able to obtain commitments to minimum or maximum utilization levels

■ 4.6 BUSINESS RELATIONSHIP MANAGEMENT

4.6.1 Introduction
Business Relationship Management (BRM) is the process that enables IT to provide links between the service provider and customers at the strategic and tactical levels. The primary measure of whether this is being achieved is the level of customer satisfaction.

The two primary **goals** of BRM are:
- To establish and maintain a business relationship between the service provider and the customer based on understanding the customer and its business needs
- To identify customer needs and ensure that the service provider is able to meet these needs as business needs change over time and between circumstances

The **objectives** of BRM include:
- Ensure that the provider understands the customer's perspective of service
- Ensure high levels of customer satisfaction
- Establish and maintain a constructive relationship between provider and customer
- Identify changes to the customer environment that could potentially impact services
- Identify technology trends that could potentially impact services provided
- Establish and articulate business requirements for new services or changes to existing services
- Ensure that the provider is meeting the business needs of the customer
- Work with customers to ensure that services and service levels are able to deliver value
- Establish formal complaints and escalation processes

Scope
For internal service providers BRM is typically executed between a senior representative from IT and senior managers from the business units. Here the emphasis is on aligning the objectives of the business with the activity of the service provider.

BRM focuses on understanding how services meet customer requirements.
- Business outcomes that the customer wants to achieve
- Services presently offered
- How customers use services
- How services are provided, including agreed levels and levels of quality
- Technology trends and the potential impact on current and future needs of the business and services

- Levels of customer satisfaction and improvement initiatives to address dissatisfaction
- How to optimize services for the future

Other processes are concerned with customer satisfaction, but they focus on the quality of services and on specific actions they can take to meet customer expectations for those services.

A good example is the difference between BRM and SLM (Service Level Management, see section 5.7). Both these processes involve regular interfaces with customers and both are concerned with ongoing reviews of service and service quality.

Table 4.4 Differences between BRM and SLM

	BRM	SLM
Purpose	To establish and maintain a business relationship between the service provider and the customer based on understanding the customer and its business needs. To identify customer needs (utility and warranty) and ensure that the service provider is able to meet these needs.	To negotiate service level agreements (warranty terms) with customers and ensure that all service management processes, operational level agreements and underpinning contracts are appropriate for the agreed service level targets.
Focus	Strategic and tactical – the focus is on the overall relationship between the service provider and their customer, and which services the service provider will deliver to meet customer needs.	Tactical and operational – the focus is on reaching agreement on the level of service that will be delivered for new and existing services, and whether the service provider was able to meet those agreements.
Primary measure	Customer satisfaction, also an improvement in the customer's intention to better use and pay for the service.	Achieving agreed levels of service (which leads to customer satisfaction).

Value to the business

The value of BRM is in the ability of the service provider to articulate and meet the business needs of its customers. BRM creates a forum for ongoing, structured communication with its customers. This enables BRM to achieve better alignment and integration of services in the future, as well as the ability to achieve the current business outcomes.

4.6.2 Policies, principles, and basic concepts

BRM and the business relationship manager

The process of BRM is often confused with the business relationship manager role. This is because the role is high profile and many customers identify the process activities with the person playing the role.

Table 4.5 BRM process activities and other service management processes

Scenario	Primary process being executed	Other processes involved
Developing high-level customer requirements for a proposed new service	BRM	SPM
Building a business case for a proposed new service	BRM	SPM
Confirming customer's detailed functionality requirements for a new service	Design Coordination	BRM
Confirming a customer requirement for service availability for a new service	SLM	BRM Availability Management
Establishing patterns of business activity	Demand Management	BRM
Evaluating business case for new service request from customer and deciding go/no go	SPM	BRM Financial Management
Report service performance against service level targets	SLM	BRM

Customer portfolio

The customer portfolio is a database or structured document used to record all customers of the IT service provider. The customer portfolio is BRM's view of the customers who receive services from the IT service provider.

Customer agreement portfolio

The customer agreement portfolio is a database or structured document used to manage service contracts or agreements between an IT service provider and its customers. Each IT service delivered to a customer should have a contract or other agreement that is listed in the customer agreement portfolio.

Customer satisfaction

BRM measures customer satisfaction and compares service provider performance with customer satisfaction targets and previous scores. Surveys are the most common form of measuring customer satisfaction. Surveys should be easy to complete in a short time.

Service requirements

BRM is involved in defining and clarifying requirements for services throughout its lifecycle. The main processes involved here are Service Portfolio Management in Service Strategy and Design Coordination and SLM in Service Design.

This type of activity is specialized and will require expertise in business analysis. Customers do not always know how to articulate requirements, especially when they have to be translated into the language and format that the service provider can understand and use to design and build the service, and to define metrics to determine success.

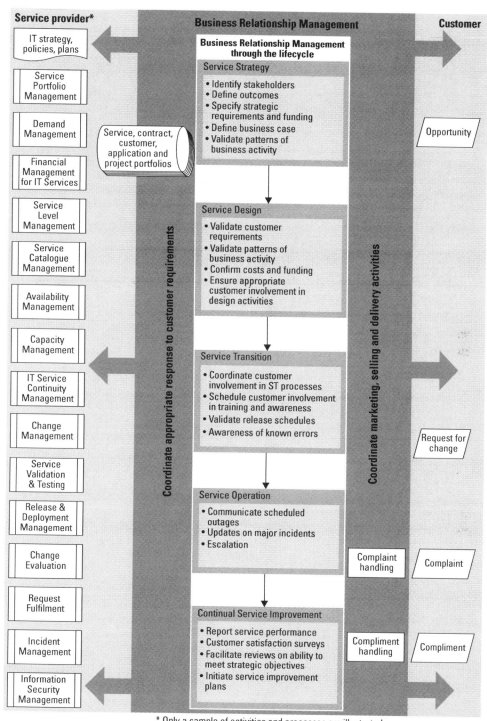

* Only a sample of activities and processes are illustrated

Figure 4.8 Overview of activities in Customer Relation Management

(source: AXELOS)

BRM as facilitator of strategic partnerships

BRM ensures that relevant information about the strategic direction of the customer is communicated to the appropriate people within the service provider organization. This will enable them to re-assess their own strategy, market spaces, future opportunities, and service portfolio.

4.6.3 Process activities, methods, and techniques
The nature of the BRM process

The BRM process consists of activities in every stage of the Service Lifecycle, but it is rarely executed as a single end-to-end process. The exact activities that are executed will depend on the situation that has caused the service provider or customer to initiate the process.

The BRM process has distinct groups and sequences of activities, even if they are not all performed from beginning to end every time the process is initiated. For example, the process can be initiated in the Service Design stage of the lifecycle by SLM, without first going through Service Strategy.

Process initiation

The BRM process is initiated either by the customer or by service management processes and functions.

Initiation by customers

Customers communicate with the service provider about their needs, opportunities, and requirements in a number of ways and for many reasons such as: *an opportunity; a request for change; other requests; a complaint; a compliment*

Initiation by the service provider

The service provider can initiate the BRM process when they require inputs from customers. The supplier may also initiate the process for the creation of a new service or for making changes to an existing service.

4.6.4 The BRM process through the lifecycle

This is the core of the BRM process, which enables the service provider's internal process to align, interface, and, where necessary, integrate with the customer's business. The activities in each stage are not always all executed, and they are not always executed in the same sequence.

Service Strategy

The main areas BRM will work with in this stage are:
- IT strategy, policies and plans
- Service Portfolio Management

- Demand Management
- Financial Management for IT Services

Service Design
- Project management
- Financial Management for IT Services
- SLM
- Demand Management
- Service Catalogue Management
- Availability Management
- Capacity Management
- ITSCM

Service Transition
The BRM will coordinate customer involvement in the processes active during Service Transition. They will ensure all changes/releases meet requirements set by the customer.
- Change Management
- Knowledge Management
- Service Validation & Testing
- Release & Deployment Management
- Change Evaluation

Service Operation
Many organizations feel that once a service has been deployed, the BRM process is no longer required for that service – until a new requirement is raised. This is not true, because this process has also relations with:
- Request Fulfilment
- Incident Management

Continual Service Improvement
Processes and activities that BRM interfaces with in this stage of the Service Lifecycle include:
- Service reporting
- SLM
- Seven-step improvement process

4.6.5 Information management
- The service portfolio
- The project portfolio
- The application portfolio
- The customer portfolio
- The customer agreement portfolio

- The service catalogue
- Customer satisfaction surveys

4.6.6 Interfaces

- **Strategy Management for IT Services** – To identify market spaces with information gleaned from customers
- **SPM** – To identify more detailed requirements and information about the customer environment required to create service models and assess proposed services
- **Financial Management for IT Services** – To obtain information about the financial objectives of the customer and helps the service provider to understand what level of funding or pricing the customer is prepared to accept
- **Demand Management** – To identify and validate patterns of business activity and user profiles
- **SLM** – To use information about customers and service requirements to understand the customer's priorities regarding service performance and deliverables
- **Service Catalogue Management** – To provide the basis for many discussions, reviews and requests that are initiated through BRM
- **Capacity Management and Availability Management** – To process, analyze and understand business outcomes and service requirements
- **ITSCM** – To provide valuable perspectives and information on business priorities and outcomes during a crisis or a disaster
- **Change Management** – To assess the impact and priority of changes
- **RDM** – To ensure the appropriate level of customer involvement with the release activities as well as with SVT and Change Evaluation
- **The 7-step improvement process** – To identity, validate, prioritize and communicate improvement opportunities and plans with the customer

4.6.7 Triggers

- A new strategic initiative
- A new service, or a change to an existing service, has been initiated
- A new opportunity has been identified
- A service has been chartered by Service Portfolio Management
- Customer requests or suggestions
- Customer complaints
- Customer compliment
- A customer meeting has been scheduled
- A customer satisfaction survey has been scheduled

4.6.8 Inputs

- Customer requirements
- Customer requests, complaints, escalations, or compliments
- The service strategy
- The customer's strategy

- The service portfolio
- The project portfolio
- Service level agreements
- Requests for change
- Patterns of business activity and user profiles

4.6.9 Outputs

- Stakeholder definitions
- Defined business outcomes
- Agreement to fund (internal) or pay for (external) services
- The customer portfolio
- Service requirements for strategy, design, and transition
- Published results of customer satisfaction surveys
- Schedules of customer activity in various service management process activities
- Schedule of training and awareness events
- Reports on the customer perception of service performance

4.6.10 Critical success factors

- The ability to document and understand customer requirements of services, and the business outcomes they wish to achieve
- The ability to measure customer satisfaction levels, and action to take with the results
- The ability to identify changes to the customer environment that could potentially impact the type, level or utilization of services provided
- The ability to identify technology trends that could potentially impact the type, level or utilization of services provided
- The ability to establish and articulate business requirements for new services or changes to existing services
- BRM must be able to measure that the service provider is meeting the business needs of the customer
- Formal complaints and escalation processes are available to customers

4.6.11 Metrics

- Business outcomes and customer requirements are documented and signed off
- Customer satisfaction levels are consistently high
- Customer satisfaction and customer retention rates are consistently high
- Changes to services and strategy, creating changes to the customer environment result in improved customer satisfaction scores/higher revenues
- Opportunities leveraging new technologies have been identified with the business and an opportunity's return on investment has been measured
- The service provider is consistently rated above a defined threshold
- Service performance is matched to business outcomes
- Numbers of complaints/escalations are measured and trended over time and by customer

4.6.12 Challenges

- The need to be involved in defining services, and tracking that they are delivered according to the agreed levels of service
- A history of poor service
- Customers not being willing to share requirements, feedback, and opportunities
- Confusion between the role of business relationship manager (BRM) and the process of BRM. Often business relationship managers are needed to do activities in other processes because they have a direct contact with the customer. However these activities are not part of the business relation management process.

4.6.13 Risks

- Confusion about the boundaries with many other processes
- A disconnect between the customer-facing processes and those focusing more on technology

5 Service Design Phase

■ 5.1 INTRODUCTION TO SERVICE DESIGN

Service Design follows the Service Strategy in the Service Lifecycle, and deals with the design and development of new or modified services and their related processes. The Service Design processes are used for two distinct purposes.

Good Service Design offers the following benefits:
- Improved synchronization of services with the needs of the business
- Improved quality of service delivery
- Improved consistency of the service
- Improved effectiveness of performances
- More simplified decision-making
- Improved IT administration
- Simpler implementation of new or modified services
- More effective service management and IT processes
- Reduced Total Cost of Ownership (TCO)

All activities in the design phase of the lifecycle result from the requirements and demands of the customer and they reflect the strategy, planning, and policy as defined in the Service Strategy phase. Each lifecycle phase is an input to the subsequent lifecycle phase. Service Strategy delivers important input for Service Design that subsequently delivers input to the Service Transition phase, and for that reason is the core of the Service Lifecycle.

In order to design effective and efficient services compliant with the customer demands, it is essential the output of other areas and processes be part of the Service Design process. The eight processes within the Service Design phase are (see Figure 5.0):
1. Design Coordination
2. Service Catalogue Management
3. Service Level Management
4. Capacity Management

5. Availability Management
6. ITSCM
7. Information Security Management
8. Supplier Management

Processes in the ITIL lifecycle

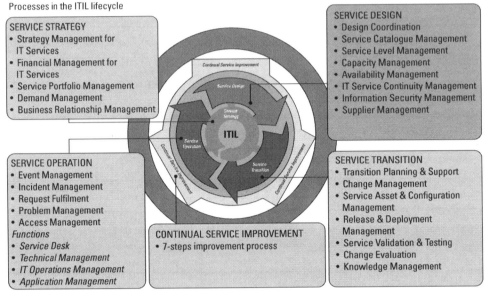

Figure 5.0 The eight processes of Service Design in relation to the ITIL lifecycle

5.1.1 Goal and objectives

The **goal** of the Service Design phase is to design new or modified IT service to realize the strategy of a service provider. It facilitates the introduction of these services into supported environments and it ensures delivery of the services to the required quality, customer satisfaction cost-effective service provision.

The primary **objective** is to design service in such a way, that during their lifecycle minimal improvements are required.

In order to ensure that the services that are developed meet the customer's expectations, the following actions must be undertaken:

- The new service must be documented from the concept phase of the service portfolio and it must be kept up-to-date throughout the process.
- The service level requirements (SLR) must be clearly defined, documented, signed off, and understood by all stakeholders before the service is delivered.
- Based on the SLR, the Capacity Management team can model these requirements within the existing infrastructure to assist in supporting the outputs from the Demand Management process.
- If it appears that a new infrastructure is needed or more support is desired, then financial management must be involved.

- Before the implementation phase begins, a business impact analysis (BIA) and a risk assessment must be performed. This will provide valuable information for ITSCM, Availability Management and Capacity Management.
- The service desk must be brought up to speed regarding the new service delivery before the new services are delivered.
- Service Transition can make a plan for the implementation of the service.
- Supplier Management must be involved if there are purchases to be made.

A holistic approach should be adopted for all aspects of the Service Design phase and related areas to ensure the effective and efficient integration between functions and process activities across the entire IT organization (including all resources and capabilities). By providing a consistent, repeatable, and measurable holistic approach, the IT organization will be better equipped in providing the required end-to-end business-related functionality and quality, thus delivering value to the customers.

To satisfy the changing needs and demands of the business, the design of effective and efficient IT services is a process of balancing among functionality, available resources (human, technical, and financial) and available time. This is a continual process in all phases of the lifecycle of IT services.

The Service Design phase in the lifecycle begins with the demand for new or modified requirements from the customer. Ultimately at the end of the design process, a service solution must be designed that satisfies the requirements before including the service in the transition process. The ultimate output of the design phase is the Service Design package – more on this later in this chapter. Good preparation and an effective and efficient infusion of *personnel, processes, products* (services, technology, and tools) and *partners* – ITIL's four Ps – is necessary if the design plans and projects are to succeed.

Table 5.1 The Four Ps of Service Design

Personnel	Ensure the personnel have the right skills, knowledge, availability, and aptitudes, and display the appropriate attitudes and behaviors
Processes	Review the existing processes to ensure they can support the new or modified service appropriately
Products	Deploy the appropriate service-assets and customer-assets
Partners	Review the existing agreements to ensure they are appropriately aligned to the new or modified service

Considering the mutual dependence of departments, IT services cannot be designed, transitioned, or implemented in isolation. Everyone in the organization must be informed of the underlying components and mutual relationships of IT service delivery (and the related involved departments). This process requires a holistic approach, clear

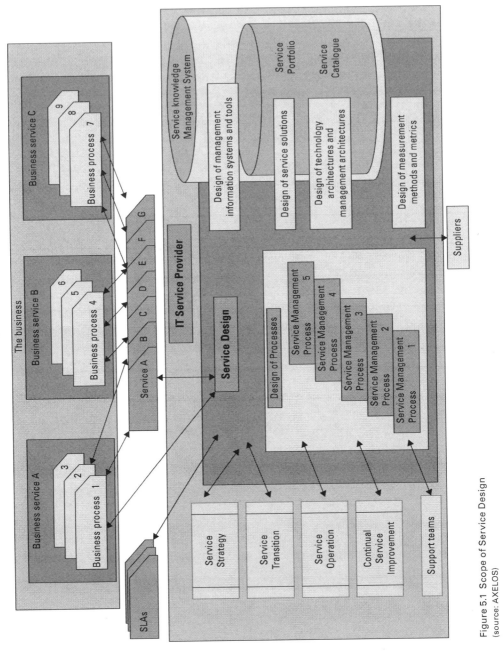

Figure 5.1 Scope of Service Design
(source: AXELOS)

communication, and the requirement that everyone has access to the correct, most recent and unambiguous IT plans, and everyone is provided with the appropriate information.

5.1.2 Scope

Service Design delivers guidelines for the design for fit and innovative services meeting the actual and future business demands. In this phase the IT services/products are identified, defined, and aligned with the business requirements. Figure 5.1 shows the detailed scope of Service Design.

■ 5.2 DESIGN ASPECTS

In order for the organization to strive to attain the highest possible quality with a continual "*improvement focus*" a structured and results-oriented approach is necessary in each of the five separate aspects of design. Results-oriented in this case means aiming "*to satisfy the wishes of the customers/users*". These five aspects are as follows:
1. Service solutions for new or changed services
2. The management information systems and tools, especially the service portfolio
3. The technology architectures and management architectures
4. The processes required
5. The measurement methods and metrics

5.2.1 The design of service solutions for new or changed services
A structured design approach is necessary in order to produce a new service against agreed costs, functionality, and quality and within the agreed time scale. The process must be iterative and incremental in order to satisfy the customers" changing wishes and requirements. The areas that need to be considered within the design of the service solution should include:
■ Analyzing the agreed business requirements
■ Reviewing the existing IT services and infrastructure and producing alternative service solutions, with a view to reusing, repurpose, recycle existing components
■ Budgets and expenditure plans for designing, transitioning, operating and improving the service
■ Timelines to complete design, develop, build, test and deploy the service
■ Reviewing ROI, VOI and TCO (where applicable)
■ Agreeing the preferred solution in terms of planned outcomes and target levels for utility and warranty
■ Ensure alignment with all strategies, policies, plans and architectural documents
■ Completing the following assessment: organizational readiness, risk analysis, risk mitigation, operational, business capability and maturity, IT capability and maturity
■ Alignment of operational level agreements and underpinning contracts with service level requirements

5.2.2 The design of the management information systems and tools, especially the service portfolio
The service portfolio is the most critical management information system used to support all processes and describes a provider's services in terms of business value. It articulates business needs and the provider's response to those needs. By definition, business value terms correspond to market terms, providing a means for comparing service competitiveness across alternative providers.

Like good project management practices, no work should start on a new or modified service until the Service Portfolio Management process has chartered the service. Once a strategic decision to charter a service is made, this is the stage in the Service Lifecycle when Service Design begins: *"designing"* the service, which will eventually become part of the service catalogue.

The service catalogue is essentially a subset of the overall service portfolio. It is organized into a structured database (or document) with information about all the live IT services, including those available for deployment. The service catalogue is the only part of the service portfolio published to customers, and is used to support the sale and delivery of IT services – more on this later in this section.

The service portfolio should contain the information relating to every service and its current status within the organization. The following is an overview of the service portfolio, highlighting the various phases. It is important to note that the customer has an insight only into the service catalogue. The other sections of the portfolio are not available to the customer.

> **Important note: The service portfolio is...**
> * ...owned and managed by the Service Portfolio Management process
> * ...designed during the Service Design phase (see the Service Catalogue Management process)
> * ...created (built/tested/implemented) during the Service Transition phase

5.2.3 The design of the technology and management architectures

The architecture design activities include preparing the blueprints for the development and deployment of an IT infrastructure, the applications, and data (according to the needs of the business). It should be noted that during this design aspect, the provision of quality, high value services is possible only by the personnel, the processes, and the partners that are involved in this production aspect.

The term *"architecture"* is used in various contexts with different meaning. In the context of ITIL, architecture is described *as the fundamental organization of a system, embodied in its components, their relationships to each other and to the environment, and the principles guiding its design and evolution.*

In the above description, the term *"system"* is used in its most general meaning, referring to *a collection of components organized to accomplish a specific function or set of functions.*

Therefore a system can range from the whole organization, to a business function, all the way to an information system. Each system in its own right has its own architecture made up of the following:
- Components of the system
- The relationships between them (such as control interfaces and data exchanges)

- The relationships between the system and its environment (political, organizational, technological, etc.)
- Design principles that inform, guide, and constrain its structure and operation

ITIL describes this architecture design as follows:

> Architecture design is the development and maintenance of IT policy, strategies, architectures, designs, documents, plans, and processes for deployment, implementation, and improvement of appropriate IT services and solutions throughout the organization.

ITIL recommends to design and develop business processes and solutions based on a Service Oriented Architecture (SOA).

Designing the relevant service-related architecture is not simple and varying – sometimes conflicting needs must be taken into account. In any case, it must be ensured that:
- It satisfies the needs of the business, its products and services
- A proper balance is found between innovation, risks and costs
- It conforms to relevant frameworks, strategies, policies, etc.
- There is coordination among the designers, planners, strategists, etc.

Every enterprise is a complex system of functions, processes, structures, and information sources. The architecture of the enterprise must offer insights into how these matters connect with each other in order to achieve the enterprise objectives. The enterprise architecture is, in its own right, both large and complex.

There are various frameworks for the development of enterprise architectures. The enterprise architecture must include the following elements:
- Service Architecture
- Application Architecture
- Information Architecture
- IT Infrastructure Architecture
  - Product architecture
  - Management architecture
- Environment Architecture

In addition to a technical component (applications, system software, information and data, infrastructure and environment systems), a management architecture must also be developed. In this regard, there are five elements that must be taken into consideration, namely: the business sector/industry (needs, requirements), personnel, processes, tools, and technology (IT products that are used in providing the services). It is important that the technology is not the primary focus, but rather the wishes and requirements of the customer.

Within the framework described earlier, it is possible to identify (at least) three architectural roles. These could all report to a senior *"enterprise architect"* in the organization:

Business/organizational architect – this role is concerned with...
- The business models, the business processes and the organizational design
- The structural and functional components of the organization and their relationship
- How the business functions and activities of the organization are distributed among them
- The governance of the organization and the roles and responsibilities required

Service architect – this role is concerned with...
- The service, the data and the application architectures
- The logical architectures supporting the business
- The relationships between logical architectures

IT infrastructure architect – this role is concerned with...
- The physical technology model
- The infrastructure components and their relationships
- The choices for technologies, interfaces and protocols
- The selection of products to implement the infrastructure

5.2.4 The design of the processes required

Working with defined processes is the basis of ITIL. By defining what the activities are and what the input and output are, it is possible to work more efficiently and effectively, and especially in a more customer-oriented way. By assessing these processes, the organization can enhance its efficiency and effectiveness even further. The next step is to establish norms and standards. In this way the organization can link the quality requirements with the output. This approach corresponds with Deming's *Plan-Do–Check–Act* Management Cycle.

Every process must have a process owner who is responsible for the process and for its improvement. Service Design offers the process owner support in the design process by standardizing terms and templates and ensuring that processes are consistent and are integrated.

Additionally it is crucial that the roles and responsibilities are clearly defined. One of the possible models that can be helpful in this regard is the RACI model; see Chapter 2.

5.2.5 The design of measurement methods and metrics

In order to lead and manage the development process effectively, regular assessments must be performed. The selected assessment system must be synchronized with the capacity and maturity of the processes that are assessed. Care should be taken as it will affect the behavior of delivering the service. Immature processes are not capable of supporting refined assessments. There are four elements that can be investigated, namely **progress, fulfilment, effectiveness,** and **efficiency** of the process. As the processes develop over time, the units of measure also must develop. Therefore, the emphasis in mature processes is more on the assessment of efficiency and effectiveness.

The reasons to measure are to direct, to justify, to intervene, and to validate. Additional information can be found in the chapter on Continual Service Improvement.

■ 5.3   DESIGN ACTIVITIES

5.3.1 Development of requirements

For each system there are three types of requirements:

1. **Functional requirements** – They describe what is necessary to support a certain business function or process (Procurement, Marketing, Operation, etc.). Functional requirements have a relation with the utility aspects of a service.

2. **Management and operational requirements** – They describe the non-functional requirements of ITSM. The requirements serve as a basis for the first systems, the estimation of costs and support for the viability of the proposed service. Management and operational requirements are related to the warranty aspects of a service.

3. **Usability requirements** – These requirements relate to a large number of quality aspects: manageability, efficiency, availability and reliability, capacity and performance, security, installation, continuity, controllability, maintainability, operability, measurability and ability to report.

These requirements ensure that the services satisfy the expectations of the users in terms of ease of use and user-friendliness.

Requirement investigation

There are various investigation techniques for arriving at clearer requirements. Considering that customers are often unsure about the requirements, the support of a developer is sometimes necessary. This person must be aware of the fact that people may see him/her as *"someone from the IT department"*, which dictates the requirements. A certain amount of care is therefore needed.

5.3.2 Problems in the development of requirements

There are various problems that can occur in developing requirements:

■ Lack of relevance to the objectives of the service
■ Lack of clarity or ambiguity in the wording
■ Duplication between requirements

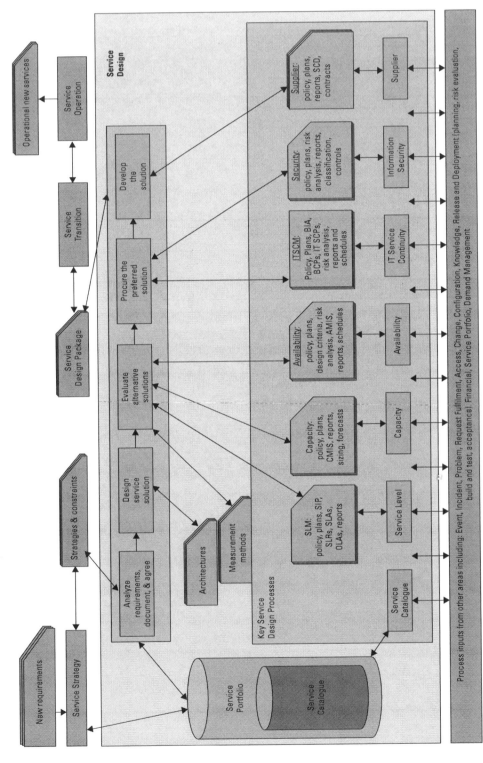

Figure 5.2 Process scheme of Service Design (based on source: AXELOS)

- Conflicts between requirements
- Uncertainty on the part of users
- Inconsistent levels of detail

In order to face these and other problems, it is important to appoint participants. Three groups need to be involved in the establishment of requirements: the customer, the end-user community, and the service development team.

Documenting requirements

The requirements document is the core of the process. This document contains every individual requirement in a standard template. The requirements that eventually come from the users must also be included. Every requirement must be SMART (*Specific, Measureable, Achievable/Appropriate, Realistic/Relevant and Timely/Time-bounded* formulated. In addition, they should be checked to make sure they are clear, unambiguous, and reasonable, synchronized with the customer's objectives, and not in conflict with any of the other requirements.

The result can then be recorded in the requirements catalogue. This should be a component of the requirements portfolio in the overall service portfolio. The end-user requirements should be included here and labelled with an identification number, the source, the owner, the priority (e.g.: according to the MoSCoW approach: *must have, should have, could have, won't have*), description, involved business process, and so on.

The requirements analysis is an iterative process. In other words, the requirements change during the course of the development process of the service. It is therefore also important that the users are involved throughout the entire process.

Following the design of the required service solution, the next steps are the following activities in the Service Design phase before the solution is moved forward to the Service Transition phase.

- Evaluation of the alternative service designs
- Designing the service solutions

5.3.3 Evaluation of alternative solutions

If external supplier services and solutions are involved additional evaluations may be necessary.

- Selecting a set of suppliers and completing a tendering process
- Evaluation and review of supplier responses and selection of the preferred supplier(s) and their proposed solution(s)
- Evaluation and costing of the alternative designs

Where external suppliers are involved in the preferred solution, the organization must:

- Complete all necessary checks on the preferred supplier
- Finalize the terms and conditions of any new contracts
- Procure the selected solution

5.3.4 Developing the service solution

The development phase consists of translating the service design into a plan. Dependent on the scope and scale of the new or modified service, a program, or project approach may be required. Regardless of the method used, the plan/project/program will be responsible for delivering one or more components of the service. This may include:

- Business needs/requirements
- The strategy for the development and/or acquisition of the solution
- The timescales involved
- The resources required, funding, architectures, applications, information, and personnel
- The development of all constituent components of the service, including management mechanisms, such as measurement, monitoring and reporting
- All test plans

Table 5.2 IT services delivery strategies

Delivery strategy	Characteristics	Advantages	Disadvantages
In-sourcing	Internal capacities are used for the design, development, maintenance, execution, and/or offer of support for the service.	− Direct control − Freedom of choice − Rapid prototyping of leading-edge services − Familiar policies and processes − Company-specific knowledge	− Scale limitations − Cost/time to market for services readily available outside − Dependent on internal resources, skills/competences
Outsourcing	Engaging an external organization for the design, development, maintenance, execution, and/or offering of support of the service.	− Economies of scale − Purchased expertise − Focus on company core competences − Test drive/trial of new services	− Less direct control − Exit barriers − Solvency risk of suppliers − Unknown supplier skills and competences − More challenging business process integration − Increased governance
Co-sourcing or multi-sourcing	Often a combination of insourcing and outsourcing, using a number of organizations. Generally involves external organizations working together in designing, developing, transitioning, maintaining, operating, and/or supporting a portion of a service.	− Time to market − Leveraged expertise − Control − Use of specialized providers	− Project complexity − Intellectual property and copyright protection − Culture clash between companies

Delivery strategy	Characteristics	Advantages	Disadvantages
Business process outsourcing (BPO)	An external organization takes over a business process, or part of one, at a cheaper location, e.g.: a call center.	– Single point of responsibility – "One-stop shop" – Access to specialist skills – Risk transferred to the outsourcer – Low-cost location	– Culture clash between companies – Loss of business knowledge – Loss of relationship with the business
Application service provision	Computer-based services are offered to the customer over a network.	– Access to expensive and complex solutions – Low-cost location – Support and upgrades included – Security and ITSCM options included	– Culture clash between companies – Access to facilities only, not knowledge – Often usage-based charging models
Knowledge process outsourcing (KPO)	This goes one step further than BPO, and rather than offering knowledge of a (part of a) process, knowledge of an entire work area is offered.	– Access to specialist skills, knowledge and expertise – Low-cost location – Significant cost savings	– Culture clash between companies – Loss of internal expertise – Loss of relationship with the business
The Cloud	Cloud service providers offer specific pre-defined services, usually on-demand. These services can be offered internally, but generally refer to outsourced service provision.	– Services are easily defined – Sourcing is straightforward – Mapping between the service and business outcome is relatively straightforward – Greater customer control of the service	– Internal clouds are still complex – Focus could mask the relationship between IT activities and business outcomes – Difficulty coordinating insourced offerings with external cloud services – Security of information business continuity management
Multi-vendor sourcing	This type of sourcing involves sourcing different sources from different vendors, often representing different sourcing options from the above.	– Less risk in that the organization is not tied to a single vendor – Leverage of specialized skills in different organizations ensures a more complete support model	– Difficulty in coordinating activities and services from different vendors – Requires a very clear understanding of the overall value chain and each vendor's role
Partnership	Formal arrangements between two or more organizations to work together on strategic initiatives that leverage critical expertise or market opportunities.	– Time to market – Market expansion/ entrance – Competitive response – Leveraged expertise – Trust, alignment and mutual benefit – "Risk and reward" agreements	– Project complexity – Intellectual property and copyright protection – Culture clash between companies

Good project management practices should be used to ensure that conflict is avoided and that the compatible components are developed from the various different development activities.

Although designers are free to design services, it must be understood that they are dependent on internal resources (including available financial resources) and external circumstances (e.g.: the impact of ISO, SOX, and COBIT).

■ 5.4   BASIC CONCEPTS OF SERVICE DESIGN

5.4.1 Delivery options for IT services
The gap (between the current and the desired situation) does not necessarily have to be bridged by the organization itself. There are various strategies that can be considered for outsourcing some or all of the services, each with advantages and disadvantages. The most common of these are summarized in Table 6.4.

The choice of one of the above delivery strategies depends on the specific situation in which the organization finds itself. Various issues play a role in the decision. The organization's available internal capacities and needs and the personnel (culture) have a significant impact on the delivery strategy. Whichever strategy is chosen, it is always essential to assess and review the performances in order to remain ultimately able to satisfy the changing demands of the market.

5.4.2 Application development and management
An application is defined by ITIL as:

> An application is a software program(s) with specific functions that offer direct support to the execution of business processes and/or procedures.

Applications, along with data and infrastructure, comprise the technical component of IT services. It is crucial that the applications that are provided correspond with the requirements of the customer. Organizations often expend a great deal of time on the functional requirements of the new service, while too little time is spent on the design of the management– and operational (non-functional) requirements of the service. This means that when the service is performed, it completely caters to the functional requirements, but not to the expectations of the business and the customer in the area of quality and performance.

Two alternative approaches are necessary to implement the Application Management function, namely:
- **Service Development Lifecycle** – (SDLC) is a systematic problem-solving approach for supporting the development of an IT service.

■ **Application maintenance** – The other approach looks globally at all of the services in order to ensure a continuing process of managing and maintaining the applications. All applications are described consistently in the application portfolio, which is synchronized with the customers" requirements.

Application frameworks

The application framework includes all management– and operational aspects and provides solutions for all of the management– and operational requirements for an application. Architecture-related activities must be planned and managed separately from the individual system-based software projects. Application designers must concentrate on one application, while application framework developers focus on more than one application and on the opportunities.

CASE tools

Development environments traditionally have their own Computer Assisted/Aided Software Engineering tools (CASE) that, for example, offer the means to specify requirements draw design diagrams or generate applications.

Application development

After the design phase, the application must be further developed. Both the application and the environment must be prepared for the launch. The application development phase includes the following issues:

■ Consistent coding conventions
■ Independent structural guidelines for applications
■ Business-ready testing
■ Management checklist for the building phase
■ Organization of the team roles for the structure

Important outputs of application development include:

■ Scripts for starting and stopping an application
■ Scripts for monitoring both hardware– and software configurations
■ Specifications of the unit of measure that can be obtained from the application
■ SLA-objectives and requirements
■ Operational requirements and documentation
■ Support requirements

Rapid Application Development

It is necessary to understand the differences between object-oriented and structured system development and the basic principles of Rapid Application Development (RAD) in order to recognize how the choice of a software solution changes the structure of the lifecycle approach.

Traditional development approaches are based on the principle that the requirements of the customer/client can be determined at the beginning of the lifecycle and that the development costs can be kept under control by managing the changes. RAD–approaches begin with the notion that change is inevitable and that discouraging change simply indicates passivity concerning the market. The RAD–approach is an incremental and iterative development approach.

The **incremental approach** implies that a service is designed bit by bit. Parts are developed separately and are delivered piecemeal. Each piece is supported by one of the business functions and together they support the whole. The big advantage in this approach is its shorter delivery time. The development of each part, however, requires that all phases of the lifecycle are continued.

The **iterative approach** implies that the lifecycle is repeated many times through the design. Prototypes of the entire process are used in order to understand the customer-specific requirements better, after which the design is adapted to it.

A combination of the two approaches is possible. An organization can begin by specifying the requirements for the entire service, followed by an incremental design and the development of the application.

Commercial off-the-shelf solutions

Many organizations choose standard software solutions to satisfy needs and demands. A framework is needed for the selection, modification and implementation of packages of this kind, and it is especially important to know at the outset what requirements are set at management and operational levels. It is equally important, concerning purchasing, to have an understanding of the advantages and disadvantages of such packages.

Besides defining the functional requirements, it is also crucial to determine the requirements concerning the product, the supplier, and the integration of the service package.

Data– and information management

Data is one of the most critical matters that must be kept under control in order to develop, deliver, and support effective IT services. Factors for successful data management include:

- The users have access to the information that they need for their work
- Information is shared in the organization
- The quality of the information is maintained at an acceptable level
- Legal aspects in the areas of privacy, security, and confidentiality are taken into account

If data assets are not effectively managed, there is a risk that people will collect information and data that are not necessary; emphasis will be placed on outdated information; a lot of information is no longer accessible; and information is made accessible to those who are not authorized to have it.

Scope

There are four management areas in the field of data and information management:

- Management of data
- Management of data– and information technology
- Management of information processes
- Management of data standards and policy

Data management and the Service Lifecycle

In order to understand the use of data in business processes, it is recommended that a lifecycle approach is followed that looks into subjects such as:

- What data do we have at this time and how are they classified?
- What data should be collected through the business processes?
- How will the data be stored and maintained?
- How are the data accessed and by whom?
- How are the data disposed of and by whom?
- How is the data quality protected?
- How can the data be made more accessible and available?

Data has an important connotation, not only for organizations for which the provision of data is a core business; consider, for example, a press bureau such as Reuters. Data is increasingly viewed as a common property with a value that can be placed in financial terms. Various opportunities for this exist:

- Valuing data by its availability
- Valuing lost data
- Valuing data by considering the data lifecycle

Classifying data

Data can be classified on three levels:

- Operational data
- Tactical data
- Strategic data

Data owner

Responsibilities of the data owner include:

- Determining who can create, revise, read and delete data
- Consent given regarding the way in which data are stored for modification
- Approving levels of security
- Agreeing business description and a purpose

Data integrity

In defining IT services, it is important that management and operational data requirements are considered. Specifically in the following areas:

- Restoration of lost data
- Controlled access to data
- Implementation of policy on archiving of data
- Periodic monitoring of data integrity

■ 5.5   DESIGN COORDINATION

5.5.1 Introduction

The **purpose** of the Design Coordination process is to ensure the goals and objectives of the Service Design stage are met by providing and maintaining a single point of coordination and control for all activities and processes within this stage of the Service Lifecycle.

The **objectives** of Design Coordination are:

- Ensure the consistent design of appropriate new or changed services, their capabilities, and their resources to meet current and evolving business outcomes and requirements
- Coordinate all design activities across programs, projects, changes, and support teams (internal and external) as well as schedules, resources, and (possibly) conflicts
- Produce Service Design Packages (SDPs) based on service charters and change requests
- Ensure that appropriate service designs and/or SDPs are produced and that they are handed over to Service Transition as agreed
- Manage the quality criteria, requirements and handover points from Service Strategy to Service Design and then to Service Transition
- Ensure that all service models, solution, and designs conform to all strategic, architectural, governance, and other corporate requirements
- Improve the effectiveness and efficiency of service design activities and processes
- Ensure that all parties involved adopt a common framework of standard, reusable design practices in the form of activities, processes and supporting systems
- Monitor and improve the performance of the Service Design lifecycle stage

Scope

The scope of the Design Coordination process includes all design activity, particularly all new or changed service solutions that are being designed for transition into (or out of, in the case of a service retirement) the live environment.

Not every design activity requires the same level of rigor to ensure success, so a significant number of design efforts will require little or no individual attention from the Design Coordination process. Some design efforts could be:

■ Part of a program and/or of a project
■ Handled through the change process
■ Extensive and complex
■ Simple and swift

Each organization should define the criteria that will be used to determine the level of rigor or attention to detail to be applied in Design Coordination for each design. Whatever perspective is adopted by an organization, the end result of the Design Coordination process should result in more successful changes. A successful change delivers the desired business outcomes with minimal disruption or other negative impacts on business operations, at the right level of quality, on time and on budget.

Value for the business
The main value of the Design Coordination process to the business is the production of a set of consistent quality solution designs and SDPs that will provide the desired business outcomes.

Through the work of Design Coordination organizations can:

■ Achieve the intended business value at acceptable risk and cost levels
■ Minimize rework and unplanned labor costs during later Service Lifecycle stages
■ Support the achievement of higher customer and user satisfaction
■ Ensure that all services conform to a consistent architecture, allowing seamless integration
■ Provide improved focus on service value and business outcomes
■ Develop improved efficiency and effectiveness of all design activities and processes
■ Achieve greater agility and better quality in the design of service solutions, within projects and major changes

Service Design Package
During the Service Design phase, Design Coordination is responsible for the production of Service Design Packages (SDP). The SDP is the documentation of all aspects of the service including the requirements in each lifecycle phase. This information is especially of importance for the Service Transition team. Examples of these documents are:

■ Business requirements
■ Functional requirements
■ Service level requirements
■ Management requirements
■ Organizational readiness test
■ Service transition plan (how to build, test, and roll out)

- Acceptation plan for Service Operation
- Service Operational acceptation plan (How to make the service operational?)

A SDP is produced for each new IT service, major change, or IT service retirement.

5.5.2 Activities, methods, and techniques

Design Coordination activities fall into two categories: overall lifecycle stage activities and individual design activities.

Overall lifecycle stage activities should include:
1. Define and maintain policies and methods
2. Plan design resources and capabilities
3. Coordinate design activities
4. Manage design risks and issues
5. Improve service design

Individual design activities should include:
1. Plan individual designs
2. Coordinate individual designs
3. Monitor individual designs
4. Review designs and ensure handover of SDP

The following work occurs during the Service Design stage and should be coordinated by the Design Coordination process:
- Requirements collection, analysis and engineering to ensure that
  - Business requirements, service provider, and technical requirements are clearly documented and agreed
  - They all support the business requirements correctly
- Design of all appropriate aspects of the service solutions
- Review, revision, and maintenance of all processes involved in Service Design, including designs, plans, architectures, policies, and documentation
- Production and maintenance of IT policies and design documents
- Review/revision of design documents for completeness and adherence to standards
- Planning for the deployment and implementation of IT strategies using *"roadmaps"*, programs, and project plans
- Risk assessment and management of all design processes and deliverables
- Ensuring alignment with all corporate and IT strategies and policies
- Production of service designs and/or SDP for new or changed services

5.5.3 Information management

The key information generated by the Design Coordination process is included in the SDP, which contains everything necessary to take the service through all other stages of the Service Lifecycle. The SDP may consist of multiple documents which should be

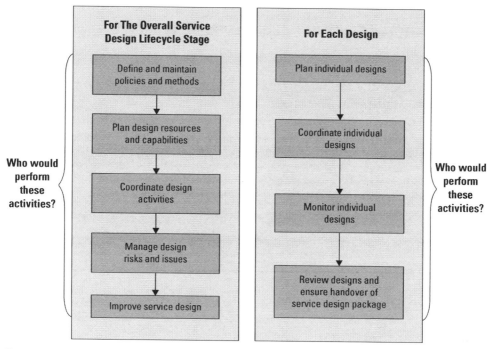

Figure 5.3 Activities within the Design Coordination process

(source: AXELOS)

included in the overall service knowledge management system (SKMS), and described by information in the CMS.

5.5.4 Interfaces

- **Service Strategy** – using information contained within the IT strategy and service portfolio
- **Service Transition** – with the handover of the design of service solutions within the SDP
- **Service Portfolio Management** – Provides the service charter and all associated documentation such as business requirements, requirements for service utility and warranty, risks, and priorities.
- **Change Management** – Collaboratively defined policies and consistent practices
- **Financial Management for IT Services** – Provides details of the value proposition for the new or changed service as well as budgets available.
- **BRM** – Provides intelligence and information regarding the business's required outcomes, customer needs and priorities, and serves as the interface with the customer at a strategic level
- **Transition Planning & Support**
  - Design Coordination provides the SDP to the Service Transition stage

- Transition Planning & Support carries out the overall planning and coordination for the Service Transition stage, in the same way that Design Coordination does for Service Design.
- **Strategy Management for IT Services** – Provides information about the current and evolving Service Strategy to ensure that design guidelines and documentation remain aligned with the strategy over time
- **RDM** – Manages the planning and execution of individual authorized changes, releases, and deployments. Planning and design for Release & Deployment is carried out during Service Design
- **SVT** – Plans and executes tests to ensure that the service matches its design specification and will meet the needs of the business
- **Change Evaluation** – Determines the performance of a service change. This includes evaluation of the service design to ensure it is able to meet the intended requirements
- **SLM** – Responsible for defining and agreeing the service level requirements for new or changed services, which must be done in a consistent manner according to practices developed cooperatively with Design Coordination
- **Availability Management, Capacity Management, ITSCM and Information Security Management processes** – Each of these processes is actively involved in Service Design and must perform these design activities consistently, according to practices developed cooperatively with Design Coordination
- **Supplier Management** –Ensures the contributions of suppliers to design activities are properly managed. This process will then build these practices into supplier contracts and agreements as appropriate, and then manage the performance of the suppliers during Service Design

5.5.5 Triggers
Triggers for the Design Coordination process are changes in the business requirements and services, and therefore the main triggers are requests for changes (RFC) and the creation of new programs and projects. Another major trigger for the review of Design Coordination activities would be the revision of the overall IT strategy.

5.5.6 Inputs
- Service charters for new or significantly changed services
- Change requests from any stages of the Service Lifecycle
- Change records and authorized changes
- Business information on their current and future requirements
- Business impact analysis
- Governance requirements
- Corporate, legal and regulatory policies and requirements
- The enterprise architecture
- The IT strategy, including constraints and resource limitations
- The program and project schedules
- The service portfolio

- The service catalogue
- The schedule of changes
- The CMS
- Feedback from all other processes
- Management systems
- Measurement and metrics methods
- Processes

5.5.7 Outputs

- Comprehensive and consistent set of service designs and SDP
- A revised enterprise architecture
- Revised management systems
- Revised measurement and metrics methods
- Revised processes
- Updated service portfolio
- Updated service catalogue
- Updated change records

5.5.8 Critical success factors

- Accurate and consistent SDPs
- Managing conflicting demands for shared resources
- New and changed services meet customer expectations

5.5.9 Metrics

- Reduction in the number of subsequent revisions of the content of SDPs
- Percentage reduction in the re-work required for new or changed service solutions in subsequent lifecycle stages
- Increased satisfaction with the service design activities, within project and staff
- Reduced number of issues caused by conflict for service design resources
- Percentage increase in the number of successful new and changed services in terms of outcomes, quality, cost and timeliness
- Improved effectiveness and efficiency in the Service Design processes, activities and supporting systems
- Reduced number/percentage of emergency change requests submitted by projects
- Percentage increase in the number of transitioned services that consistently achieve the agreed service level targets

5.5.10 Challenges

- Maintaining high quality designs and SDPs consistently across all areas of the business, services and infrastructure
- Ensuring that sufficient time and resources are devoted to Design Coordination activities and that the roles and responsibilities of the process are assigned to the appropriate individuals and/or groups to ensure completion

■ Developing common design practices that produce the desired high-quality designs without introducing unnecessary bureaucracy

5.5.11 Risks
■ Potential lack of skills and knowledge
■ Reluctance of the business to be involved
■ Poor direction and strategy
■ Lack of information on business priorities and impacts
■ Poorly defined requirements and desired outcomes
■ Reluctance of project managers to communicate and get involved
■ Poor communication
■ Lack of involvement from all relevant stakeholders
■ Insufficient interaction with and input from other lifecycle stages
■ Trying to save time and money during the design stage

■ 5.6   SERVICE CATALOGUE MANAGEMENT

5.6.1 Introduction
The **purpose** of Service Catalogue Management (SCM) is to provide a single source of consistent information on all of the agreed services, and ensure that it is widely available to those who are approved to access it.

The **goal** of Service Catalogue Management is the development and upkeep of a service catalogue that contains all accurate details, the status, possible interactions, and mutual dependencies of all current services and those being prepared to run operationally.

Scope
Offering and maintaining accurate information about all services that are in transition or that have been transferred to Service Operation. These will be part of the service catalogue, individually or as service packages.

Value for the business
The service catalogue is the central resource of information on the IT services delivered by the service provider organization. This ensures that all areas of the business can view an accurate, consistent picture of the IT services, their details, and their status. It contains a customer-facing view of the IT services in use, how they are intended to be used, the business processes they enable, and the level of quality of service the customer can expect for each service.

Basic concepts
Over the years, the IT infrastructures of organizations grow at a rapid pace and there may not be a clear picture of the services offered by the organizations and whom they

are offered to. To get a clearer picture, a service portfolio is developed (with a service catalogue as part of it), and maintained.

- **Service portfolio** – The portfolio contains information about each service and its status. As a result, the portfolio describes the entire process, starting with the customer requirements for the development, building, and execution of the service. The service portfolio represents all active and inactive services in the various phases of the lifecycle.
- **Service catalogue** – The catalogue is a subset of the service portfolio and consists only of active and approved services (at retail level) in Service Operation. The catalogue divides services into components. It contains policies, guidelines and responsibilities, as well as prices, service level arrangements and delivery conditions. The customer gets to review the largest part of the service catalogue.

Many organizations integrate and maintain the portfolio and catalogue as a part of their CMS. By defining every service, a Configuration Item (CI) must be defined and, when possible, incorporated into a hierarchy; the organization can relate the incidents and requests for change to the services in question. It is for this reason that changes in both service portfolio and service catalogue must be part of the Change Management process.

The service catalogue can also be used for a business impact analysis (BIA) as part of ITSCM, or as a starting point for the re-distribution of the workload as part of Capacity Management. These benefits justify the investment (in time and money) involved in preparing a service catalogue and making it worthwhile.

Table 5.3 A service catalogue with two views

View	Definition
Business/ customer	This contains details of all the IT services delivered to the customers (customer-facing services), together with relationships to the business units and the business processes that rely on the IT services. This is the customer view of the service catalogue.
Technical/ supporting	This contains details of all the supporting IT services, together with relationships to the customer-facing services they underpin and the components, CI and other supporting services necessary to support the provision of the service to the customers.

Table 5.4 A service catalogue with three views

View	Definition
Wholesale customer	This contains details of all the IT services delivered to wholesale customers (customer-facing services), together with relationships to the customers they support.
Retail customer	This contains details of all the IT services delivered to retail customers (customer-facing services), together with relationships to the customers they support.
Supporting services	This contains details of all the supporting IT services, together with relationships to the customer-facing services they underpin and the components, CI and other supporting services necessary to support the provision of the service to the customers.

5.6.2 Activities, methods, and techniques

The service catalogue is the only resource that contains constant information about all services of the service provider. The catalogue should be accessible to every authorized person.

Activities in this process include:
- Agreeing and documenting a service definition with all relevant parties
- Interfacing with Service Portfolio Management to agree the contents of the service portfolio and service catalogue
- Producing and maintaining an accurate service catalogue and its contents in conjunction with the service portfolio
- Interfacing with the business and ITSCM on the dependencies of business units and their business processes with the supporting IT services, contained within the business service catalogue
- Interfacing with support teams, service providers and configuration management on interfaces and dependencies between IT services and the supporting services, components and CI contained within the *technical/supporting services view* of the service catalogue
- Interfacing with BRM and SLM to ensure that the information is aligned to the business and business process

5.6.3 Information management

The key information for this process is contained within the service catalogue. The Service Portfolio Management, the BRM, and/or the SLM processes are the main sources of information for the service catalogue. The service catalogue is considered a configuration item and thus falls under the scope of the Change Management process. Change Management is discussed later in this book. There are many different approaches to managing service catalogue information including:
- Intranet solutions built by the service provider organization, leveraging technology already in place
- Commercially available solutions designed for Service Catalogue Management
- Solutions that are part of a more comprehensive service management suite

The personnel of the organization will be entitled to view and use portions or the entire service catalogue, based on their job description and their user profile. The user profiles are defined in the Service Strategy phase; they are designed using the Information Security Management and are primarily used by the Access Management process.

This highlights the necessity of good cooperation and coordination of activities between the lifecycle phases and the activities in the four functions (Service Desk, IT Operations Management, Technical Management and Application Management).

5.6.4 Interfaces

- **SPM** – Determines which services will be chartered and therefore move forward for eventual inclusion in the service catalogue, as well as defining critical information regarding each service or potential service, including any agreed service packages and service options
- **BRM** – Ensures that the relationship between the service and the customer(s) who require it is clearly defined in terms of how the service supports the customer(s) needs
- **SACM** – Works collaboratively to ensure that information in the CMS and in the service catalogue are appropriately linked together to provide a consistent, accurate and comprehensive view of the interfaces and dependencies between services, customers, business processes and service assets, and CI
- **SLM** – Negotiates specific levels of service warranty to be delivered, which will be reflected in the service catalogue
- **Demand Management** – Determines how services will be composed into service packages for provisioning and assists Service Catalogue Management in ensuring that these packages are appropriately represented in the service catalogue

5.6.5 Triggers

- The triggers for the Service Catalogue Management process are changes in the business requirements and services, so one of the main triggers is RFC and the Change Management process. This will include new services, changes to existing services or services being retired.

5.6.6 Inputs

- Business information from the organization's business and IT strategy plans and financial plans etc.
- Business impact analysis
- Service portfolio
- CMS
- Feedback from other processes

5.6.7 Outputs

- Documentation and agreement of a *"definition of the service"*
- Updates to the service portfolio
- Updated to the service catalogue

5.6.8 Critical success factors

- Accurate service catalogue
- Business end-user awareness of the services being provided
- IT staff awareness of the technology supporting the services

5.6.9 Metrics

- The number of services recorded and maintained within the service catalogue as a percentage of those being delivered and transitioned in the live environment
- The number of differences discovered between the information from the service catalogue and reality
- Percentage increase in the completeness of the business service catalogue, compared with the operational services
- Percentage increase in the completeness of *the technical/supporting services view* of the service catalogue, compared with the IT components in support of the services
- Access of the service desk to information in support of the services, expressed by the percentage of incidents without the appropriate service-related information

5.6.10 Challenges

- Maintaining an accurate service catalogue as part of a service portfolio, incorporating all catalogue views as part of an overall CMS and SKMS

5.6.11 Risks

- Inaccurate information in the catalogue and it not being under Change Management control
- Poor acceptance of the service catalogue and its use in the operational processes
- Inaccuracy of the information supplied by the business, IT and service portfolio
- Tools and resources needed to keep the information up-to-date
- Poor access to accurate change management information and processes
- Circumvention of the use of the service portfolio and service catalogue
- Information too detailed to maintain accurately or at too high level to be of any value

■ 5.7   SERVICE LEVEL MANAGEMENT

5.7.1 Introduction

The **goal** of the Service Level Management (SLM) process is to ensure that an agreed level of IT service is provided for all current IT services, and that future services are delivered to agreed achievable targets.

The **objectives** of SLM are:

- Defining, documenting, agreeing, monitoring, measuring, reporting and executing a review of the service level
- Delivering and improving the relation and communication with the business and the customers
- Ensuring that specific and measurable targets are being developed
- Monitoring and improving customer satisfaction with the quality of service being delivered

- Ensuring that the IT organization and the customers have a clear and unambiguous expectation of the level of service to be delivered
- Ensuring that proactive measures to improve levels of service delivered are implemented wherever it is cost-justifiable to do so

Scope

SLM represents the IT service provider to the business, and the business to the IT service provider. There is regular bi-directional contact, whereby both the present service and the future service are discussed. SLM has to manage the expectations of both parties (both internal and external). In addition, SLM assures the quality of service delivered meets the expectations of the business.

The SLM process should include the following items:
- Development of business relationships
- Development and management of Operational Level Agreements (OLA)
- Reviewing underpinning supplier contracts
- Proactive prevention of service failures, reduction of service risks and improvement in service quality
- Reporting and managing all services and review of SLA breaches and weaknesses

Value for the business

SLM provides a consistent interface to the business for all service-related issues. It provides the business with the agreed service targets and the desired management information to ensure that those targets have been met. Where targets are breached, SLM should provide feedback on the cause of the breach and details of the actions being taken to prevent the breach recurring.

The SLM process entails planning, coordinating, drafting, agreeing, monitoring, and reporting on service level agreements (SLA), and the ongoing review of service achievements to ensure that the desired and cost-justifiable service quality is maintained and gradually improved.

The SLA is a written agreement between the IT service provider and its customers, defining service targets and the responsibilities of both parties.
On the other hand, an operational level agreement (OLA) is an agreement between an IT service provider and another part of the same organization that assists with the provision of services.

Also part of the SLM is the on-going review of service achievements to ensure that the desired and cost justifiable service quality is maintained and gradually improved.

Table 5.5 Sample overview of realized service level results

Period > Goal	January	February	March	April	May	June	July	August
A								
B								
C								
D								
E								
F								
Legend:								
Goal achieved:								
Goal not achieved:								
Goal threated:								

The Supplier Management process is responsible for reviewing contracts with external suppliers. These are also known as underpinning contracts (UC).

5.7.2 Activities, methods, and techniques
The activities within this process are:
1. Design of SLA Frameworks including defining SLA structure *(service-based SLA; customer-based SLA; multi-level SLA)*
2. Determining, documenting and agreeing on the requirements for new services and production of service level requirements (SLR)
3. Monitoring the performance with regard to the SLA and reporting the outcome
4. Improving customer satisfaction
5. Review and revise underpinning contracts (UC)
6. Produce service reports
7. Reviewing and improving services
8. Review and revise SLA
9. Developing contacts and relations

5.7.3 Information management
- Provides key information on all operational services, their expected targets and the service achievements and breaches for all operational services
- Provides information on the quality of IT service provided to the customer, and information on the customer's expectation and perception of that quality of service

5.7.4 Interfaces
- **BRM** – Ensures that the service provider has a full understanding of the needs and priorities of the business and that customers are appropriately involved/represented in the work of SLM

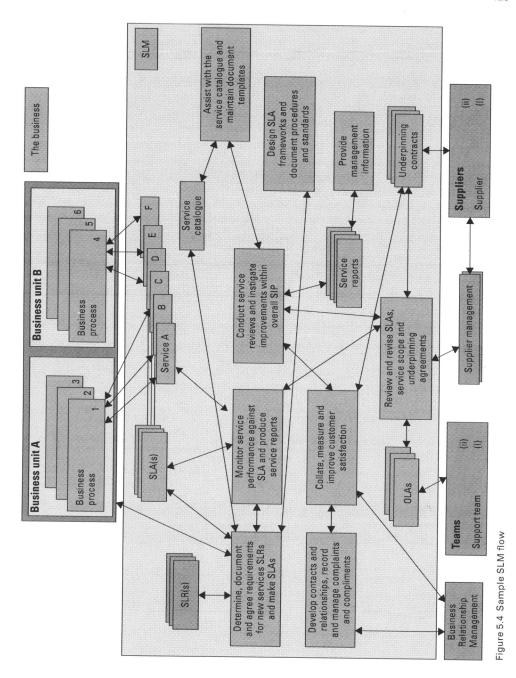

Figure 5.4 Sample SLM flow

- **Service Catalogue Management** – Provides accurate information about services and their interfaces and dependencies to support determining the SLA framework, identifying customers/business units that need to be engaged by SLM and to assist SLM in communicating with customers regarding services provided
- **Incident Management** – Provides critical data to SLM to demonstrate performance against many SLA targets, as well as operating with the fulfilment of SLA targets as

a CSF. SLM negotiates support-related targets such as target restoration times, and then the fulfilment of those targets is embedded into the operation of the Incident Management process

- **Supplier Management** – Works collaboratively with SLM to define, negotiate, document, and agree terms of service with suppliers. Also manages the performance of suppliers and contracts against these terms of service to ensure related SLA targets are met
- **Availability, Capacity, IT Service Continuity and Information Security Management** – These processes contribute to SLM by helping to define service level targets that relate to their area of responsibility and to validate that the targets are realistic. Once targets are agreed, the day-to-day operation of each process ensures achievements match targets
- **Financial Management for IT Services** – Works with SLM to validate the predicted cost of delivering the service levels required by the customer to inform their decision-making process, and to ensure that actual costs are compared to predicted costs as part of overall management of the cost effectiveness of service
- **Design Coordination** – Responsible for ensuring that the overall activities of Service Design are completed successfully. SLM develops agreed SLR and their associated targets

5.7.5 Triggers
- Changes in the service portfolio,
- New or changed agreements, SLR, SLA, OLA, or contracts
- Service review meetings and actions
- Service breaches or threatened breaches
- Customer compliments and complaints
- Periodic activities such as reviewing, reporting and customer satisfaction surveys
- Changes in strategy or policy

5.7.6 Inputs
- Business information arising from the organization's business strategy, plans and financial plans
- Business requirements
- Service portfolio and service catalogue
- Change information
- CMS

5.7.7 Outputs
- Service reports
- Service improvement plan (SIP)
- Service quality plan (SQP)
- Standard document templates

- SLA, SLR and OLA
- Service review meeting minutes

5.7.8 Critical success factors

- Managing the overall quality of IT services required, both in the number and level of services provided and managed
- Delivering the service as previously agreed at affordable costs
- Managing the interface with the business and users

5.7.9 Metrics

Objective metric:

- Number or percentage of service targets being met
- Number and severity of service breaches
- Number of services with up-to-date SLA
- Number of services with timely reports and active service reviews

Subjective metrics:

- Improvements in customer satisfaction

5.7.10 Challenges

- Identifying suitable customer representatives with whom to negotiate
- No previous experience with SLM
- Staff at different levels within the customer community may have different objectives and perceptions

5.7.11 Risks

- A lack of accurate input, involvement and commitment from the business and customers
- Lack of appropriate tools and resources required to agree, document, monitor, report and review agreements and service levels
- The process becomes too bureaucratic
- Problems with access to and support of appropriate and up-to-date CMS and SKMS. Or that the support from these systems is insufficient because they are not kept up-to-date
- Bypassing the SLM process
- Measurements from the business and customer are too difficult to execute, so are not recorded
- Inappropriate business and customer contacts and relationships are developed. This makes it impossible to make and adjust agreements about service delivery
- High customer expectations, but the customer has a low perception of the service offered
- Poor and inappropriate communication with the business and customers

■ 5.8   CAPACITY MANAGEMENT

5.8.1 Introduction

The **goal** of Capacity Management is to ensure that cost-justifiable IT capacity in all areas of IT always exists and is matched to the current and future agreed needs of the business in a timely manner.

Capacity Management is supported initially in Service Strategy where the decisions and analysis of business requirements and customer outcomes influence the development of patterns of business activity (PBA), lines of service (LOS), and Service Level Packages (SLP). This provides the predictive and on-going capacity indicators need to align capacity to demand.

The **objectives** of Capacity Management are:
- Creating and maintaining an up-to-date capacity plan that reflects the current and future needs of the customer
- Internal and external consulting on services in terms of capacity and performance
- Ensuring that the services provided comply with the defined objectives by managing both the performance and the capacity of services
- Contributing to diagnosis of performance and capacity-related incidents and problems
- Investigating the impact of all changes to the capacity plan
- Taking proactive measures to improve performance

Scope

The Capacity Management process should be the focal point for all IT performance and capacity issues. Network and server support or operation management may take on the majority of day-to-day operational duties, but will provide performance information to the Capacity Management process. In addition, Capacity Management also considers space planning and environmental systems capacity. It may also have a task in certain human resource aspects but only where a lack of human resources could result in a breach of OLA or SLA. However, human resource management (HRM) is the main responsibility of line management, though the staffing of a service desk could use identical capacity management techniques.

Capacity Management should have input to the service portfolio and procurement process to ensure that the best deals with IT service providers are negotiated. Capacity Management provides the necessary information on current and planned resource utilization of individual components to enable organizations to decide with confidence:
- Which components to upgrade
- When to upgrade
- How much the upgrade will cost

Capacity Management has a close two-way relationship with Service Strategy since the latter is based on the organization plans, which in turn are derived from the strategy. In other words, it must understand the short, medium, and long-term plans of the organization in order to function properly.

Value for the business

Capacity Management is responsible for planning and scheduling IT resources to provide a consistent service level that matches the current and future requirements of the customer. Capacity Management delivers a capacity plan in consultation with the customer. The plan specifies the IT and financial resources that are necessary to support the business, including a cost justification of expenditure.

The Capacity Management process involves balancing cost against resources needed and balancing supply against demand.

Capacity Management processes and planning must be involved in every phase of the Service Lifecycle, from Service Strategy and Service Design through Service Transition and Service Operation to Continual Service Improvement.

5.8.2 Activities, methods, and techniques

The Capacity Management process consists of:

Proactive activities, such as:
1. Pre-empting performance issues
2. Producing trends of the current component utilization and estimating the future requirements
3. Modeling and trending the predicted changes in IT services and identifying the changes that need to be made to services
4. Ensuring that upgrades are budgeted, planned and implemented
5. Actively seeking to improve service performance wherever it is cost-justifiable
6. Producing and maintaining a capacity plan
7. Tuning (optimizing) the performance of services and components

Reactive activities, such as:
1. Monitoring, measuring, reporting and reviewing
2. Responding to all capacity-related "*threshold*" events and instigating corrective action
3. Reacting to and assisting with specific performance issues

The more proactive the Capacity Management process, the lesser the need for reactive activities. Capacity Management is an extremely technical, complex, and demanding process that comprises three sub-processes (Figure 5.6).

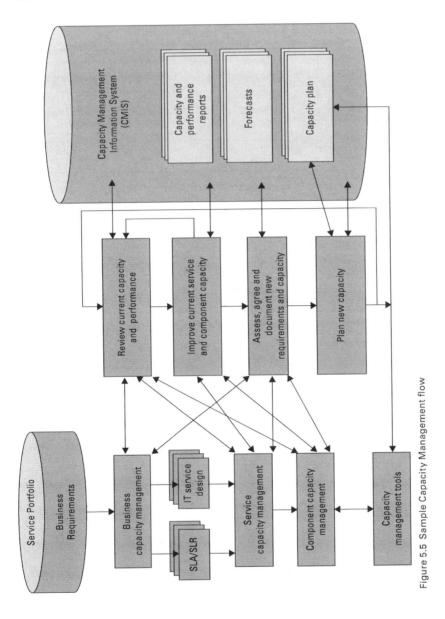

Figure 5.5 Sample Capacity Management flow

1. Business capacity management

The first supports the Design Coordination process by:

- Assisting with agreeing service level requirements
- Designing, procuring, or amending service configuration
- Verifying service level agreements
- Supporting service level agreement negotiation
- Control and implementation

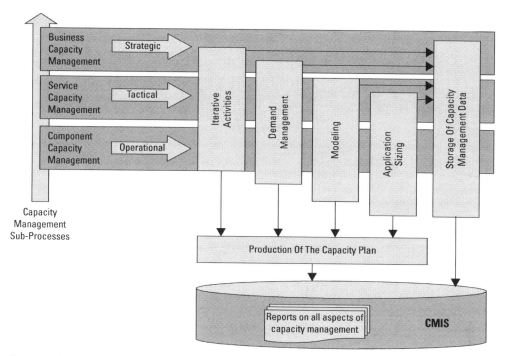

Figure 5.6 Sample sub-processes of Capacity Management

(source: AXELOS)

The second aspects support the Service Operation phase by:

■ Translating business needs and plans into requirements for service and IT infrastructure
■ Ensuring that the future business requirements for IT services are quantified, designed, planned and implemented in a timely fashion
■ Trend, forecast, model or predict future requirements

2. Service capacity management

■ Focuses on the management, control, and prediction of the end-to-end performance, capacity, usage, and workloads live IT services
■ Ensures that the performance of all services is monitored and measured
■ Ensures that the collected data is recorded, analyzed and reported
■ Instigates proactive and reactive action
■ Uses automated thresholds to manage all operational services
■ Ensures threatened or breached service targets are rapidly identified and apply cost-effective actions to reduce or avoid their (potential) impact

3. Component capacity management

■ Focuses on the management, control and prediction of the performance, utilization, and capacity of individual IT technology components
■ Ensures that the performance of all components is monitored and measured

- Ensures that the collected data is recorded, analyzed and reported
- Instigates proactive and reactive action
- Uses automated thresholds to manage all operational components
- Ensures threatened or breached components targets are rapidly identified and apply cost-effective actions to reduce or avoid their (potential) impact

Supporting activities of Capacity Management
Some activities must be executed repeatedly (proactively or reactively). They provide basic information and triggers for other activities and processes in Capacity Management. These activities include:

- Tuning and optimization
- Utilization monitoring
- Response time monitoring
- Analysis
- Implementation
- Exploitation of new technology
- Designing resilience

Capacity Management also includes:

- Threshold management and control
- Demand Management
- Predicting "*the behavior*" of IT services
- Application sizing, estimating the requirements for resources to support proposed changes

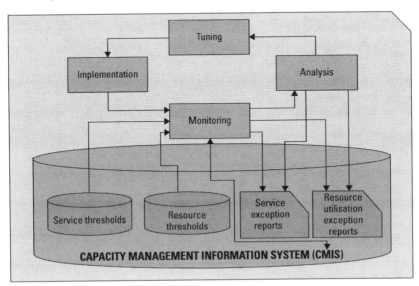

Figure 5.7 Iterative activities in Capacity Management

Design-related activities

The three sub-processes of Capacity Management deliver benefits from researching new technology and in designing resilience into services and infrastructure.

- Exploitation of new technology
- Designing resilience; this is the ability of a configuration item or IT service to resist failure or to recover quickly following a failure

5.8.3 Information management

The Capacity Management process should maintain a Capacity Management Information System (CMIS) that contains all of the measurements and information required to complete the Capacity Management process and provide the appropriate information to the business on the level of IT service provided. This information, covering services, components and supporting services, provides the basis for regular, ad hoc and exception capacity reporting and the identification of trends within the data for the instigation of improvement activities. These activities and the information contained within the CMIS provide the basis for developing the content of the capacity plan.

Capacity Management Information System (CMIS)

- The CMIS is a set of tools, data, and information that is used to support Capacity Management and is the cornerstone of a successful Capacity Management process. The information is stored and analyzed by all the sub-processes of Capacity Management.
- The CMIS is a federated repository that holds a number of different types of data, including business, service, resource, financial, and utilization from all areas of technology. It is part of the CMS.
- The CMIS can be used to record and store selected data and information required to support key activities such as report generation, statistical analysis, and capacity forecasting and planning.

Capacity plan

- In order to provide structure and focus to a wide range of initiatives that may need to be undertaken to improve capacity, a capacity plan should be formulated and maintained. It is recommended that the capacity plan is considered complementary to the availability plan and financial plan, and that publication is aligned with the availability and business budgeting cycle.

5.8.4 Interfaces

- **Availability Management** – To determine the resources needed to meet current and future agreed availability target
- **SLM** – To determine capacity targets, to investigate and resolve capacity-related issues
- **ITSCM** – To assist with the assessment of business impact and risk and determining the capacity needed to support risk reduction measures and recovery options

- **Incident Management and Problem Management** – To assist with incident resolution, problem investigation and justification for addressing capacity-related issues
- **Demand Management** – To anticipate the demand for services based on user profiles and patterns of business activity, and identify ways to influence customer behaviors

5.8.5 Triggers
- New and changed services requiring additional capacity
- Service breaches, capacity or performance events, warnings and alerts
- Exception reports
- Request from SLM to assist with explanation of achievements for capacity and/or performance targets

5.8.6 Inputs
- Business information
- Service and IT information
- Component performance and capacity information
- Service performance issue information
- Service information
- Financial information
- Change information
- Performance information
- CMS
- Workload information

5.8.7 Outputs
- CMIS
- Capacity plan
- Service performance information and reports
- Workload analysis and reports
- Ad hoc capacity and performance reports
- Forecasts and predictive reports
- Thresholds, alerts and events
- Improvement actions

5.8.8 Critical success factors
- Accuracy of business predictions
- Knowledge of current and future technologies
- Ability to demonstrate cost-effectiveness
- Ability to plan and implement appropriate IT capacity to meet business needs

5.8.9 Metrics
- Reduction in business disruption caused by a lack of adequate IT capacity
- Accurate forecasts of planned expenditure

- Percentage accuracy of forecasts of business trends
- Percentage reduction in lost business due to inadequate capacity
- Production of workload forecasts on time
- Increased ability to monitor performance and throughput of services and components
- Timely justification and implementation of new technology
- Reduction in use of old technology
- Reduction in incidents and problems related to inadequate capacity

5.8.10 Challenges

- Persuading the business to provide information on its strategic business plans, to enable the IT service provider organization to provide effective business capacity management
- Combining all of the component capacity management data into an integrated set of information that can be analyzed in a consistent manner
- Difficulty in sifting and analyzing the huge amount of data gathered by Capacity Management

5.8.11 Risks

- A lack of…
  - Commitment from the business to the Capacity Management process
  - Appropriate information from the business on future plans and strategies
  - Senior management commitment
  - Resources and/or budget for the Capacity Management process
- Capacity Management sub-processes conducted in isolation; there is a lack of appropriate and accurate business information
- The processes become too bureaucratic or manually intensive
- Too much focus on one of the sub-processes to the detriment of the others
- The reports and information are too bulky or too technical

■ 5.9   AVAILABILITY MANAGEMENT

5.9.1 Introduction

The **goal** of Availability Management is to ensure that the level of service availability delivered in all services is matched to or exceeds the current and future agreed needs of the business, in a cost effective manner.

Its **objectives** are:

- Creating and maintaining an up-to-date availability plan that reflects the current and future needs of the customer
- Advising on availability-related issues
- Guiding the customer and IT service provider
- Ensuring that availability results meet or exceed the defined requirements

■ Providing assistance in diagnosis and resolution of availability-related incidents and problems
■ Assessing the impact that changes have on the availability plan and the performance and capacity of the services and resources
■ Taking proactive measures to improve availability

Scope
Availability Management includes designing, implementing, measuring, managing, and improving IT services and the components availability. It must understand the service and component availability requirements from the business perspective in terms of the:
■ Current business processes (their operation and requirements)
■ Future business plans and requirements
■ Service targets and the current Service Operation and delivery
■ IT infrastructure, data, applications and the environment (including performance)
■ Business impacts and priorities in relation to the services and their usage

By understanding these issues, Availability Management is able to ensure that all services and components are designed and delivered in order to meet their targets in terms of agreed business need. Availability Management should be applied to all operational services, new, modified, and supporting services. It covers all service aspects that have an impact on availability, such as training, competences, procedures, and tools.

Value for the business
The availability and reliability of IT services has a direct impact on customer satisfaction and company reputation. Availability Management is vital. It should therefore be included (just like Capacity Management) in all stages of the Service Lifecycle.

5.9.2 Activities, methods and techniques
The main activities of Availability Management are:
1. Determining the availability requirements of the business
2. Determining the vital business functions (VBFs). However, the business determines and validates the VBFs
3. Determining the impact of failing components
4. Defining the targets for availability, reliability and maintainability of the IT components
5. Monitoring and analyzing IT components
6. Establishing measures and reporting of availability, reliability, and maintainability that reflect the business user and IT support organization perspectives. At the same time these reports and metrics need to supply sufficient information and support the technical specialists who are responsible for supporting the services to be delivered
7. Investigating the underlying reasons for unacceptable availability
8. Creating and maintaining an availability plan

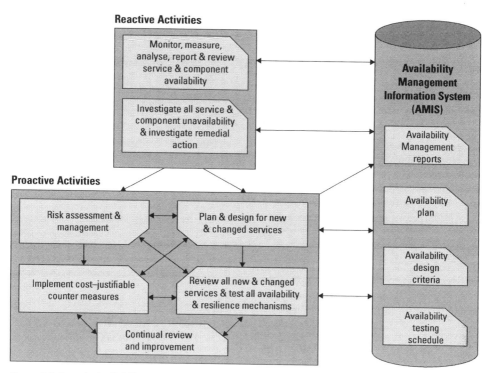

Figure 5.8 Sample Availability Management flow

Availability Management monitors, measures, analyzes, and reports on the following aspects: *Availability, Reliability, Maintainability,* and *Serviceability.*

■ Availability – the service, component or CI ability to perform its agreed function when required. Availability is usually calculated as a percentage. In most cases this calculation is based on the agreed opening hours and failure times

■ Reliability – the length of time a service, component or CI can perform its agreed function without interruption

■ Maintainability – how quickly and effectively a service, component or CI can be restored to normal working after a failure

■ Serviceability – the ability of an external IT service provider to meet the terms of their contract

Measuring is extremely important. It can be done from three perspectives:
■ *Business perspective*
■ *User perspective* and
■ *The IT service provider's perspective*

Availability Management must ensure that all services meet their agreed targets. New or changed services must be designed in such a way that they will meet their agreed targets. To achieve this, Availability Management can perform reactive and proactive activities.

Reactive activities – are executed in the operational phase of the lifecycle:

- Monitoring, measuring, analyzing and reporting the availability of services and components
- Unavailability analysis
- The expanded incident lifecycle
- Service failure analysis (SFA)

Proactive activities – must be executed in the design phase of the lifecycle:

- Identifying vital business functions
- Designing for availability
- Component failure impact analysis (CFIA)
- Single point of failure (SPOF) analysis
- Fault tree analysis (FTA)
- Modeling
- Risk analysis and management
- Availability testing schedule
- Planned and preventive maintenance
- Production of the projected service availability (PSA) document
- Continual review and improvement

Leading principles

Effective Availability Management consists of both reactive and proactive activities. It is important not to lose sight of the following things:

- The availability of services is one of the most important aspects to satisfy customers.
- In the event of failures, an effective response can still result in high customer satisfaction.
- Improving availability is possibly only by understanding how the services support the customer's operations.
- Availability can only be managed as well as the weakest link in the chain.
- It is not just a reactive process, but also – and particularly – proactive.
- It is wiser and more cost-effective to build in the right availability level from the start, i.e.: in the design of new services.

Starting points for Availability Management

Figure 5.9 illustrates a number of starting points for Availability Management. The unavailability of services can be reduced by aiming to reduce each of the phases distinguished in the extended incident lifecycle.

Services must be restored quickly when they are unavailable to users. The **Mean Time to Restore Service (MTRS)** is the time within which a function (service, system, or component) is restored to operational use after a failure. The MTRS depends on a number of factors, such as:

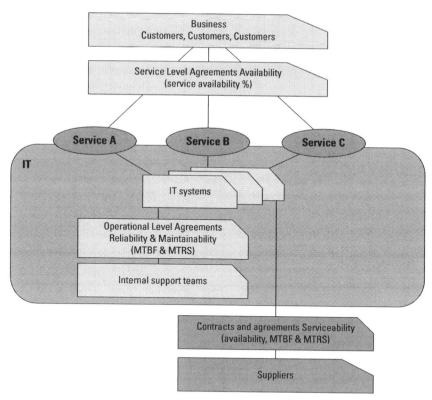

Figure 5.9 Availability terms and measurements

(source: AXELOS)

- Configuration of service assets
- MTRS of individual components
- Competences of support personnel
- Available resources
- Policy plans
- Procedures
- Redundancy

Analysis of the MTRS in relation to each factor is useful to improve the performance and design of services.

Other metrics for measuring availability include:

- **Mean Time Between Failures (MTBF)** – The average time that a CI or service can perform its agreed function without interruption.
- **Mean Time Between Service Incidents (MTBSI)** – The mean time from when a system or service fails, until it next fails.
- **Mean Time To Repair (MTTR)** – The average time taken to repair a CI or service after a failure. MTTR is measured from when the CI or service fails until it is repaired. MTTR does not include the time required to recover or restore.

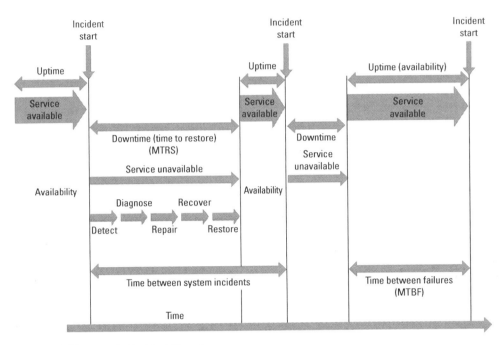

Figure 5.10 The extended incident lifecycle

(source: AXELOS)

Redundancy

Redundancy is a way of increasing reliability and sustainability of systems.

ITIL defines four types of redundancy:

- **Active redundancy** – This type is used to support essential services that absolutely cannot be interrupted. The productive capacity of redundancy assets is always available. With active redundancy all redundant units are operating simultaneously. An example would be a set of "*mirrored*" disks (RAID 1 through x configurations) in a server computer.
- **Passive redundancy** – The use of redundant assets that are left inoperative until the event of a failure (reactive). For example stand-by servers or clustered systems.
- **Diverse redundancy (heterogeneous redundancy)** – Redundancy through various types of service assets that share the same capabilities (spreading the risk). This type is used when the cause of the failure is difficult to predict. For example, use of different storage media, programming languages, or development teams.
- **Homogeneous redundancy** – Refers to using extra capacity of the same type of service assets. With this type there is a high certainty about the causes of failure. For example use of two identical processors.

The active and passive redundancy types can be used individually or in combination with the homogeneous and heterogeneous types. For example: redundancy that is both active and homogeneous has a low tolerance of failure and a high certainty about the causes of failure.

5.9.3 Information management

The Availability Management process should maintain an AMIS that contains all of the measurements and information required to complete the Availability Management process and provide the appropriate information to the business on the level of IT service provided. This information, covering services, components and supporting services, provides the basis for regular, ad hoc and exception availability reporting and the identification of trends within the data for the instigation of improvement activities. These activities and the information contained within the AMIS provide the basis for developing the content of the availability plan.

Availability Management Information System (AMIS)

- The AMIS is a set of tools, data, and information that is used to support and is the cornerstone of a successful Availability Management process. The information is stored and analyzed by all the activities of Availability Management.
- The AMIS is a federated repository that holds a number of different types of data, including business, service, resource, financial, and utilization from all areas of technology. It is part of the CMS.

Availability plan

The availability plan formulates a wide variety of initiatives for improving availability.

The information system constitutes the basis for the availability plan. The availability plan is not the same as an availability management implementation plan, while it can initially be developed jointly with the implementation plan. Availability management changes all the time, which is why the availability plan must contain the following elements:

- Current levels of availability compared against the agreed levels (from the customer's perspective)
- Actions taken to resolve shortcomings in availability
- Details of changed availability requirements for existing and future services
- A forward looking schedule for service failure analysis (SFA) assignments
- Regular review of the SFA assignments
- Benefits and opportunities of planned upgrades

The plan should complement the capacity plan and the financial plan and cover a period of two years. The first six months should be covered in more detail. The plan should be updated with minor revisions every quarter, and major revisions occurring every six months.

5.9.4 Interfaces

- **SLM** – To determine availability targets, to investigate and resolve availability-related issues
- **ITSCM** – To assist with the assessment of business impact and risk and determining the availability needed to support risk reduction metrics and recovery options

ITSCM and Availability Management collaborate on the provision of resilience, fail-over, and recovery mechanisms. Availability Management focuses on normal business operation and ITSCM focuses on the extraordinary interruption of service.

- **Incident Management and Problem Management** – To assist with incident resolution, problem investigation and justification for addressing availability-related issues
- **Demand Management** – To anticipate the demand for services based on user profiles and patterns of business activity, and identify ways to influence customer behaviors
- **Capacity Management** – To support resilience and overall service availability
- **Change Management** – To assist with the creation of the projected service outage report (PSO). The PSO report is a document formulated when a service is expected to be not available (cannot be delivered). For example because of scheduled change, test or recovery activities.
- **Information Security Management** – To define the security measures and policies to include in the design for availability and in the design for recovery. If the data is unavailable, the service is unavailable.
- **Access Management** – To provide the methods for appropriately granting and revoking access

5.9.5 Triggers
- New or changed: business needs, services, targets within agreements, such as SLR, SLA, OLA or contracts
- Service or component breaches, availability events and alerts, including threshold events, exception reports
- Periodic review and revision of Availability Management forecasts, reports and plans; business and IT plans and strategies; and designs and strategies
- Recognition/notification of a change of risk or impact for a business process, VBF, a service, or component
- Request from SLM to assist with explanation of achievements for availability targets

5.9.6 Inputs
- Business information
- Business impact information
- Reports and registers
- Service information
- Financial information
- Change and release information
- SACM
- Service targets
- Component information
- Technology information
- Past performance

- Unavailability and failure information
- Planning information

5.9.7 Outputs
- The AMIS
- The availability plan
- Availability and recovery design criteria
- Reports on the availability, reliability and maintainability of services
- Availability, reliability and maintainability reports of achievements against targets
- Updated risk register
- Monitoring, management and reporting
- Availability management test schedule
- Planned and preventive maintenance schedule
- The PSO
- Revised risk assessment reviews and reports and an updated risk register
- Contributions for the PSO to be created by change in collaboration with Release & Deployment Management
- Details of the proactive availability techniques and measures
- Improvement actions for inclusion within the service improvement plan

5.9.8 Critical success factors
- Managing the availability and reliability of IT services
- Availability of IT infrastructure (as agreed in the SLA) provided at optimal costs
- Satisfying business needs for access to IT services

5.9.9 Metrics
- Percentage reduction in the unavailability of services and components
- Percentage increase in the of reliability of services and components
- Percentage improvement in overall end-to-end availability of service
- Percentage reduction of the cost of unavailability
- Percentage increase in customer satisfaction

5.9.10 Challenges
- Persuading the business to provide information on its strategic business plans, to enable the IT service provider to provide effective availability management
- Combining all of the component availability management data into an integrated set of information that can be analyzed in a consistent manner
- Difficulty in analyzing the huge amount of data gathered by Availability Management
- Determining the components making up the end-to-end service
- Computing end-to-end availability

5.9.11 Risks

- A lack of…
  - Commitment from the business to the Availability Management process
  - Appropriate information from the business on future plans and strategies
  - Senior management commitment
  - Resources and/or budget for the Availability Management process
- Availability Management activities, methods, and techniques conducted in isolation; there is a lack of appropriate and accurate business information
- The processes become too bureaucratic or manually intensive
- Too much focus on component/system versus end-to-end service availability
- The reports and information are too bulky or too technical

■ 5.10 IT SERVICE CONTINUITY MANAGEMENT

5.10.1 Introduction

The **goal** of IT Service Continuity Management (ITSCM) is to support the overall business continuity process by ensuring that the required IT technical and service facilities can be resumed within required and agreed business timescales.

Objectives of ITSCM include:

- Maintaining a set of continuity plans and recovery plans
- Performing regular business impact analysis (BIA)
- Conducting regular risk estimates and management exercises
- Providing advice and guidance to all other areas of the business and IT on all continuity and recovery-related issues
- Ensuring that the appropriate continuity and recovery mechanisms are put in place to meet or exceed the agreed business continuity targets
- Assessing the impact of all changes on the continuity and recovery plans
- Implementing proactive measures to improve the availability of services
- Negotiating agreements with IT service providers in relation to the desired recovery capability to support continuity plans

Scope

ITSCM focuses on those events that the business considers a disaster. The Incident Management process handles less significant events. ITSCM primarily considers the IT assets and configurations that support the business processes. The ITSM is a subset of the overall Business Continuity Management (BCM) strategy.

ITSCM does not usually directly cover longer-term risks such as those from changes in business direction. While these can have a huge impact, there is generally enough time to identify them and take action. Minor technical problems, such as non-critical disk failures, are not covered by this process – they are handled by Incident Management.

ITSCM is about:

- Agreements on ITSCM's scope
- A business impact analysis to quantify the impact of disasters
- Risk analysis (RA); risk identification and risk assessment to identify potential threats to business continuity and the likelihood of the threats becoming reality
- Creating an overall ITSCM strategy that must be integrated into the business continuity management strategy
- Creating continuity plans
- Testing the plans
- On-going operation and maintenance of the plans

Value for the business

ITSCM has a valuable role in supporting the business continuity planning process. Organizations often use it to create awareness of continuity and recovery requirements and justify their decision to implement the process of business continuity planning (including plans).

5.10.2 Activities, methods, and techniques

ITSCM is a cyclic process. It keeps the developed service continuity plans and recovery plans in line with the business continuity plans as these are updated.

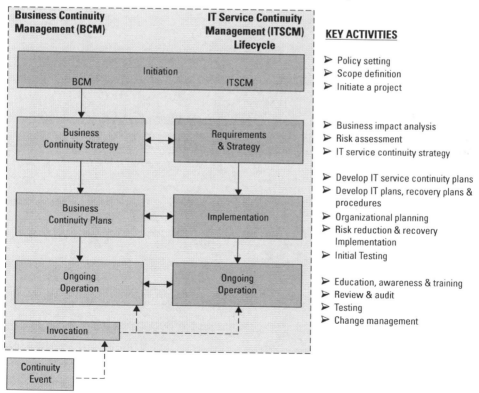

Figure 5.11 The lifecycle of ITSCM in relation to the activities of BCM

The process consists of four phases (Figure 5.11):

1. **Initiation** – This phase covers the entire organization and includes the following activities:
   - Defining the policy
   - Specifying terms of reference and scope
   - Allocating resources (people, resources and funds)
   - Defining the project organization and control structure
   - Agree project and quality plans.

2. **Requirements and strategy** – Determining the business requirements for ITSCM is vital when investigating how well an organization can survive a disaster. This phase includes *requirements* and *strategy*. The *requirements* involve undertaking a business impact analysis and risk analysis:
   - *Requirement 1*: Business Impact Analysis – (BIA) – Its purpose is to quantify the impact caused by the loss of services. If the impact can be determined in detail, it is called "*hard impact*" – e.g.: financial losses. "*Soft impact*" is less easily determined. It represents, for instance, the impact on public relations, morale, and health. The BIA identifies the most important services for the organization and as such provides important input for the strategy. Among other things, the analysis identifies:
     – The type of damage or loss (e.g.: income, reputation)
     – How the damage could escalate
     – The required competences, facilities and services to continue important processes
     – The timeframe within which partial (the most vital processes) and full recovery must occur
     – Determination of recovery periods for every individual service
     – Generally speaking, more preventive measures need to be taken with regards to those processes and services with earlier and higher impacts. Greater emphasis should be placed on continuity and recovery measures for those where the impact is lower and takes longer to develop.
   - *Requirement 2*: Risk estimate – There are various risk analysis and management methods.
     Risk analysis is an assessment of risks that may give rise to service disruption or security violation. Risk management identifies the response and cost-justifiable counter-measures that can be taken.

   A standard method like Management of Risk (M_o_R) can be used to investigate and manage the risks.
   - *Strategy 1*: Risk response measures – Measures to reduce risks must be implemented in combination with Availability Management since failure reduction has an impact on service availability. Measures may include: fault tolerant systems, good IT security controls, and offsite storage.

- *Strategy 2*: ITSCM recovery options – The continuity strategy is a balance between the cost of risk reduction measures and recovery options to support the recovery of critical business processes within agreed timescales. A number of recovery options are possible:
  - *Manual workarounds*: temporary manual solution for a limited period of time
  - *Reciprocal arrangements*: support agreements between parties with similar infrastructures (not used often these days)
  - *Gradual recovery (or cold standby)*: method that makes basic facilities such as accommodation and computer space available at limited costs within several days
  - *Intermediate recovery (warm standby)*: recovery within two to three days, generally based on a prepared facility that is often shared with several other parties
  - *Fast recovery (hot standby)*: recovery within 24 hours that focuses on the main services, involving e.g.: shadow sites that can be operational very quickly and with very low data loss
  - *Immediate recovery (also hot standby)*: option for the immediate recovery of mainly business-critical services with the aid of mirroring techniques, dual sites, and other redundancy solutions; no data loss involved

3. **Implementation** – The ITSCM plans can be created once the strategy is approved. You should remember, however, that the organization structure (leadership and decision-making processes) changes in the event of a disaster recovery process. Set this up around a senior manager generally in charge, with a coordinator below them and the recovery teams below that. Test the plans in full, e.g.: using the following test types:
   - Walkthrough tests
   - Full tests
   - Partial test (e.g.: a single service or server)
   - Scenario test (testing for specific responses/scenarios)

4. **On-going operation** – This phase includes:
   - Education, awareness and training of personnel
   - Review
   - Testing
   - Change Management (ensures that all changes have been assessed for their potential impact)
   - Ultimate test (invocation)

5.10.3 Information management

Information management records all of the information that is required to maintain the ITSCM plans, and aligns the plan with the BCM information.

- The most recent version of the BCM strategy and business impact analysis
- Risks within a risk register including, risk assessment and possible responses to these
- Executed and planned tests
- Details of the ITSCM and related plans
- Existing recovery facilities, suppliers, partners and agreements
- Details on backup and restore processes
- Information from the latest version of the BIA
- Comprehensive information on risk within a risk register, including risk assessment and risk responses
- The latest version of the BCM strategy and business continuity plans

Each critical business area is responsible for the development of a plan detailing the individuals who will be in the recovery teams and the tasks to be undertaken on invocation of recovery arrangements.

5.10.4 Interfaces

- **Change Management** – To assess changes against ITSCM plans and activities. The plan itself must be under Change Management control
- **Incident Management and Problem Management** – Incidents can evolve into major incidents or disasters
- **Availability Management** – To coordinate risk assessment and implementing risk responses
- **SLM** – Recovery requirements will be agreed and documented in the SLA
- **Capacity Management** – To ensure that there are sufficient resources to enable recovery onto replacement computers following a disaster
- **SACM** – The CMS documents the components that make up the infrastructure and the relationship between the components
- **Information Security Management** – A major security breach could be considered a disaster, so security aspects are included when conducting BIA and risk assessment

5.10.5 Triggers

- The occurrence of a major incident that requires assessment for potential invocation of either business or IT continuity plans
- Assessment of changes and attendance at change advisory board meetings
- Lessons learned from previous continuity events and associated recovery activities.
- New or changed: business needs; services; targets within agreements, such as SLR, SLA, OLA or contracts
- Service or component breaches, availability events and alerts, including threshold events, exception reports
- Periodic review and revision of…
  - Business impact analysis
  - Risk assessment activities
  - Results of continuity and recovery testing

- Continuity management forecasts, reports and plans
- Business and IT plans and strategies
- Designs and strategies
■ Recognition/notification of a change of risk or impact for a business process, VBF, a service, or component

5.10.6 Inputs
■ Business information
■ A business continuity strategy and a set of business continuity plans
■ IT information
■ Service information
■ Financial information
■ Change information
■ SACM verification and audit reports
■ Business continuity management and Availability Management testing schedules
■ Capacity Management information
■ IT service continuity plans and test reports from supplier and partners

5.10.7 Outputs
■ Revised ITSCM policy and strategy
■ Business impact analysis exercises and reports
■ Risk analysis and management reviews and reports
■ A set of ITSCM plans
■ Testing schedule
■ Test scenarios
■ Test reports and reviews

5.10.8 Critical success factors
■ IT services are delivered and can be recovered to meet business objectives
■ Awareness throughout the organization of the business and ITSCM plans

5.10.9 Metrics
■ Increase in…
- Validated awareness of business impact, needs and requirements throughout IT
- Successful test results
- Success of regular audits of the ITSCM plans
■ Periodical and regular…
- Validated communication of the ITSCM objectives and responsibilities
- Successful validation that all service recovery targets are agreed, achievable
- Comprehensive testing of ITSCM plans achieved consistently
- Reviews of all plans
■ Overall reduction in the risk and impact of possible failure of IT services

5.10.10 Challenges
- Providing appropriate plans when there is no BCM process
- Changing the perception that continuity is an IT responsibility, and therefore the business assumes IT services will continue to run under any circumstances.
- Alignment and integration with an existing BCM process

5.10.11 Risks
- A lack of…
  - A BCM process
  - Commitment from the business to ITSCM
  - Appropriate information from the business on future plans and strategies
  - Senior management commitment
  - Resources and/or budget for ITSCM
- Too much focus on technology issues to the detriment of the needs and the priorities of the business and/or IT services
- Risk assessment and management conducted in isolation without input from other Service Design processes
- Out of date and/or misalignment of ITSCM plans and information with the business and BCM information and plans
- ITSCM activities, methods, and techniques conducted in isolation; there is a lack of appropriate and accurate business information
- The processes become too bureaucratic or manually intensive
- The reports and information are too bulky or too technical

■ 5.11 INFORMATION SECURITY MANAGEMENT

5.11.1 Introduction
The **goal** of Information Security Management is to align IT and business security and ensure that information security is managed effectively in all services and service management activities.

Its **objectives** of Information Security Management are:
- Information is available and usable when required (availability)
- Information is available exclusively to authorized persons (confidentiality)
- The information is complete, accurate and protected against unauthorized changes (integrity)
- Transactions and information exchange between companies and partners can be trusted (authenticity and non-repudiation)

Scope
Information Security Management needs to understand the total IT and business security environment. This means, among other things:

- The current and future business security policy and plans
- Security requirements
- Legal requirements
- Obligations and responsibilities
- Business and IT risks (and their management)

This enables Information Security Management to manage the current and future security aspects of the business cost effectively. The process should include the following elements:

- Production, maintenance, distribution and enforcement of an information security policy
- Understanding agreed current and future security requirements of the business
- Implementing (and documenting) controls that support the information security policy and manage risks
- Managing IT service providers and contracts concerning access to the system and services
- Management of security breaches and incidents
- Proactive improvement of the security control systems

Value for the business
Information Security Management ensures that the information security policy complies with the overall business security policy of the organization and the requirements of corporate governance. It raises internal awareness of the need for security within all services and assets. Executive management is responsible for the organization's information and is tasked with responding to issues that affect its protection. Boards of directors are expected to make information security an integral part of corporate governance.

Basic concepts
The Information Security Management process and framework include:

- Information security policy
- Information security management system (ISMS)
- Security management information system (SMIS)
- Comprehensive security strategy (related to the business objectives and strategy)
- Effective security organizational structure
- Set of security controls to support the policy
- Risk management
- Monitoring processes
- Communication strategy
- Training and awareness strategy

5.11.2 Activities, methods, and techniques

The key activities within the Information Security Management process are:

- Production and maintenance of an overall information security policy and a set of supporting specific policies
- Communication, implementation and enforcement of the security policies
- Assessment and classification of all information assets and documentation
- Implementation, review, revision and improvement of a set of security controls and risk assessment and responses
- Monitoring and management of all security breaches and major security incidents
- Analysis, reporting, reduction of volumes and impact of security breaches/incidents
- Schedule and completion of security reviews, audits, and penetration tests

Information security management system (ISMS)

The ISMS provides the basis for cost-effective development of an information security program that supports the business objectives. Use the four Ps of Personnel, Processes, Products (including technology), and Partners (including service providers) to ensure high levels of security are in place.

This system will generally consist of:

- An information security policy and specific security policies
- The SMIS
- A comprehensive security strategy
- An effective security organizational structure
- A set of security controls to support the policy
- The management of security risks
- Monitoring processes to ensure compliance and provide feedback on effectiveness
- Communications strategy and plan for security
- Training and awareness strategy and plan

ISO 27001 is the international standard against which organizations may seek certification of their ISMS. Figure 5.13 is based on various recommendations, including ISO 27001, and provides insight into the five elements and their objectives.

Security governance

When IT security governance has been properly implemented it can deliver six outcomes:

1. Strategic alignment (of IT and business)
2. Value delivery
3. Risk management
4. Performance management
5. Resource management
6. Business process assurance

Customers – Requirements – Business Needs

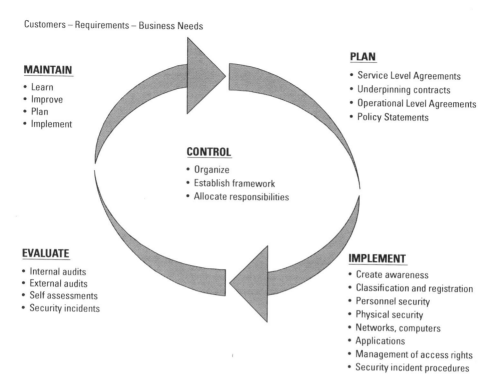

MAINTAIN
- Learn
- Improve
- Plan
- Implement

PLAN
- Service Level Agreements
- Underpinning contracts
- Operational Level Agreements
- Policy Statements

CONTROL
- Organize
- Establish framework
- Allocate responsibilities

EVALUATE
- Internal audits
- External audits
- Self assessments
- Security incidents

IMPLEMENT
- Create awareness
- Classification and registration
- Personnel security
- Physical security
- Networks, computers
- Applications
- Management of access rights
- Security incident procedures

Figure 5.12 Framework for managing IT security

(source: AXELOS)

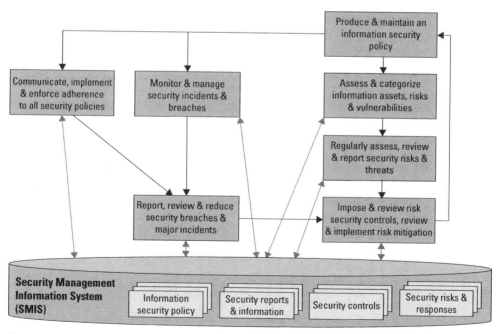

Figure 5.13 Sample security controls for threats and incidents management

(source: AXELOS)

The information security manager must understand that security is not merely a step in the lifecycle and that it cannot be solved by technology alone. Information security must be an integral part of all services (and systems) and is an on-going process that needs to be continually managed. Figure 5.13 describes controls that can be used in the process.

The Figure 5.14 shows that a risk may result in a **threat** that in turn causes an **incident**, the consequence of which is damage.
- **Preventive measures** – prevent effects (e.g.: access management)
- **Reductive measures** – limit effects (e.g.: backup and testing)
- **Detective measures** – detect effects (e.g.: monitoring)
- **Repressive measures** – suppress effects (e.g.: blocking)
- **Corrective measures** – repair effects (e.g.: rollback)

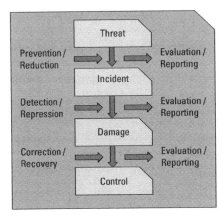

Figure 5.14 Security controls for threats and incidents

(source: AXELOS)

5.11.3 Information management
All the information required by Information Security Management should be contained within the SMIS. This should include all security controls, risks, breaches, processes, and reports necessary to support and maintain the information security policy and the SMIS. The SMIS will also provide the input to security audits and reviews and to the continual improvement activities.
- The SMIS is a set of tools, data, and information that is used to support Information Security Management and is the cornerstone of a successful process.
- The SMIS can be used to record and store selected data and information required to support key activities such as report generation, statistical analysis, and security forecasting and planning.

5.11.4 Interfaces
- **Incident Management and Problem Management** – Information Security Management provides support in the decision-making process relating to and the correction of security incidents and problems

- **SLM** – This provides support for the establishment of security requirements and responsibilities and their inclusion in the SLR and SLA
- **Access Management** – To perform the actions to grant and revoke access and applies the policies defined by Information Security Management
- **Change Management** – Information Security Management supports Change Management in determining the possible impact of changes on security
- **ITSCM** – To collaborate with ITSCM on the assessment of business impact and risk, and the provision of resilience, fail-over and recovery mechanisms
- **SACM** – To provide accurate asset information to assist with security classifications
- **Availability Management** – Data that is unavailable or lacking in integrity compromises the ability of the service to perform its agreed function
- **Capacity Management** – For consideration when procuring and/or introducing any new technology or software
- **Financial Management for IT Services** – To provide adequate funds to finance security requirements
- **Supplier Management** – To assist with the joint management of suppliers and the terms and conditions to be included within contracts concerning supplier security responsibilities
- **Legal and human resources issues** – To investigate security issues. ISM should be integrated with these corporate processes and functions

5.11.5 Triggers

- New or changed:
  - Corporate governance guidelines
  - Business security policy
  - Corporate risk management processes and guidelines
  - Business needs
  - Services
  - Targets within agreements, such as SLR, SLA, OLA or contracts
- Service or component security breaches, security events and alerts, including threshold events, exception reports
- Periodic review and revision of… business and IT plans and strategies; designs
- Recognition/notification of a change of risk or impact for a business process, VBF, a service, or component
- Requests from other areas, particularly SLM for assistance with security issues

5.11.6 Inputs

- Business information
- Corporate governance and business security policies and guidelines
- IT information
- Service information
- Risk analysis processes and reports
- Details of security events and breaches

- Change information
- Information from the configuration management system
- Details of partner and service provider access

5.11.7 Outputs
- Overall Information Security Management policy
- A security management information system (SMIS)
- Revised security risk assessment processes and reports
- Security controls, audits and reports
- Security test schedules and plans
- A set of security classifications
- A set of classified information assets
- Reviews and reports of security breaches and major incidents
- Policies, processes, and procedures for managing partners and suppliers and their access to services and information

5.11.8 Critical success factors
- The business is protected against *security violations*
- Determination of a clear and agreed policy, integrated with the needs of the business
- Security procedures that are justified, appropriate and supported by senior management
- Effective marketing and education in security requirements
- A mechanism for improvement
- An integral part of IT services, ITSM processes, and business security management
- The availability of services is not compromised by security incidents
- Clear ownership and awareness of the security policies among the customer community

5.11.9 Metrics
- Percentage decrease in security breaches
- Percentage decrease in the impact of security breaches and incidents
- Percentage increase in SLA conformance to security clauses
- Decrease in the number of non-conformances with security policy and process
- Increase in the acceptance and conformance of security procedures
- Increased support and commitment of senior management
- Increased awareness of the security policy throughout the organization

5.11.10 Challenges
- Ensuring there is adequate support from the business, business security and senior management
- Changing the perception that continuity is an IT responsibility, and therefore the business assumes IT services will continue to run under any circumstances.
- Alignment and integration with an existing BCM process

5.11.11 Risks
- Risks factors can be both internal and external, including
  - Widespread use of technology
  - Increasing dependence of the business on IT
  - Increasing complexity and interconnectivity of systems
  - Disappearance of the traditional organizational boundaries
  - Increasingly onerous regulatory requirements
  - Increasing requirements for availability and robustness
  - External dangers from hackers, malware, extortion, industrial espionage, and leakage of organizational or private data
- A lack of commitment from…
  - The business to the Information Security Management process and procedures
  - The business on future plans and strategies
  - Senior management
  - Resources and/or budget for the Information Security Management process
- Focusing too much on technology issues instead of needs/priorities of the business.
- Out-of-date and misaligned policies, plans, risks, and information to the business and business security.

◼ 5.12 SUPPLIER MANAGEMENT

5.12.1 Introduction
The **goal** of the Supplier Management process is to manage suppliers and the services they supply, to provide seamless quality of IT service to the business, ensuring value for money.

The **Objectives** of Supplier Management are:
- Obtain value for money from suppliers and contracts
- Ensure that underpinning contracts and agreements with suppliers are aligned to business needs
- Manage relationships with suppliers and their performance
- Negotiate and agree contracts with suppliers
- Maintain a supplier policy and a supporting supplier and contract database (SCMIS)

Scope
The Supplier Management process includes the management of all suppliers and contracts needed to support the provision of IT services to the business. The greater the contribution of a supplier, the more effort the service provider must put in managing the (relationship with the) supplier, and the more they should be involved with the development and implementation of the strategy. The smaller the supplier's value contribution, the more likely it is that the relationship will be managed mainly at an operational level. The process should include the following aspects:

- Implementation and enforcement of the supplier policy
- Maintenance of SCMIS
- Categorizing of suppliers and contracts and risk assessment
- Evaluation of contracts and suppliers
- Developing, negotiating, and agreement of contracts
- Revising, renewing, and terminating contracts

Value for the business
One of the most important goals of Supplier Management is to get value for money from suppliers and contracts and to ensure that all targets in underpinning contracts and agreements are aligned to business needs and agreed targets within the SLA. This ensures the delivery of end-to-end seamless, quality IT services that are aligned to the business expectation. The Supplier Management process should align with all corporate requirements and the requirements of all other IT and service management processes, particularly Information Security Management and ITSCM.

Basic concepts
All activities in this process should be driven by a supplier strategy and the policy from Service Strategy. A SCMIS should be created to achieve consistency and effectiveness in implementing policy. Ideally, the SCMIS would be an integrated element of CMS or SKMS. The SCMIS should contain all details regarding suppliers and contracts, together with details about the type of service or product, and any information and relationship to other configuration items.

The data will provide important information for activities and procedures such as:
- Categorizing of suppliers
- Maintenance of supplier and contract database
- Evaluation and set-up of new suppliers and contracts
- Establishing new suppliers
- Supplier and contract management and performance
- Renewed and terminated contracts

5.12.2 Activities, methods, and techniques
For external suppliers, it is recommended to draw up a formal contract with clearly defined, agreed upon, and documented responsibilities and goals. This contract should be managed during its entire lifecycle.

The activities that are executed within this process are:
1. Definition of new supplier and contract requirements
2. Evaluation of new suppliers and contracts
3. Supplier and contract categorization and maintenance of the SCMIS
4. Establishment of new suppliers and contracts

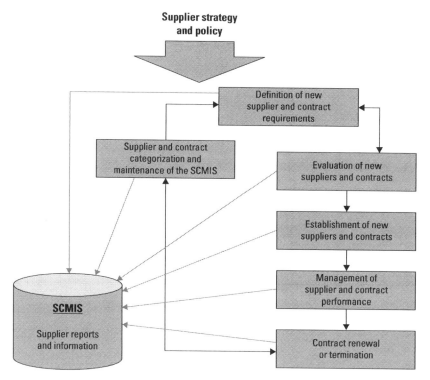

Figure 5.15 Sample Supplier Management flow

(source: AXELOS)

5. Manage the supplier and contract performance
6. Contract renewal or termination

5.12.3 Information management

All the information required by Supplier Management should be contained within the SCMIS. This should include all information relating to suppliers and contracts, as well as all the information relating to the operation of the supporting services provided by suppliers. Information relating to these supporting services should also be contained within the service portfolio, together with the relationships to all other services and components. This information should be integrated and maintained in alignment with all other IT management information systems, particularly the service portfolio.

5.12.4 Interfaces

- **Service Portfolio Management** – Ensures that the service portfolio accurately depicts all supporting systems and details
- **Financial Management for IT Services** – Funds supplier management requirements and contracts, provides financial advice, and guidance on procurement
- **SLM** – Assists in determining goals, requirements and responsibilities
- **ITSCM** – Works with Supplier Management with regard to the management of continuity service suppliers

- **Information Security Management** – Manages suppliers and their access to services
- **Change Management** – Supplier contracts and agreements are subject to change management procedures. Involvement of suppliers should be assessed and reflected in planning for changes

5.12.5 Triggers
- New or changed... corporate governance guidelines; business and IT strategies, policies or plans; business needs; services; requirements within agreements, such as SLR, SLA, OLA or contracts
- Periodic review and revision of the designs and strategies, and Supplier Management policies, reports and plans
- Requests from other areas, particularly SLM and Information Security Management, for assistance with supplier issues
- Requirements for new contracts, contract renewal or contract termination
- Re-categorization of suppliers and/or contracts

5.12.6 Inputs
- Business information
- Supplier and contracts strategy
- Supplier plans and strategies
- Supplier contracts, agreements and targets
- Supplier and contract performance information
- IT information
- Performance issues
- Financial information
- Service information
- CMS

5.12.7 Outputs
- SCMIS
- Supplier and contract performance information and reports
- Supplier and contract review meeting minutes
- Supplier SIPs
- Supplier survey reports

5.12.8 Critical success factors
- Business protected from poor supplier performance or disruption
- Supporting services and their targets align with business needs and targets
- Availability of services is not compromised by supplier performance
- Clear ownership and awareness of supplier and contractual issues

5.12.9 Metrics

- Increase in the number of...
  - Suppliers meeting the targets within the contract
  - Service and contractual reviews held with suppliers
  - Supplier and contractual targets aligned with SLA and SLR targets
  - Suppliers with nominated supplier managers
  - Contracts with nominated contract managers
- Reduction in the number of
  - Service breaches caused by suppliers
  - Threatened service breaches caused by suppliers
  - Breaches of contractual targets

5.12.10 Challenges

- Constantly changing business and IT needs
- Existing imperfect contracts
- Legacy issues, especially with services recently outsourced
- Insufficient expertise retained within the organization
- Being tied into long-term contracts
- Disputes over charges
- Interference by either party in the running of the other's operation
- Being caught in a daily fire-fighting mode, losing the proactive approach
- Poor communication
- Personality conflicts and/or cultural conflicts
- One party using the contract to the detriment of the other party
- Losing the strategic perspective, focusing on operational issues

5.12.11 Risks

- Lack of...
  - Commitment from the business to the Supplier Management process
  - Commitment from senior management to the Supplier Management process
  - Appropriate information on future business and IT policies, plans and strategies
  - Resources and/or budget for the Supplier Management process
  - Clarity and integration by supplier with service management processes, policies and procedures of the service provider
- Legacy of badly written and agreed contracts
- Suppliers fail or are incapable of meeting the terms and conditions of the contract
- Misaligned culture between provider and supplier
- Uncooperative/unwilling suppliers in supporting the Supplier Management process
- Suppliers are taken over and relationships, personnel and contracts are changed
- Excessive and bureaucratic demands

■ 5.13 ORGANIZATION

5.13.1 Roles and responsibilities

Well performing organizations can quickly and accurately make the right decisions and execute them successfully. In order to achieve this, it is crucial that the roles and responsibilities are clearly defined. This is also an essential issue in the Service Design process. One of the possible models that can be helpful in this regard is the RACI model, as explained in Chapter 2.

Skills

Despite the fact that every position brings with it specific skills/competences (see "*Roles*" below), the responsible person must:

■ Be aware of the business priorities and objectives
■ Be aware of the role that IT plays
■ Possess customer service skills
■ Be aware of what IT can provide to the customer
■ Have the competences and knowledge that are needed in order to perform the function well
■ Have the ability to use, understand and interpret best practice policies and procedures to ensure adherence

Roles

In this section is a description of the roles and responsibilities of the most important positions in the Service Design process. Depending on the size of organizations these roles can be combined. The most important roles are:

■ **The process owner** is responsible for ensuring that the process is implemented as agreed and that the established objectives will therefore be achieved. Tasks are:
  • Documenting and recording the process
  • Defining the KPI and if necessary revising them
  • Improving the effectiveness and efficiency of the process
  • Providing input to the service improvement plan
  • Reviewing the process, the roles and responsibilities

■ **The service design manager** is responsible for the overall coordination and inputting of the service designs. Tasks include:
  • Ensure that the Service Strategy corresponds with the design process and that the designs satisfy the established requirements
  • Design the functional aspects of the services
  • Produce and maintain the design documentation
  • Assess the effectiveness and efficiency of the design process

■ **The service catalogue manager** is responsible for the production and maintenance of the service catalogue. In addition, the service catalogue manager must:
- Ensure that the services are recorded in the service catalogue
- Ensure that the information that has been included is up-to-date and is consistent with the information in the service portfolio
- Ensure that the service catalogue is secure and that there are backups

■ **The service level manager** has as their most important responsibilities to:
- Have an insight into the changing demands of the customer and the market
- Ensure that the customers" existing and future requirements have been identified
- Negotiate and make agreements on the delivery of services
- Assist in the production and maintenance of an accurate service portfolio
- Ensure that the objectives that have been ratified in underlying contracts are synchronized with the SLA

■ **The availability manager** is responsible for:
- Ensuring that the existing services are available as agreed
- Assisting in investigating and diagnosing all incidents and problems
- Contributing to the design of the IT infrastructure
- Proactively improving the availability of services

■ **The information security manager** has as his most important tasks to:
- Design and maintain the information security policy
- Communicate with the involved parties on matters pertaining to the security policy
- Assist in the business impact analysis
- Perform risk analyses and risk management together with Availability Management and ITSCM

In addition, there are still the following responsible positions to recognize in this process:
- IT planner
- IT designer/architect
- Service continuity manager
- Capacity manager
- Supplier manager

■ 5.14 METHODS, TECHNIQUES AND TOOLS

5.14.1 Technological considerations

It is extremely important that someone ensures that the tools to be used support the processes and not the other way around. There are various tools and techniques that can be used for supporting the service and component designs. They not only make the

hardware and software designs possible, but also enable the development of environment designs, process designs and data designs. The great variety of tools and techniques offer the following benefits:
- Attainment of speed in the design process
- Adherence to standards
- The development of prototypes and models
- Take into account diverse scenarios (what if…?)

The design process can be simplified by making use of tools that give a graphic image of the service and its components, from the business processes to the service and the SLA, through the infrastructure, environment, data and applications, processes, OLA (operational level agreements), teams, contracts and suppliers. If the tool also contains financial information and is coupled with a *"metrics tree"*, the service can be guarded and managed through all of the phases in its lifecycle.

These tools not only facilitate the design process, they also support all of the phases in the Service Lifecycle, including:
- Management of all levels of the Service Lifecycle
- All aspects of the service and its performance
- Management of costs
- Management of the service portfolio and service catalogue
- A CMS and a SKMS

The following generic activities must be performed:
- Ensure that there is a generic lifecycle for IT assets
- Formalize relationships between different types of IT assets
- Define the roles and responsibilities
- Ensure that a study is performed in order to understand the total cost of ownership (TCO) of an IT service

Even more can be added for application assets:
- Define an acquisition strategy for IT assets and analyze how this can be synchronized with both the IT– and the business strategy
- Document the role that the application plays in the provision of IT services
- Determine standards for the use of various approaches to the design of applications

For data/information assets still more can be added:
- Ensure that data designs are made in the light of:
  - The importance of standardization
  - The need for qualitatively valuable data
  - The value of data to the organization

For IT infrastructure assets more can be added:

- Establish standards for the acquisition and management of IT– and environmental infrastructure (electricity, space, middleware, database systems etc.)
- Determine activities for the optimum use of the IT infrastructure assets
- Specify the need for tools and describe how they would be used

For skills assets more can be added:

- Formalize how competences could be considered as assets in the organization
- Ensure that the competences are documented

In order to establish interfaces and dependencies the following can be added:

- Formalize the interfaces that the acquisition and management of IT assets have with functions and processes outside the IT sphere
- Formalize quality control in the acquisition and management of IT assets

5.14.2 Service management tools

Many service management processes and activities cannot be effectively executed without proper support aids, mostly known as **tools**. With these tools the management tasks can be automated, e.g.: controlling tasks or software distribution tasks. There are various tools and techniques available that have enhanced the performance abilities of the IT organizations.

Tools help ensure that Service Design processes can function effectively. They enhance efficiency and provide valuable management information on the identification of possible weak points. The long-term benefit is that the use of tools serves to reduce costs and increase productivity, in the interest of improving the quality of IT service delivery. In addition, the use of tools makes possible the centralization of essential processes, as well as the automation and integration of "*core*" service management processes.

Considerations in the evaluation of service management tools include:

- Data structure, data handling and integration
- Conformity with international standards
- Flexibility in implementation, use, and sharing of data
- Support in the monitoring of service levels

The tool serves to support the process rather than the other way around. If possible, it is recommended that a completely integrated tool is acquired, that supports the many service management processes. If this is not possible, then interfaces among the various tools should be taken into consideration. During the selection process it is advisable to employ a statement of requirements (SoR). The requirements should be considered using the MoSCoW analysis:

- **M** – must have this
- **S** – should have this

- **C** – could have this
- **W** – won't have this now, but would like in the future

The tool must be flexible so that it can support individual access rights. It is necessary to determine who has access to the data and with what objective. In addition, it must be decided as to which platform the tool can work on. During the first consideration it is wise to look into the credit-worthiness of the supplier and find out if they offer support (training) for a few months or years. In this process it is important to realize that a solution almost never satisfies 100 percent of the requirements. The 80/20 rule is perhaps more realistic in this framework. In other words, the tool is likely to satisfy closer to 80 percent of the established requirements.

5.15 IMPLEMENTATION CONSIDERATIONS

In this section the implementation considerations for Service Design are addressed. In addition, the interfaces of Service Design with the other phases of the Service Lifecycle will be discussed.

5.15.1 Business impact analysis (BIA)
The BIA is a valuable source of information for establishing the customer's needs, and the impact and the risk of a service. The BIA is an essential element in the business continuity process and dictates the strategy to be followed for risk reduction and recovery after a catastrophe. The BIA consists of two parts: on the one hand is the investigation of the impact of the loss of a business process or function; on the other hand is the stopping of the effect of that loss.

5.15.2 Implementation of Service Design
The process, policy, and architecture for the design of IT services, as described in this book, must be documented and used in order to design and implement appropriate IT services. In principle, it is recommended that all of the processes are implemented at the same time, since all of the processes are related to each other and often are also dependent on each other. What is ultimately needed is an integrated set of processes that IT Services can manage and oversee throughout the entire lifecycle. Since organizations can rarely implement everything at once, the process for which there is the greatest need should be the first to be done, realizing that all processes are interlinked. In addition, this also depends on the maturity of the organization's ITSM. The implementation priorities must correspond with the objectives of the SIP.

5.15.3 Prerequisites
There are various prerequisites for new or revised processes. They are often requirements of other processes. For example, before SLM can design the SLA a business service catalogue and a *technical/supporting services view* of the service catalogue are necessary.

Problem Management depends on a mature Incident Management process. These things are much bigger than just ITSM: Availability Management and Capacity Management need information from the business plan. There are more of these examples which need to be considered first before high process maturity can be achieved.

5.15.4 Critical success factors

The critical success factors, which change over time, for the Service Design phase may include but are not limited to the following:

- Management support
- Business support
- Hiring and retaining personnel
- Service management training
- Appropriate tools
- Test validity
- Measuring and reporting

5.15.5 KPI for Service Design

- Percentage of specifications of the requirements of Service Design produced on time
- Percentage of specifications of the requirements of Service Design produced within budget
- Percentage of Service Design Packs produced on time
- Accuracy of Service Design
- Accuracy of the SLA, OLA, and contracts

5.15.6 Challenges

- The need for synchronization of existing architecture, strategy, and policy
- The use of various technologies and applications
- Unclear or changing customer requirements
- Lack of awareness and knowledge of service delivery
- Resistance to working systematically
- Inefficient use of resources

5.15.7 Risks

- If the level of maturity in one of the processes is low, it is impossible to reach a high level of maturity in other processes
- Business requirements are not clear for the IT personnel
- Too little time is allotted for service design
- Synchronization among infrastructure, customer, and partners is not good, which means the requirements cannot be satisfied
- The Service Design phase is not clear or on the whole is not available

5.15.8 Interfaces with other phases in the lifecycle

All activities in the Service Design phase originate from the customer's needs and requirements, and are then also a reflection of the strategy, plans, and policy produced by the first phase of the lifecycle: the Service Strategy.

The Service Design phase in the lifecycle begins with the new or changed requirements of the customer. Ultimately, by the end of the design process, a service solution must be designed which satisfies those requirements before they begin the Service Transition process together with the service package. In the Service Transition phase, the service will be evaluated, structured, tested and deployment will take place after which the implementation will be transferred to Service Operation.

The output of each phase forms the input for each subsequent phase in the lifecycle. For example Service Strategy delivers important input to Service Design, that subsequently delivers input to the Service Transition phase.

The service portfolio provides information to every process in every phase of the lifecycle. In this respect it is in fact the backbone of the Service Lifecycle. The service portfolio must be a component of the service knowledge management system and be included as a document in the configuration management system. This will be described in greater detail in Chapter 6 "Service Transition".

6 Service Transition Phase

■ 6.1 INTRODUCTION TO SERVICE TRANSITION

This chapter explains how the specifications from Service Design can be effectively converted to a new or changed service. An effective Service Transition ensures that the new or changed services are better aligned with the customer's business operation. Specifically:

- The capacity of the business to react quickly and adequately to changes in the market
- Changes in the business as a result of takeovers, contracting, etc. are well managed
- More successful changes and releases for the business
- Better compliance of business and governing rules
- Less deviation between planned budgets and the actual costs
- Better insight into the possible risks during and after the input of a service
- Higher productivity of customer personnel

The seven processes in Service Transition are (see Figure 6.0):
1. Transition Planning & Support
2. Change Management
3. Service Asset & Configuration Management
4. Release & Deployment Management
5. Service Validation & Testing
6. Change Evaluation
7. Knowledge Management

6.1.1 Goal and Objectives
The **goal** of Service Transition is assuring that new or revised or phased out services meet to the expectations of the business, as documented in the Service Charter and the Service Design Package during the Service Strategy and Service Design phases of the lifecycle.

Processes in the ITIL lifecycle

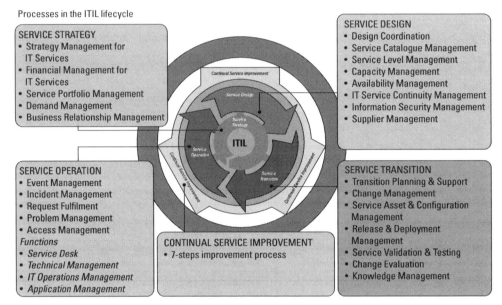

SERVICE STRATEGY
- Strategy Management for IT Services
- Financial Management for IT Services
- Service Portfolio Management
- Demand Management
- Business Relationship Management

SERVICE DESIGN
- Design Coordination
- Service Catalogue Management
- Service Level Management
- Capacity Management
- Availability Management
- IT Service Continuity Management
- Information Security Management
- Supplier Management

SERVICE OPERATION
- Event Management
- Incident Management
- Request Fulfilment
- Problem Management
- Access Management
Functions
- *Service Desk*
- *Technical Management*
- *IT Operations Management*
- *Application Management*

CONTINUAL SERVICE IMPROVEMENT
- 7-steps improvement process

SERVICE TRANSITION
- Transition Planning & Support
- Change Management
- Service Asset & Configuration Management
- Release & Deployment Management
- Service Validation & Testing
- Change Evaluation
- Knowledge Management

Figure 6.0 The seven processes of Service Transition in relation to the ITIL lifecycle

The **objectives** of Service Transition include:
- Planning and managing service changes in an efficient and effective manner
- Managing the risks connected to new, changed or phased out services
- Rolling out service releases successfully into production
- Creating the correct expectations regarding the performance and use of new and changed services
- Ensuring that service changes result into the expected business value
- Delivering high quality knowledge and information on services and service assets

6.1.2 Scope
ITIL defines the **scope** of Service Transition as follows:

> **Service Transition** includes the management and coordination of the processes, systems and functions required for the packaging, building, testing, and deployment of a release into production, and establish the service specified in the customer and stakeholder requirements.

A Service Transition generally comprises the following steps:
- Planning and preparation
- Building and testing
- Any pilots
- Planning and preparation of the deployment
- Deployment and transition
- Review and closing of Service Transition

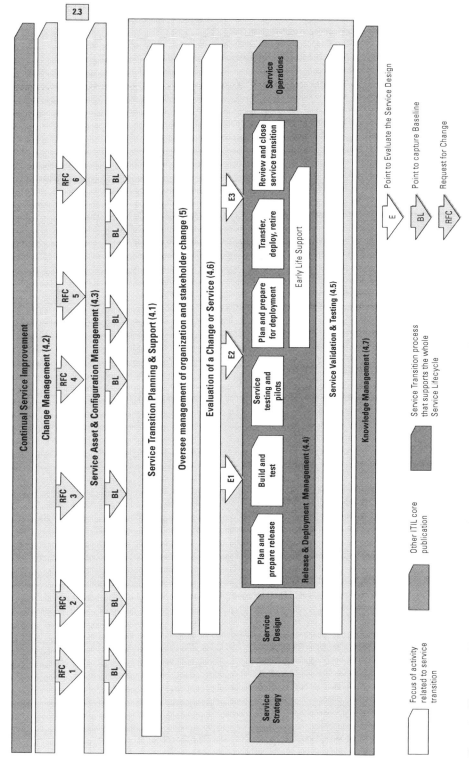

Figure 6.1 The scope of Service Transition

Although Change Management, SACM and Knowledge Management support all phases of the Service Lifecycle, the ITIL Service Transition book covers these. Release & Deployment Management, Service Validation & Testing, and Change Evaluation are included in the scope of Service Transition.

■ 6.2   BASIC CONCEPTS

The following policies are important for an effective Service Transition and apply to every organization. The approach must still be adjusted to the conditions, which differ from organization to organization:
■ Define and implement guidelines and procedures for Service Transition
■ Always implement all changes through Service Transition
■ Use frameworks and standards
■ Re-use existing processes and systems
■ Align service transition plans with the needs of the business
■ Create relations with stakeholders and maintain these.
■ Set up effective "*controls*"
■ Deliver systems for knowledge transfer and decision support
■ Plan releases and deployment packages
■ Anticipate and manage changes in direction
■ Manage resources proactively
■ Ensure involvement at an early stage in the Service Lifecycle
■ Assure the quality of a new or changed service
■ Proactively improve service quality during a Service Transition

■ 6.3   TRANSITION PLANNING & SUPPORT

6.3.1 Introduction
The **goal** for Transition Planning & Support is the transition of services and coordinating the required resources.

The **objectives** for Transition Planning & Support include:
■ Coordinating activities related to all projects, suppliers and service teams, when necessary
■ Implementing new or changes services according to budget, with the desired quality and within the agreed time frame
■ Implementing new or changed management information systems, processes, and metrics
■ Follow up on plans that enable customers and business to align their activities with the Service Transition plans
■ Identifying, managing and controlling risks

Scope

The following activities are included in the scope of Transition Planning & Support:

- Guarding the guidelines (policies), standards and models for the Service Transition activities and processes
- Coordinating all new and changed services throughout all processes
- Coordinating all efforts required to manage several transitions during the same time frame
- Creating the budget and resource planning for future transition activities
- Monitoring and improving Service Transition achievements
- Aligning Service Transition activities with the program and project management, service design and service development activities

Value for the business

An integrated approach to planning improves the alignment of transition plans with the customer, service provider, business and change project plans.

Basic concepts

Transition Planning & Support produces the **release guidelines and policy**. Herein the following subjects are addressed:

- Naming conventions, distinguishing release types, such as: **major release**, **minor release** and **emergency release**
- Roles and responsibilities – many people from different organizations can be involved with a release; it is useful to set up a responsibility matrix for this purpose
- Release frequency, the expected frequency of each type of release
- Approach for accepting and grouping changes in to a release
- How the configuration baseline for the release is captured and verified against the actual release contents e.g.: hardware, software, documentation and knowledge
- Entry and exit criteria and authority for acceptance of the release into each Service Transition stage and into the controlled test, training, disaster recovery and production environments
- The criteria authorization for leaving early life support (ELS) and handover to Service Operations

6.3.2 Activities, methods, and techniques

The activities for planning and support consist of:

1. Set up transition strategy
2. Prepare Service Transition
3. Plan and coordinate Service Transition
4. Transition process support

1. Set up transition strategy

The transition strategy defines the overall approach to organizing Service Transition and allocating resources. Aspects that may be addressed in the transition strategy are:

- Purpose, goals and objectives
- Context and scope
- Applicable standards, agreements, legal, regulatory and contractual agreements
- Organizations and stakeholders involved in the Service Transition
- Framework for Service Transition
- Criteria for success and failure
- People: roles and responsibilities
- Approach including transition model, plans for managing changes, assets, configurations and knowledge, transition estimation, preparation, evaluation, error handling, KPI
- The products (deliverables) that are the result of the transition activities such as transition plans, schedule of milestones, financial requirements

The SDP defines the various phases of Service Transition. These may consist of: acquiring and testing components, testing service release, Service Operation readiness test, rollout, ELS, review, and close Service Transition.

2. Prepare Service Transition
Preparatory activities consist of:
- Review and acceptance of inputs from other Service Lifecycle phases review and check the input deliverables e.g.: SDP, service acceptance criteria (SAC) and evaluation report
- Identifying, raising and scheduling RFC
- Checking the configuration baselines are recorded in configuration management before the start of Service Transition
- Checking transition readiness of both customer and IT organization.

3. Plan and coordinate Service Transition
A **service transition plan** describes the tasks and activities required to release and deploy a release into the test environments and into production including:
- Work environment and infrastructure
- Schedule of milestones
- Activities and tasks to be performed
- Personnel, resource requirements, budgets and timescales at each stage
- Lead times and contingency

Good **integrated planning** and management are essential to deploy a release across distributed environments and locations into production successfully. An **integrated set of transition plans** should be maintained that is linked to lower level plans such as release, build, and test plans.

It is *best practice* to manage several releases in a **program**, with each significant deployment run as a **project**.

Quality reviews should be implemented for all Service Transition, release, and deployment plans. Questions that might be asked are:

- Are the service transition plans and release plans up-to-date, authorized and are the release dates known?
- Were any risks related to impact on costs, organization, and technology taken into account?
- Are new CI compatible with each other and with configuration items in the target environment?
- Are the people who need to work with IT sufficiently trained?
- Have potential changes in the business environment been taken into account?

4. Service Transition process support

Service Transition advises and **supports** all stakeholders. The planning and support team will provide insight for the stakeholders regarding Service Transition processes and supporting systems and tools. In addition, the team will perform **management/ administration** of changes, work orders, issues, risks, communication, and deployment. The team will also update stakeholders regarding planning and process.

Finally, Service Transition activities are **monitored**: the implementation of activities is compared with the way they were intended (as formulated in the transition plan and model).

Service Transition lifecycle stages

The SDP should define the lifecycle stages for Service Transition, and the move from one stage to the next should be subject to formal checks. For each stage there will be exit criteria, entry criteria, and mandatory deliverables. Each criterion or *"quality gate"* defines a set of standards which must be met before moving on to the next stage. Typical stages in the life of a transition might include:

- Acquire and test new CI and components
- Build and test
- Service release test
- Service Operational readiness test
- Deployment
- Early life support
- Review and close Service Transition

6.3.3 Information management

- The Transition Planning & Support process makes heavy use of the service knowledge management system, to provide access to the full range of information needed for short-, medium- and long-range planning.

6.3.4 Interfaces

Like all processes, the Transition Planning & Support process has relationships with all other processes. However, some of the most visible relationships include but are not limited to:

- **Demand Management** – To provide long-term information about likely resource requirements
- **Service Portfolio Management** process – To engage Transition Planning & Support to provide input to their planning and decision-making. For change proposals to trigger longer-term planning within Transition Planning & Support
- **BRM** – To manage appropriate two-way communication with customers
- **Service Design** stage – In the form of a Service Design Package
- **Supplier Management** – During Service Transition to ensure that appropriate contracts are in place
- **Service Transition phase** – All processes in this phase are coordinated by Transition Planning & Support
- **Pilots, handover, and early life support** – To be coordinated with the Service Operation functions
- **Various groups within the organization** – To provide the personnel needed to carry out many aspects of Service Transition

6.3.5 Triggers

- For planning a single transition: An authorized change
- Longer-term planning: Receipt of a change proposal from Service Portfolio Management
- Budgeting for future transition requirements: The organization's budgetary planning cycle

6.3.6 Inputs

- Service Design Package
- Service Design
- Change proposal
- Authorized change

6.3.7 Outputs

- Transition strategy and budget
- Integrated set of Service Transition plans

6.3.8 Critical success factors

- Understanding and managing the trade-offs between cost, quality and time
- Effective communication with stakeholders
- Identifying and managing risks of failure and disruption
- Coordinating activities of multiple processes involved in each transition
- Managing conflicting demands for shared resources

6.3.9 Metrics

Increase in...
- The number of releases implemented that meet the customer's agreed requirements in terms of cost, quality, scope and release schedule
- Customer and user satisfaction
- Project and service team satisfaction

Improved...
- Service Transition success rates
- Efficiency and effectiveness of the processes and supporting systems

Reduced...
- Business disruption
- Number of issues, risks and delays
- Variation of actual versus predicted scope, quality, cost and time
- Time and resource to develop and maintain integrated plans and coordination activities
- Number of issues caused by conflicting demands for shared resources

6.3.10 Challenges
- Building up the relationships needed to manage and coordinate the many stakeholders
- Coordinating and prioritizing many new or changed services concurrently
- Understanding the risks and issues for each project to proactively manage resource planning

6.3.11 Risks
- Lack of information from Demand Management and Service Portfolio Management
- Poor relationships with projects and programs
- Delays to one transition having a subsequent effect on future transitions, due to resource constraints
- Insufficient information to address conflicts

■ 6.4   CHANGE MANAGEMENT

6.4.1 Introduction
There is always a reason for implementing a change. We distinguish proactive or reactive reasons. Examples of a proactive reason are cost reduction or service improvement. Examples of reactive changes are solving service disruptions or adapting the service to a changing environment.

The **goal** of Change Management **is** to control the entire lifecycle of a change. It ensures that the severity of the impact and service interruption is minimized.

The **objectives** of Change Management are:
- Enabling to react on changes in business requirements
- To be able to respond on change requests from business and the IT, in such a way that the services align with business demands
- Ensuring that changes are recorded, assessed, authorized, prioritized, planned, tested, implemented and documented and reviewed in a controlled manner
- Ensuring that all changes are recorded in CI in the CMS
- Optimizing the overall business risks

The Change Management process must:
- Use standardized methods and procedures
- Record all changes in the CMDB
- Take account of risks for the business

Scope
The scope of service management covers changes to base-lined service assets and CI across the whole Service Lifecycle. Section 6.5 "Service Asset & Configuration Management" discusses these issues in greater detail.

Every organization must define for itself which changes its Change Management process does and does not cover. For instance, changing a defective hard drive of a PC may not be part of the Change Management process.

Figure 6.2 shows the scope of the Change Management process as well as the interfaces of the process with the business at the strategic, tactical, and operational levels.

Value for the business
Service and infrastructure changes can have a negative impact on the business through service disruption and delay in identifying business requirements, but Change Management enables the service providers to add value to the business. For example:
- Changes relating to financial regulations, such as SOX, or other rules of good governance
- Timely implementation of changes so that the business's deadlines are achieved
- Reducing the number of failed changes, thereby reducing the number of service interruptions
- Prioritizing changes and responding adequately to change requests from the customer
- Reducing the mean time to restore services (MTRS)

Thanks to the increased dependency on IT services, and because the underlying information technology has become so complex, significant efficiency benefits can be realized by means of well-structured and planned changes and releases. Some indicators of inadequate Change Management are:

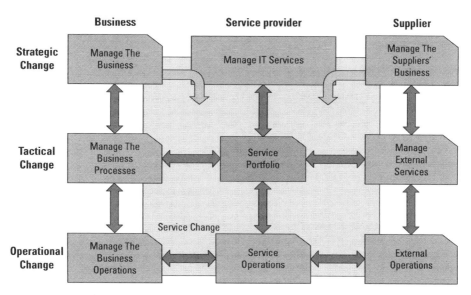

Figure 6.2 The scope of Change Management

- Unauthorized changes
- Unplanned downtime
- Implemented changes with little success
- High number of "*emergency changes*"
- Delayed project implementations

Policies
Policies for supporting Change Management are:
- Creating a zero tolerance culture in relation to unauthorized changes
- Aligning the Change Management process with other change processes in the organization
- Effective prioritization, e.g.: innovative versus preventive versus detective versus corrective changes
- Establishing accountability and responsibilities for changes through the lifecycle
- Establishing a single focal point for changes
- Ensuring integration with other service management processes
- Setting up "*change windows*", performance and risk assessments, performance measures

Design and planning
The change management process is planned in combination with release and configuration management. This makes it possible to assess the impact of changes on services and releases.

The requirement and design for the Change Management processes include:
- Requirements relating to relevant laws and regulations
- An approach to eliminate unauthorized changes
- Identification and classification
- Organization, roles, responsibilities
- Stakeholders
- Grouping and relating changes
- Procedures
- Interfaces with other service management processes

Basic concepts
The ITIL definition of a change is:

> A **change** is the addition, modification, or removal of an authorized, planned, or supported service or service component and its associated documentation.

The terms *"change"*, *"change record,"* and *"RFC"* are often used inconsistently, thus leading to confusion and misunderstanding. ITIL defines them as follows:
- ***Change proposal*** – *A document to communicate a high-level description of a possible service introduction or significant change, together with the related business case and expected implementation schedule.*
- ***Request for change* (RFC)** – *a formal proposal for a change to be made. It may be recorded on paper or electronically*
- ***Change record*** – *A record (in a database, usually as part of an integrated service management suite) containing the details of a change. Each change record documents the lifecycle of a single change.*

Change advisory board (CAB)
This is a consultation body that meets at fixed intervals to assess changes and help Change Management prioritize the changes. It may include representatives from all key stakeholders and departments, including:
- Customers
- End users
- Application developers
- System administrators
- Experts
- Service desk representatives
- Production
- Service provider representatives

The CAB must have a number of standard agenda items, including:
- Unauthorized changes
- Authorized changes not handled by the CAB

- RFC that must be reviewed by the CAB members
- On-going or closed changes
- Assessment of implemented changes

Change proposals

Change proposals are submitted to Change Management before chartering new or changed services in order to ensure that potential conflicts for resources or other issues are identified. Authorization of the change proposal does not authorize implementation of the change but simply allows the service to be chartered so that Service Design activity can begin.

A change proposal is used to communicate a high-level description of the change. This change proposal is normally created by the Service Portfolio Management process.

Request for Changes (RFC)

Requests for change often originate from various service management processes or from various groups e.g.: customers and suppliers. A RFC is a formal proposal for a change to be made.

Change models and workflows

A change model is a way of predefining the steps that should be taken to handle a particular type of change in an agreed way. This helps ensuring that changes of all types are handled in a predefined path and to predefined timescales.

The change model includes:
- Steps, describing the steps to be followed in chronological order
- Responsibilities
- Timescales and thresholds for completion
- Escalation procedures

ITIL defines three types of change: **normal, emergency** and **standard.**

Normal change

A normal change is requested via a RFC and follows the normal change process, including discussion and review in the CAB.

Emergency change

An **emergency change** is intended to repair a failure (ASAP) in an IT service that has a large negative impact on the business. If this requires permission from the CAB, but the full CAB cannot be convened, it is necessary to identify a smaller group to make emergency decisions: the **Emergency CAB (ECAB)**. The ECAB assists the change manager in deciding if the situation is an emergency then authorizing the change. An emergency change must be tested and documented to the greatest possible extent.

Standard changes (pre-authorized)

A standard change is a change to a service or other configuration item for which the approach is pre-authorized by Change Management, and this approach follows an accepted and established procedure. The following are characteristics of standard changes.

- The tasks are well known, documented, and proven to work
- The change authority may the submitter's immediate manager
- The budget approval usually lies with the submitter's immediate manager
- The risk is usually minimal, well understood, and accepted
- They may be used as workarounds by the Incident Management process
- They may be used to fulfil service requests by the Request Fulfilment process
- They may be automated to handle events by the Event Management process

Remediation planning

No change should be approved without having an answer to the following question: *"What will we do if the change is unsuccessful"*? An organization must always ensure that a *fallback (back-up) option* is available.

Remediation is a set of actions taken to recover after a failed change or release. Remediation may include back-out, invocation of service continuity plans, or other actions designed to enable the business process to continue.

Change implementation plans should include milestones and other triggers for invoking and implementing remediation in order to ensure that there is sufficient time in the agreed change window for back-out or other remediation when necessary.

6.4.2 Activities, methods, and techniques

Overall the Change Management activities include:

- Change planning and control
- Change and release scheduling
- Communications
- Change decision making and authorization
- Ensuring there are remediation plans
- Measurement and control based on KPI
- Management reporting
- Understanding impact
- Continual improvement

The specific activities to manage individual changes are discussed in subsequent sections:

1. Create and record RFC
2. Review the RFC and change proposal
3. Assess and evaluate the change
4. Authorize the change

5. Plan updates
6. Coordinate change implementation
7. Review and close change

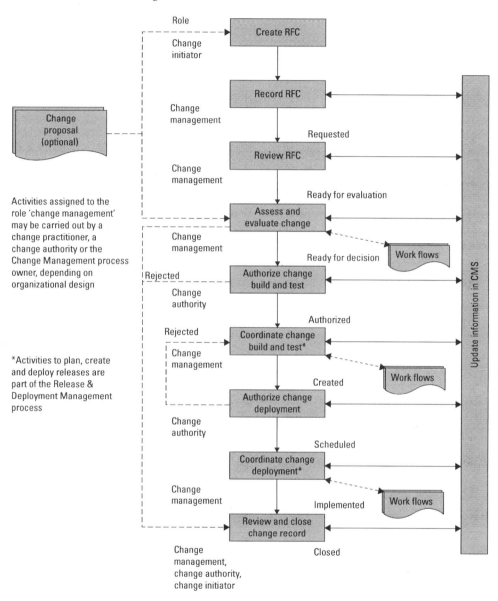

Figure 6.3 Example process flow of a regular change (based on source: AXELOS)

This section outlines the aspects followed within a *"normal"* change. The general principles set out apply to all changes and the *"normal"* change procedure is modified accordingly to deal with standard and emergency changes for example.

1. Create and record the RFC

The change is raised by a request from the initiator – the individual or organizational group that requires the change. For example, this may be a business unit that requires additional facilities, or Problem Management personnel instigating an error resolution from many other sources.

All RFC are registered and it must be possible to identify them via a unique identification number. The scope and impact of the eventual change determine how much information is required for the change.

2. Review the RFC and change proposal

After registration, the stakeholders verify whether the RFC is:
- Totally impractical
- Repeats earlier RFC (that are already accepted)
- Rejected, or still under consideration
- Complete (e.g.: adequate description, with necessary budgetary approval)

Such requests are rejected and returned to the initiator with details of the reason for the rejection. The initiator should have a right of appeal against rejection.

3. Assess and evaluate the change

This step starts with **categorizing** the change. The issue of risk must be considered before the authorization of any change. The **likelihood** that the risk will occur and its possible **impact** determine the **risk category** of the change. In practice, a risk categorization matrix is generally used for this purpose.

After the change has been categorized, it is **evaluated**. Based on the impact, risk assessment, potential benefits, and costs of the change, the **change authority** (e.g.: the change manager and/or CAB) determines whether the change is supported or not.

The following questions must be answered for all changes. Without this information, the impact assessment cannot be completed, and the balance of risk and benefit to the live service will not be understood. The **seven "R" of Change Management** represent a good starting point for impact analysis:
1. Who raised the change? (**Raised**)
2. What is the reason for the change? (**Reason**)
3. What is the return required from the change? (**Return**)
4. What are the change's risks? (**Risk**)
5. What resources does it require? (**Resources**)
6. Who is responsible for build, testing, and implementation? (**Responsible**)
7. Which relationships exist between this and other changes? (**Relationship**)

Determine the change's **priority** to establish the order in which the changes put forward must be considered. Priority is derived from the agreed impact and urgency. **Impact** is based on the beneficial change to the business that will result or on the degree of damage and cost to the business if it fails. **Urgency** indicates how long implementation can be delayed.

Change planning and scheduling
Change Management schedules the changes on the change calendar: the **Schedule of Change** (SC). The SC contains the details for all approved changes and their planning e.g.: implementation dates.

Changes can be bundled into a release. In consultation with the relevant IT departments, the CAB may set up fixed times to implement changes – moments where services will be hindered as little as possible by changes. A recovery plan must be prepared in case a change implementation is unsuccessful.

4. Authorize the change
Formal authorization from a change authority is required for every change. This may be a role, person, or group of people. The level at which approval is required depends on the change type. An example is shown in Figure 6.4.

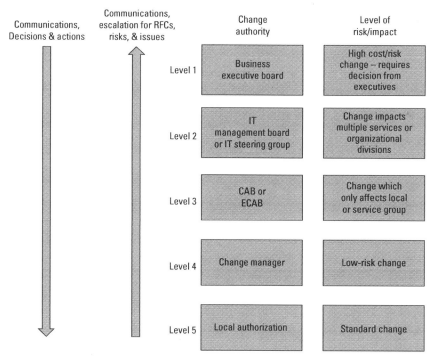

Figure 6.4 Example of an authorization model

5. Coordinate the change implementation

When changes are bundled into a release, the activities (implanting a change into a release and testing the release) are coordinated in the RDM process. Building and creating a release are issues discussed in Section 6.6 "Release & Deployment Management".

Simple changes, not being part of a release, will be coordinated in the Change Management process. Authorized RFC should be passed on to the relevant technical and/or application specialists for building and testing of the changes.

You should **test** the changes, the remediation, and the implementation method for the changes thoroughly. Section 6.7 "Service Validation & Testing" discusses testing in detail.

6. Review and close the change

Implemented changes – perhaps with the exception of standard changes – are evaluated after some time. The CAB then determines whether further follow-up is required.

If the change is successful, it can be closed. The outcome should be included in the **Post Implementation Review (PIR)**: the change evaluation. If the change is unsuccessful, Change Management or the CAB decides what should be done. A new or modified RFC may result.

6.4.3 Information management

- All change requests must be associated with services and other CI. This means they must be included within the CMS
- Correlate changes with incidents and review the history of changes to any CI as part of Incident Management or Problem Management
- Change management must have access to the CMS and to information and documents within the SKMS in order to plan and manage changes, to identify stakeholders in any change, and to predict the potential impact of changes

6.4.4 Interfaces

- **Transition Planning & Support** – to ensure that there is a coordinated overall approach to managing Service Transitions
- **IT change processes** – To define clear boundaries, dependencies, and rules
- **Change Evaluation** – To deliver the change evaluation report be to Change Management in time for the CAB (or other change authority) to use it to assist in their decision-making
- **Business change processes** – To ensure that change issues, aims, impacts and developments are exchanged and cascaded throughout the organization where applicable

- **Service Portfolio Management** – To submit change proposals before chartering new or changed services, in order to identify potential conflicts for resources or other issues
- **All service management processes**
  - To implement process improvements
  - To participate with impact assessment and implementation of service changes
  - To assess for the impact of a change on the policies, plans, or initiatives, of that process
- **SACM**
  - To provide reliable, quick and easy access to accurate configuration information
  - To enable stakeholders and personnel to assess the impact of proposed changes and to track changed workflow.
  - To identify related CI that will be affected by the change
- **Problem Management** – To implement workarounds and to fix known errors
- **Service Portfolio Management** – To assess whether a service should move to another section of the service portfolio

6.4.5 Triggers

Strategic changes
- Legal/regulatory change
- Organizational change
- Policy and standards change
- Change after analyzing business, customer and user activity patterns
- Addition of new service to the market space
- Updates to the service portfolio, customer portfolio or customer agreement portfolio
- Change of sourcing model
- Technology innovation

Operational change
- Standard changes as defined by the Request Fulfilment process
- Implementation of corrective and preventative changes

Change to one or more services
- Service catalogue
- Service package
- Service definition and characteristics
- Release package
- Capacity and resource requirements
- Service level requirements
- Warranties
- Utilities
- Cost of utilization
- Service assets

- Acceptance criteria
- Predicted quality of service
- Predicted performance
- Predicted value
- Organizational design
- Stakeholder and communications plans
- Physical change in the environment
- Measurement system
- Plans from capacity, ITSCM, change, transition, test, and release and deployment
- Decommission/retire services
- Procedures, manuals, service desk scripts

Changes to deliver continual improvement
- Some strategy and service changes will be initiated by CSI

6.4.6 Inputs
- Policy and strategy for change and release
- Request for change
- Change proposal
- Plans – change, transition, release, test, evaluation, and remediation
- Current change schedule and PSO
- Evaluation reports and interim evaluation reports
- Current assets or configuration items
- As-planned configuration baseline
- Test results, test report, and evaluation report

6.4.7 Outputs
- Rejected and canceled RFC
- Authorized changes
- Authorized change proposals
- Change to the service or infrastructure resulting from authorized changes
- New, changed, or disposed configuration items
- Revised change schedule
- Revised PSO
- Authorized change plans
- Change decisions and actions
- Change documents and records
- Change management reports

6.4.8 Critical success factors
- Responding to business and IT requests for change that will align the services with the business needs while maximizing value
- Optimizing overall business risk

■ Ensuring that all changes to configuration items are well managed and recorded in the configuration management system

6.4.9 Metrics

■ Increase in…
  • The percentage of changes that meet the customer's agreed requirements
  • Accuracy of predictions for time, quality, cost, risk, resource, and commercial impact
■ Reduction in the…
  • Backlog of change requests
  • Number of disruptions to services, defects and re-work caused by inaccurate specification, poor or incomplete impact assessment
  • Percentage of changes that are categorized as emergency changes
  • Number of unauthorized changes identified
  • Number of incidents attributed to changes

6.4.10 Challenges

■ Ensuring that every change is recorded and managed
■ Ensuring there is active and visible sponsorship from executives and senior management
■ Changing the perception that the process is bureaucratic and time-wasting, and will not be valued
■ Migrating from operational change control to a true Change Management process involved early enough in the Service Lifecycle, includes assessment of benefits and costs, and helps to plan and manage changes
■ Agreeing and documenting the many levels of change authority and communicating effectively between these change authorities

6.4.11 Risks

■ Lack of commitment to the Change Management process…
  • By the business / business sponsorship
  • By IT management / IT management sponsorship
  • By IT personnel
■ Lack of clarity on interaction with…
  • Other service management processes
  • Project management or Service Design activities
■ Implementation of changes without the use of Change Management
■ Change assessment being reduced to "*box-ticking*"
■ Introduction of delays to change implementation without adding sufficient value
■ Excessively bureaucratic change management processes that introduce excessive delay to required changes.

■ Insufficient…
- Time for proper assessment and pressure to expedite decisions
- Time for implementation of changes, trying to fit too many changes into change window
- Resources for assessment, planning, and implementation

■ 6.5   SERVICE ASSET & CONFIGURATION MANAGEMENT (SACM)

6.5.1 Introduction

The **goal** of Service Asset & Configuration Management (SACM), required for delivering services, is to control the assets (knowing what is in which place) and to provide accurate and reliable information about these assets, when and where this information is needed. This information includes details about the configuration of these assets and the internal relations between the assets.

The **objectives** of SACM are:
- To assure that the assets are identified, that all changes in status (e.g.: from storage to usage, and from use to archive) are executed in a controlled manner and that the actual status and use of IT assets are reported
- To identify, control, store, report, control and verify services and other CI
- To record, manage and protect the integrity of the service assets and CI during their lifecycle
- To build and maintain an accurate and complete CMS
- To maintain accurate configuration information on the historical, planned and current status of services and other CI
- To support other service management processes.

Scope
All assets that are used during the Service Lifecycle fall within the scope of asset management. The process offers a complete overview of all assets, and shows who is responsible for the control and maintenance of these assets.

Configuration management ensures that all CI that form part of the service or product are identified, **baselined** (the configuration) and maintained. It ensures that releases into controlled environments and operational use are on the basis of formal approvals. The process also provides a logical model of all services, assets, the physical infrastructure, and the mutual relations.

SACM also relates to non-IT assets and CI, such as work products used to develop the services and CI required to support the service that are not formally classified as assets. The scope of the process also includes assets and CI of other suppliers ("*shared assets*"), to the extent that they are relevant to the service.

Value for the business
SACM makes visible how a service, a release or (component of) an IT infrastructure is put together and which performance is delivered by a release or (component of) an IT infrastructure.

Among other things this results in:
- Better forecasting and planning of changes
- Changes and releases to be assessed, planned and successfully delivered
- Incidents and problems to be resolved within the service level targets
- Better adherence to standards, legal and regulatory obligations (fewer non-conformances)
- Ability to identify the costs for a service

Policies
The first step is to develop and maintain the SACM policies that set the objectives, scope and principles and critical success factors for what is to be achieved by the process. There are significant costs and resource implications to implementing SACM and therefore strategic decisions need to be made about the priorities to be addressed. Many IT service providers focus initially on the basic IT assets (hardware and software) and services that are business critical or covered by legal and regulatory compliance e.g.: SOX, software licensing.

Design and planning
The policies describe the starting points for the development and control of assets and CI, for instance:
- The costs of SACM are proportionate to the potential risks to the service if SACM were not implemented
- The need to provide specifications for "*corporate governance*"
- The need to guarantee the agreements in the SLA and other contracts
- The specifications for available, reliable and cost-effective services
- The specifications for performance criteria
- The transition from reactive maintenance to proactive control
- The requirement to maintain adequate asset and configuration information for stakeholders

Basic concepts
Service assets, configuration items, configuration records, the CMS and the SKMS
It is important to distinguish between service assets, configuration items and configuration records, as these concepts are often confused.

Service asset
A service asset is any resource or capability that could contribute to the delivery of a service.

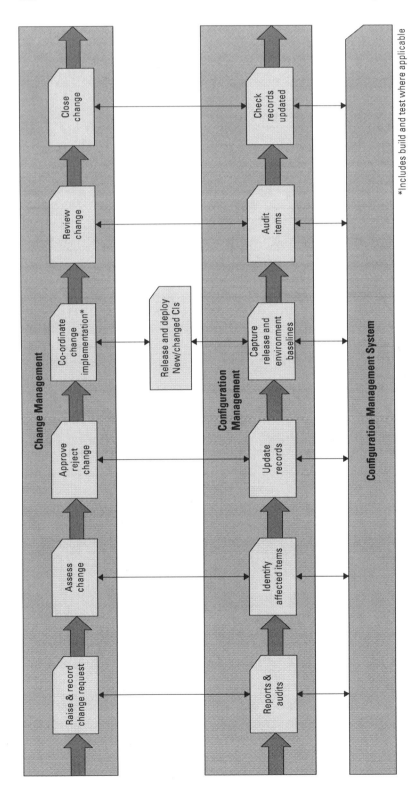

Figure 6.5 The workflow of Change Management and SACM
(source: AXELOS)

Note: service assets and customer assets are essentially defined the same way. The primary difference is that *service-assets* are used by the service provider while *customer-assets* are used by the customers (within the business).

Configuration item

A CI is a service asset that needs to be managed in order to deliver an IT service. Every CI is under the control of the Change Management process. Note that a change considered as a "*pre-approved standard change*" is part of the Change Management process, even if it does not have to be submitted to the CAB.

Configuration record

A configuration record is stored in a CMDB and managed with a CMS. The CI record contains a set of attributes and relationships about a CI – either parent-child or peer-to-peer. It is important to note that a CI is not stored in a CMDB; the configuration *records* in the CMDB describe the CI.

The configuration management database (CMDB)

The CMDB is a set of tools and databases that are used to manage data and information about configuration items. The CMDB is a federated and logical model where multiple individual databases are linked together.

The configuration management system (CMS)

The CMS is a set of the tools, files, and databases that are used to manage the data, information, and knowledge used by the service provider to run itself and support the business. The SACM process is responsible for managing the CMS. The SACM process owns some items in the CMS, but others items such as incident, problem, known error, change, release databases, and the management information systems of the Service Design processes (to name but a few) will be owned and managed by the respective processes.

The service knowledge management system (SKMS)

The SKMS is a set of the tools, files, and databases delivered and supported by the service provider to manage the data, information, and knowledge used by the business to accomplish their outcomes. The SACM process is *not* responsible for managing the SKMS. As with the CMS, various items will be owned and managed by various processes. The Knowledge Management process is responsible for managing the SKMS.

The CMS and the SKMS generally consists of four logical layers:
1. **Presentation layer (top layer)**: To provide different "*views*" of the three previous layers to the service provider and to the business
2. **Knowledge layer**: To process the information into meaningful reports and queries for analysis purposes.

3. **Information layer**: To collate, structure, and integrate the data into meaningful information.
4. **Data layer (bottom layer)**: To collect the data and information from different sources in different file formats

The configuration model
SACM delivers a model of the services, assets, service-assets, customer-assets, and the infrastructure by recording the relationships between configuration items to:
- Assess the impact and cause of incidents and problems
- Assess the impact of proposed changes
- Plan and design new or changed services
- Plan technology refresh and software upgrades
- Plan releases
- Optimize asset utilization and costs

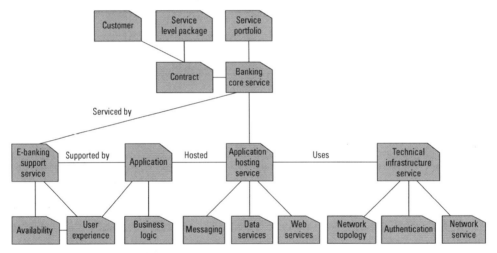

Figure 6.6 Sample logical configuration model

CI types
There are many types of CI, such as: service lifecycle CI; service CI; organizational CI; internal CI; external CI; interface CI.

Where possible, automated tools (such as discovery, inventory and audit tools) are used to populate and maintain the CMDB, CMS and SKMS. This minimizes the opportunity for error and saves costs.

Libraries and stores
ITIL defines various **libraries** to support the CMDB, the CMS, and the SKMS. The libraries will of course be referenced to in the CMDB in the form of CI records. They are also considered part of the CMS or the CKMS.

Definition	Example	
A **secure media library** is a collection of software, electronic or document CI of a known type and status.	Definitive Media Library (DML)	This is a secure store where the definitive, authorized (approved) versions of all media CI are stored and protected.
A **secure hardware store** is a secure location (storage space) where IT assets are stored.	Definitive spares	These are areas set aside for secure storage of definitive hardware spares.

Configuration baseline

A *configuration baseline* is a configuration of a service, or part of a service, that has been formally reviewed, agreed, and signed-off. It serves as the basis for further activities, and that can only be changed through formal change procedures. Configuration baselines are included in the CMS. A baseline is also used to:

■ Mark a milestone in the lifecycle of a service
■ Build a service component from a defined set of inputs
■ Change or rebuild a specific version at a later stage
■ Assemble all relevant components in readiness for a change or release
■ Fall-back to a previous known state in the case of issues during or after a change

Snapshot

A *snapshot* (moment in time) is the most recent status of a CI or environment. A snapshot is stored in the CMS and is kept as a read-only historical record. A snapshot can be used to assist:

■ Problem Management in analyzing the situation at the time incidents occurred
■ Information Security Management in facilitating system restore for security scanning software

6.5.2 Activities, methods, and techniques
The basic SACM process activities consist of:
1. Management and planning
2. Configuration identification
3. Configuration control
4. Status accounting and reporting
5. Verification and audit

1. Management and planning
The management team and configuration management decide what level of configuration management is needed and how this level will be achieved. This is documented in a **configuration management plan**.

2. Configuration identification
Configuration identification focuses on determining and maintaining the naming and version numbering of assets and CI, the mutual relations and the relevant attributes.

Create a **configuration structure** for each IT service. This structure shows the relations and hierarchy between CI for a certain service. The configuration structure has a top-down approach.

Document **naming conventions** and apply them in the identification of CI, documents and changes, but also, for instance, in basic configurations, releases, and compilations.

Each CI must be uniquely identifiable by means of a version number, as there may be several versions of the same CI; for example different versions of software. During the planning of the naming conventions, allow for future growth. The names must also be short but meaningful, and correspond with the existing conventions as much as possible.

Provide all physical CI, such as hardware, with **labels**, so that they are easy to identify. The labels must be easy to read and accessible, so that a user can pass the information on the label on to the service desk. Labels with a barcode are very efficient for physical audits of the CI. During such audits it is checked whether the CI in the organization correspond with those within the CMS.

With the aid of **attributes** information is stored that is relevant for the CI in question. Note that different CI types require different attributes. This is one of the reasons why there are many CMDB. A common attribute must be identified and used to link the various CI types found in various CMDB. A relationship attribute is one such way to accomplish this. The following is a list of *potential* attributes.

Table 6.1 Potential CI attributes

CI unique identifier (number/label or barcode)	Related software
CI type	Historical data (verification or audit trail)
Name	Relationship type
Description	Applicable agreements (SLA, OLA, UC)
Version	Purchase date
Location	Acceptance date
License details (type, expiry date)	Current status
Owner	Planned status
Status	Purchase value
Supplier/source	Residual value after depreciation
Related documents	Comments

The characteristics of a CI or CI type are often recorded in **configuration documentation**.

Table 6.2 RACI table for configuration documentation in the lifecycle

Service Lifecycle Phase	Examples of Service Lifecycle Assets and CI impacted	Service Strategy	Service Design	Service Transition	Service Operations	CSI
Service Strategy	– Portfolios – service contract, customer – Service Strategy requirements – Service Lifecycle Model	A	C	C	R	C
Service Design	– Service Package – (including SLA) – Service Design Package e.g.: – Service Model, Contract, supplier's service management plan, Process interface definition, Customer Engagement plan, – Release Policy – Release Package definition	I	A	C	R	C
Service Transition	– Service Transition model – Test plan – Controlled environments – Build/Installation plan – Build specification – Release plan – Deployment plan – CMS – SKMS – Release Package – Release baseline – Release documentation – Test report	I	C	A	R	C
Service Operations	– Service Operations model – Service Support model – Service Desk – User assets – User documentation – Operations documentation – Support documentation	I	C	C	A/R	R

Relationships describe how CI work together to provide a service. The CMDB maintains these relations to demonstrate the interdependencies between CI, for instance:

- A CI **is part of** another CI – a software module is part of an application (parent-child relation)
- A CI **is connected to** – a workstation is connected to the local area network (LAN)
- A CI **uses** another CI – a business application uses a database
- A CI **is installed on** another CI – word processor is installed on a PC

Relationships are also the mechanism for associating RFC, incidents, problems, known errors, and releases to CI. Relations can be one-to-one, one-to-many and many-to-one.

Configuration items are classed by means of a **classification**, for instance: service, hardware, software documentation, personnel.

3. Configuration control
Configuration control ensures that the CI is adequately managed. No CI can be added, modified, replaced, or removed without following the agreed procedure.

4. Status accounting and reporting
The lifecycle of a component is classified into different stages and the stages that different types of CI go through must be properly documented. For instance, a release goes through the following stages: registered, accepted, installed, and withdrawn.

Status reports give an insight into the current and historical data of each CI and the status changes that have occurred.

Different types of **service asset and configuration reports** are needed for configuration management. The reports may relate to individual CI, but also to a complete service. Such reports may consist of:
- A list of CI and their baseline
- Details on the current status and change history
- A list of unauthorized CI detected
- Reports on the unauthorized use of hardware and software

5. Verification and audit
SACM conducts verifications and audits to ensure that:
- There are no discrepancies between the documented baselines and the actual business environment to which they refer
- CIs physically exist in the organization or DML and spares stores, the functional and operational characteristics of CI can be verified and checks can be made that records in the CMDB match the physical infrastructure
- Release and configuration documentation is present before the release is rolled out

Verification	Regular (ongoing) activity responsible for ensuring that information in the CMDB is accurate and that all configuration items have been identified and recorded in the CMDB
Audit	Periodical formal inspection to check whether a standard or set of guidelines is being followed, that records are accurate, or that efficiency and effectiveness targets are being met. An audit may be carried out by internal or external groups

Document all exceptions resulting from the verifications and audits and report them. Corrective actions (CIs that need to be added, changed, or deleted) are handled via the Change Management process.

Audit tools can perform checks at regular intervals, for instance weekly. For example, a desktop audit tool compares the configuration of an individual's desktop against the "master" configuration that was installed.

6.5.3 Information management
- Backup copies of the CMS should be taken regularly and stored securely. It is advisable for one copy to be kept at a remote location for use in the event of a disaster
- The CMS contains information on backup copies of CI. It will also contain historical records of CI and CI versions that are archived, and possibly also of deleted CI or CI versions
- Typically, the CMS should contain records only for items that are physically available or could be easily created using procedures known to, and under the control of SACM
- The CMS includes pointers to knowledge and information assets that are stored in the SKMS, and it is important to maintain these links and to verify their validity as part of regular audits
- SACM is responsible for the maintenance of many knowledge and information assets within the SKMS, and these must be maintained with the same level of control as the CMS

6.5.4 Interfaces
- **Change Management** – identifying the impact of proposed changes
- **Financial Management for IT Services** – To capture key financial information such as cost, depreciation methods, owner and user, maintenance and repair costs
- **ITSCM** – For increased awareness of the assets on which the business services depend, control of key spares and software
- **Incident Management and Problem Management** – To provide and maintain key diagnostic information
- **Availability Management** – To assist in the detection of points of failure
- **Change Management and Release & Deployment Management** – To benefit from a single coordinated planning approach
- **Configuration control is synonymous with change control** – Understanding and capturing updates to the infrastructure and services
- **SACM** also has close relationships with some business processes, especially fixed asset management and procurement

6.5.5 Triggers
- Updates from Change Management
- Updates from Release & Deployment Management
- Purchase orders
- Acquisitions
- Service requests

6.5.6 Inputs
- Designs, plans and configurations from Service Design Packages
- Requests for change and work orders from Change Management
- Actual configuration information collected by tools and audits
- Information in the organization's fixed asset register

6.5.7 Outputs
- New and updated configuration records
- Updated asset information for use in updating the fixed asset register
- Information about attributes and relationships of CI
- Configuration snapshots and baselines
- Status reports and other consolidated configuration information
- Audit reports

6.5.8 Critical success factors
- Accounting for, managing and protecting the integrity of CI throughout the Service Lifecycle
- Supporting efficient and effective service management processes by providing accurate configuration information at the right time
- Establishing and maintaining an accurate and complete CMS

6.5.9 Metrics
- Improved accuracy regarding the assets used by each customer or business unit
- Increase in re-use and redistribution of under-utilized resources and assets
- Reduction in the use of unauthorized service- and customer-assets
- Reduced number of exceptions reported during configuration audits
- Reduction in time and cost of diagnosing and resolving incidents and problems
- Improved ratio of used licenses against paid-for licenses
- Reduction in risks due to early identification of unauthorized change
- Improved audit compliance
- Shorter audits as quality configuration information is easily accessible

6.5.10 Challenges
- Persuading technical support personnel to adopt a checking in/out policy
- Attracting and justifying funding for SACM
- An attitude of "*just collecting data because it is possible to do*"
- Lack of commitment and support from management

6.5.11 Risks
- The temptation to focus on technology rather than service and business needs
- Degradation of the accuracy of configuration information over time
- Setting the scope too wide

- Setting the scope too narrow
- The CMS becomes out of date due to the movement of hardware assets by non-authorized personnel

6.6 RELEASE & DEPLOYMENT MANAGEMENT

6.6.1 Introduction
ITIL defines Release & Deployment Management as follows:

> **Release & Deployment Management** aims to build, test, and deliver the capability to provide the services specified by Service Design and that will accomplish the stakeholders' requirements and deliver the intended objectives.

The **goal** of Release & Deployment Management (RDM) is to make plans and schedules for and to hold the governance of:
- Building,
- Testing and
- Deployment of releases and
- Delivery of a new desired functionality needed by the business and the protection of the integrity of the existing services.

The **objectives** of RDM are:
- To make and agree upon release and deployment plans with customers and other stakeholders
- To make and test release packages
- To guarantee the integrity of release packages during all transition activities
- To deploy release packages from the DML to the operation phase based on the agreed plan and schedule
- To ensure that release packages can be traced, installed, tested, verified and/or can be reset when necessary
- To guarantee that changes from the business and from the service management organization are managed during release and deployment activities
- To ensure that the new service offers the desired utility and warranty
- Recording and managing the disruptions, risks and issues and taking the desired action
- Ensure that knowledge transfer to the customers and managers takes place

Scope
The processes, systems, and functions for packaging, building, testing, and deployment of a release into production and establishment of the service specified in the SDP before final handover to Service Operations.

The process is responsible for testing the changes, the remediation, and the implementation method for the changes thoroughly. But testing is an activity within the process Service Validation & Testing, see Section 6.7.

The authorization for implementing changes comes from the Change Management process.

Value for the business
Effective RDM contributes to the business because:
- Changes are realized faster, cheaper and with fewer risks, and the operational objectives are supported better
- The implementation approach is more consistent and the traceability requirements (e.g.: audits, legislation etc.) are complied with more closely

Basic concepts

A **release** is a set of new or changed configuration items that are tested and will be implemented into production together.

A **release unit** is the portion of the service or infrastructure that is included in the release, in accordance with the organization's release policy and guidelines. Releases are documented in the CMS for the support of the Release & Deployment process.

It is important to determine the correct level of the release. For a business critical application it may make sense to include the complete application in the release unit, but for a website it may only have to be the HTML page that is changed.

Releases can be classified into the following **release categories**: *major releases; minor releases;* and *emergency releases.*

In the **release design** different considerations apply in respect of the way in which the release is deployed. The most frequently occurring options for the rollout of releases are:
- Big bang versus phased
- Push and pull
- Automated or manual

A **release package** is a single release unit or a structured set of release units. In the case of a new or a changed service all the elements of which the service consists – the infrastructure, hardware, software, applications, documentation, knowledge, etc. – must be taken into account.

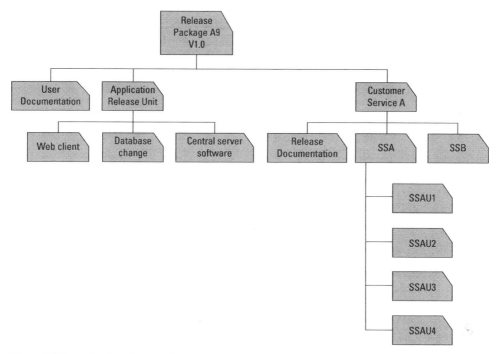

Figure 6.7 Example of a release package

(source: AXELOS)

Release and deployment models

Release and deployment models define:

- Release structure
- The exit and entry criteria
- Controlled environments for builds and tests
- The roles and responsibilities for each CI
- The release promotion and configuration baseline model
- Template release and deployment schedules
- Supporting systems, tools and procedures for documenting activities

6.6.2 Activities, methods, and techniques

RDM is divided into four phases. See Table 6.2 for a detailed description.

Table 6.3 The four phases of Release & Deployment Management

Release & deployment planning	Plans for creating and deploying the release are created
Release build & test	The release package is built, tested and checked into the DML
Deployment	The release package in the DML is deployed to the live environment
Review and close	Experience and feedback are captured, performance targets and achievements are reviewed and lessons are learned

1. Release and deployment planning

Before a deployment goes into production different plans are formulated. The type and number depends on the size and complexity of the environment and the changed or new service. Release and deployment plans form part of the overall Service Transition plan. Change Management will approve or reject the plans.

The following (sub) plans are relevant for release and deployment:
- Pass/fail criteria
- Building and test plans
- Controlled environments
- Planning release packaging and build
- Preparations for release build and test
- Deployment planning
- Logistics and delivery planning
- Planning of pilots
- Financial/commercial planning

2. Release build and test

During the release build and test stage, the common services, and infrastructure need to be managed carefully, since they can significantly affect the build and test of a technology-enabled service and its underlying technology infrastructure.
- Release and build documentation
- Acquire and test input configuration items and components
- Release packaging
- Build and manage the test environments
- Service testing and pilots
- Service rehearsals
- Pilots

3. Deployment
- Plan and prepare for deployment
- Assess readiness of target group
- Develop plans
- Perform transfer, deployment, and retirement
- Change/transfer financial assets
- Transfer/transition business and organization
- Deploy processes and materials
- Deploy service management capability
- Transfer service
- Deploy service
- Decommissioning and service retirement
- Remove redundant assets
- Verify deployment

- Remediate/back out release
- Early life support

4. Review and close

To finalize the Service Transition as a whole a formal change evaluation must be performed that is tailored to the scale and scope of the change.

6.6.3 Information management

Throughout the RDM process, appropriate records will be created and maintained. As configuration items are successfully deployed, the CMS will be updated with information such as:

- New, changed, or removed configuration items
- Relationships between requirements and test cases
- New, changed, or removed locations and users
- Status updates
- Change in ownership of assets
- License holding

Other data and information will also be captured and recorded within the broader SKMS. This could include:

- Release packages in the DML
- Installation/build plans
- Logistics and delivery plans
- Validation and test plans, evidence and reports
- Deployment information, deployment history, who was involved, timings, etc.
- Training records
- Access rules and levels
- Known errors

6.6.4 Interfaces

- **Design coordination**
  - The Design Coordination process creates the SDP that defines the new service, including all aspects of how it should be created
  - Plans and packages should be developed and documented during the Service Design stage, and Design Coordination will ensure that these are documented in the SDP
- **Transition Planning & Support**
  - Provides the framework for RDM to operate in, and transition plans provide the context for release and deployment plans
- **Change Management**
  - Provides the authorization for the work
  - RDM provides the execution of many changes
  - Release and deployment plans are a significant part of the change schedule
  - Deployment review is often combined with the review and closure of the change

- **SACM**
  - RDM depends on data and information in the CMS, and provides many updates to the CMS.
- **Service Validation & Testing**
  - To ensure that testing is carried out when necessary
  - To ensure that builds are available when required by Service Validation & Testing

6.6.5 Triggers

The activities start with receipt of an authorized change to plan, build, and test a production-ready release package. Deployment starts with receipt of an authorized change to deploy a release package to a target deployment group or environment. As a result the service is available for the intended user group.

6.6.6 Inputs

- Authorized change
- SDP
- IT service continuity plan and related business continuity plan
- Service management and operations plans and standards
- Technology and procurement standards and catalogues
- Acquired service assets and components and their documentation
- Build models and plans
- Environment requirements and specifications for build, test, release, training, disaster recovery, pilot and deployment
- Release policy and release design from Service Design
- Release and deployment models including template plans
- Exit and entry criteria for each stage of Release & Deployment Management

6.6.7 Outputs

- New, changed or retired services
- Release and deployment plan
- Updates to Change Management for the Release & Deployment activities
- Service notification
- Notification to Service Catalogue Management to update the service catalogue with the relevant information about the new or changed service
- New tested service capability and environments
- New or changed service management documentation
- SLA, underpinning OLA, and contracts
- New or changed service reports
- Tested continuity plans
- Complete and accurate configuration item list with an audit trail for the CI in the release package and also the new or changed service and infrastructure configurations
- Updated service capacity plan aligned to the relevant business plans

- Baselined release package – checked in to DML and ready for future deployments
- Service Transition report

6.6.8 Critical success factors
- Defining and agreeing release plans with customers and stakeholders
- Ensuring integrity of a release package and its constituent components throughout the transition activities
- Ensuring that the new or changed service is capable of delivering the agreed utility and warranty
- Ensuring that there is appropriate knowledge transfer

6.6.9 Metrics
Increased…
- Number and percentage of releases that make use of a common framework of standards, re-usable processes and supporting documentation
- Number and percentage of releases that meet customer expectations for cost, time and quality
- Score in surveys of customer, user, and Service Operation function satisfaction with Release & Deployment Management
- Customer and user satisfaction with the services delivered

Reduced…
- Number of CMS and DML audit failures related to releases
- Number of deployments from sources other than the DML
- Number of incidents due to incorrect components being deployed
- Variance from service performance required by customers
- Number of incidents against the service
- Customer dissatisfaction
- Resources and costs to diagnose and fix incidents and problems in deployment and live use
- Number of incidents categorized as *user knowledge*

6.6.10 Challenges
- Developing standard performance measures and measurement methods across projects and suppliers
- Dealing with projects and suppliers where estimated delivery dates are inaccurate and there are delays in scheduling Service Transition activities
- Understanding the different stakeholder perspectives that underpin effective risk management for the change impact assessment and test activities
- Building a thorough understanding of risks that have impacted or may impact successful Service Transition of services and releases
- Encouraging a risk management culture where people share information and take a pragmatic and measured approach to risk

6.6.11 Risks

- Poorly defined scope and understanding of dependencies in earlier lifecycle stages
- Using personnel who are not dedicated to the activities of the process
- Failing to use the process to manage service retirement
- Lack of...
  - Integration with the appropriate financial cycles and activities
  - Integration with the appropriate corporate governance, regulatory controls, and requirements regarding licensing and security
  - Operational support
  - Consideration for all capabilities and resources
  - Consideration for people, process, products and partner aspects
- Not managing or addressing organizational and stakeholder change:
- Poor commitment and decision-making
- Failure to obtain appropriate authorization at the right time
- Indecision or late decision-making
- Inadequate or inaccurate information
- Health and safety compromised
- Inadequate time allowed for Release & Deployment Management
- Not managing suppliers/sourcing/partnering relationships during transition:
- Inadequate "*back-out*" or "*contingency*" plan if sourcing/partnering fails

■ 6.7   SERVICE VALIDATION & TESTING

6.7.1 Introduction

Testing of services is an important contribution to the quality of IT service provision. Testing ensures that new (or changed) services are **fit for purpose** and **fit for use**.

"Fit for purpose" means that the service does what the customer expects of it, so that the service supports the business. "*Fit for use*" addresses such aspects as availability, continuity, capacity and security of the service.

Insufficient attention to testing may result in: increase of incidents, issues, and errors, extra service desk phone calls with questions regarding the functioning of the service, higher costs, and a service that is improperly used.

The **goal** of Service Validation & Testing (SVT) is to provide a service that adds value to the customers and their business.

The **objectives** of SVT are to ensure that:
- Offering confidence that a release results into a new or changed service, that creates the expected results and value for customers, within the budget, desired capacity and conditions

- To ensure the quality of a release, the service components of the release and the ability of service provision delivered by the release
- To validate that a service is "*fit for purpose*", that it will deliver the agreed utility
- To validate that a service is "*fit for use*" that it will deliver the agreed warranty
- To ensure that a new or changed service meets to the specifications of the customers and other stakeholders. And that these specifications are documented in a correct manner so that improving errors can take place at an early stage in the lifecycle
- To plan and implement a structured validation and testing process. This process has to prove that the new or changed service supports the business of the customer and complies with the specifications of the stakeholders, including the agreed service levels
- To identify, assess and address issues, errors and risks during the Service Transition phase

Scope

SVT is applied during the entire Service Lifecycle, and is aimed at testing the quality of service (units), and intended to verify whether the service provider has sufficient capacity and resources in order to provide a service or service release successfully.

Testing is also particularly supportive of the release and deployment processes. In addition, the Change Evaluation process will be using test results.

Value for the business

Service interruptions may be damaging to business operations of service provider and customers who are recipients of the services. They may result in damage to reputation, financial loss and even (fatal) accidents. For example, the role of IT in hospitals, the automotive or aerospace industries can mean injury or death if service delivery fails.

Basic concepts

The **service model** (see Figure 6.8) describes the structure and dynamics of a service provided by Service Operation. The structure consists of core and supporting services and service assets needed. When a new (or changed) service is designed, developed, and built, these service assets are tested in relation to design specifications and requirements. Activities, flow of resources, coordination, and interactions describe the dynamics.

Policies for SVT are:
- Service Transition policies
- Change Management policies
- Service quality policies
- Risk policies
- Reusability policies
- Release policies
- Mandatory integral testing and involving all stakeholders herein

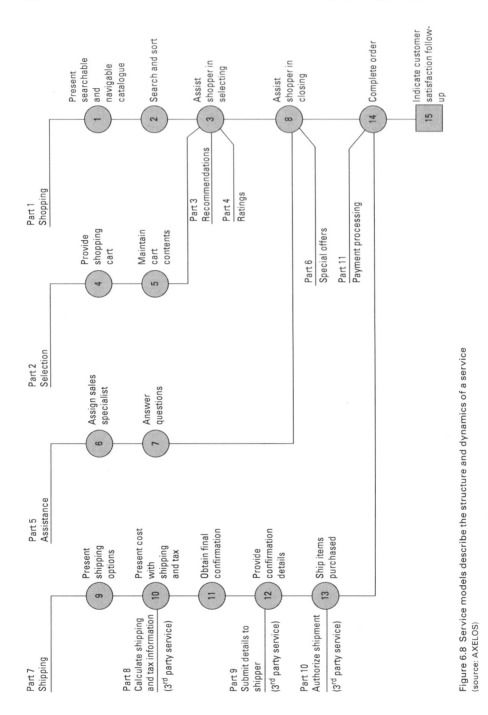

Figure 6.8 Service models describe the structure and dynamics of a service
(source: AXELOS)

The **test strategy** defines the overall testing approach and the allocation of desired resources. This strategy might be applicable to the entire organization, a collection of services or an individual service. All test strategies are developed in collaboration with the stakeholders. Attention is paid to objectives, scope, standards, test processes, test metrics, test approach, requirements, and "*deliverables*".

A **test model** consists of a test plan, what is to be tested and test scripts that indicate the method by which each element must be tested. In order to ensure that the process can be repeated, test models must be structured in such a way that:
- The specification or design criteria being tested can be traced
- Test activities, evaluation and reports can be audited
- Test elements can be maintained and changed

There are very many different **test techniques** and **test approaches**. The technique and approach depends on the service type, risk profile, test goal and test level. Examples include: document review, modeling, simulation, scenario testing, role play and laboratory testing, live pilot.

Design considerations that are important for testing relate to:
- Finances (is the budget big enough?),
- Documentation (is everything available, and in the correct format?),
- Composition (build),
- Testability (think of resources, time and facilities),
- Traceability (traceable to specifications),
- When and where testing is to take place, and
- Remediation (is there a backup plan?).

6.7.2 Activities, methods, and techniques
The activities below are not necessarily performed in this order; they might also take place parallel to each other. The following activities can be distinguished:
1. Validation and test management
2. Planning and design
3. Verification of test plan and design
4. Prepare test environment
5. Testing
6. Evaluate exit criteria and report
7. Clean up and closure

Figure 6.9 schematically displays the testing process.

1. Validation and test management
Test management consists of planning and managing (control), and reporting on the activities taking place during all test phases of the Service Transition.

2. Planning and design
Test planning and design activities take place early in the Service Lifecycle.

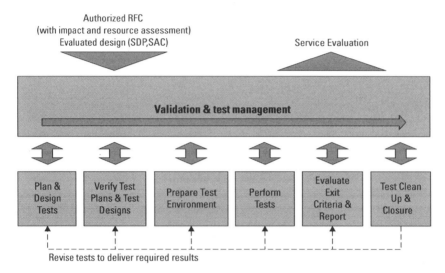

Figure 6.9 Schematic display of the test process

(source: AXELOS)

3. Verification of test plan and design
Test plans and designs are verified to make sure that everything (including scripts) is complete, and that test models sufficiently take into account the risk profile of the service in question and all possible interfaces.

4. Preparation of test environment
Prepare the test environment and make a baseline configuration of the test environment.

5. Testing
The tests are executed using manual or automated testing techniques and procedures. Testers register all results. If a test fails, the reason is documented.

6. Evaluate exit criteria and report
The actual results are compared with projected results (exit criteria). Test results can be interpreted in terms of "*pass/fail*" (approval or not), any risks the tested object may contain for service provider or client, or in terms of costs required to reach the projected goal.

7. Clean up and closure
Make sure that the test environment is cleaned up. Review the test approach and identify improvements.

Critical success factors for implementation are:
- Issues are identified in an early stage of the lifecycle
- Quality is built into every phase of the lifecycle, for example by using the "V" model

- Reusable test models are designed, and testing provides the proof that all configurations have been built and implemented according to customer requirements

Risks for implementation are:
- Unclear expectations and objectives, lack of understanding that testing is a critical process in relation to quality of service provision
- Lack of resources

6.7.3 Information management

Testing benefits greatly from re-use of test scripts and test files and to this end it is advisable to create and maintain a library of relevant tests and an updated and maintained data set for applying and performing tests. Also record the way in which these tests should be executed and implemented. No matter how well a test is designed, without good test data, the test is useless. Therefore, take the upkeep of test data seriously. For this purpose, it is important that:
- Test data is separated from live data
- Data protection regulations are taken into account
- Backup and recovery procedures are in place

6.7.4 Interfaces

- Testing supports all of the RDM steps within Service Transition
- **RDM** is responsible for ensuring that appropriate testing takes place
- The output of SVT is a key input to **Change Evaluation**, and must be provided at an appropriate time and in a suitable format to enable changes to be evaluated in time for Change Management decision-making
- The **test strategy** will ensure that the testing process works with all stages of the lifecycle
- Working with **Design Coordination** to ensure that designs are inherently testable and providing positive support in achieving this
- Working closely with **CSI** to feed failure information and improvement ideas resulting from testing exercises
- **Service Operation** will use maintenance tests to ensure the continued efficacy of services
- **Service Strategy** should accommodate testing in terms of adequate funding, resource, profile, etc.

6.7.5 Triggers

The trigger for testing is a scheduled activity on a release plan, test plan, or quality assurance plan.

6.7.6 Inputs
- RFC
- The SDP, which includes:
  - The service charter
  - Service provider interface definitions
  - Operation models
  - Capacity/resource model and plan
  - Financial/economic/cost models
  - Service management model
  - Test conditions and expected results
  - Design and interface specifications
  - Release and deployment plans
  - Acceptance criteria

6.7.7 Outputs
- The direct output from testing is the report delivered to Change Evaluation:
  - Configuration baseline of the testing environment
  - Testing carried out
  - Results from those tests
  - Analysis of the results
- Other outputs include:
  - Updated data, information and knowledge to be added to the service knowledge management system
  - Test incidents, problems and error records
  - Entries in the CSI register to address potential improvements in any area that impacts on testing
  - Third-party relationships, suppliers of equipment or services, partners, users and customers or other stakeholders

6.7.8 Critical success factors
- Understanding the different stakeholder perspectives that underpin effective risk management for the change impact assessment and test activities
- Building a thorough understanding of risks that have impacted or may impact successful Service Transition of services and releases
- Encouraging a risk management culture where people share information and take a pragmatic and measured approach to risk
- Providing evidence that the service assets and configurations have been built and implemented correctly, in addition to the service delivering what the customer needs
- Developing re-usable test models
- Achieving a balance between the cost of testing and effectiveness of testing

6.7.9 Metrics

■ Roles and responsibilities for…
  • Impact assessment and test activities have been agreed and documented
  • Customers, users and service provider personnel have been agreed and documented
■ Increase in…
  • The percentage of impact assessments and test activities where the documented roles have been correctly involved
  • The number of risks identified in Service Design or early in Service Transition compared to those detected during or after testing
  • Ratio of errors detected in Service Design compared to Service Transition, and of errors detected in Service Transition compared to Service Operation
  • Percentage of service acceptance criteria that have been tested for new and changed services
  • The effective use of resources and increased customer involvement
  • A better understanding from stakeholders of the roles and responsibilities connected with the new or changed service
  • The number of test data that can be reused
  • The number of known errors that is discovered and documented in an early stage of the testing

■ Reduction in…
  • The impact of incidents and errors for newly transitioned services
  • The variance between test budget and test expenditure
  • The cost of fixing errors, due to earlier detection
  • The business impact due to delays in testing
  • The effort and cost to set up a test environment
  • The effort required to detect errors, and to decrease the number of *"repeated errors"*

6.7.10 Challenges

■ Inability to maintain a test environment and test data that matches the live environment
■ Insufficient personnel, skills and testing tools to deliver adequate testing coverage
■ Projects overrunning and allocated testing time frames being squeezed to restore project go-live dates but at the cost of quality
■ Development of standard performance measures and measurement methods across projects and suppliers
■ Projects and suppliers estimating delivery dates inaccurately and causing delays in scheduling Service Transition activities

6.7.11 Risks

■ Unclear expectations/objectives
■ Lack of understanding of the risks, resulting in testing that is not targeted at critical elements that need to be well controlled and therefore tested

■ Resource shortages which introduce delays and have an impact on other Service Transitions

■ 6.8   CHANGE EVALUATION

6.8.1 Introduction

The **goal** of Change Evaluation is to provide a consistent and standardized means of determining the performance of a service change, its (potential) impacts on business outcomes, on existing and proposed services, and the IT infrastructure. The actual performance of a change is assessed against its predicted performance. Risks and issues related to the change are identified and managed.

The **objectives** of the Change Evaluation process are:
■ Ensure that the expectations of the stakeholders are met with and that accurate information is delivered to Change Management. Delivering the right information to Change Management may prevent that changes that have a negative impact on service delivery, and causing certain risks, have access to the Service Transition phase
■ Evaluate the intended and non-intended (as is reasonably practical) effects of a service change
■ Delivering high quality and accurate information to Change Management, so that it is able to make the right decisions regarding the authorization of a service change

Scope
The scope covers the evaluation of new or changed services at regular intervals during the lifecycle of a change as required by the change model or business requirements.

Value for the business
Change Evaluation delivers an important piece of input for CSI and the future improvement of service development and Change Management.

Policies, starting points and basic concepts
The following **policies** apply:
■ service designs or service changes are evaluated before being transitioned
■ All deviations between predicted and actual performance are managed by the customer (agent), e.g.: acceptance yes/no
■ All changes will be assessed as required
■ Identify risks and issues related to the service that is being changed
■ The customer is involved with change evaluation

The following **starting points** are important in the execution of the process:
■ The unintended effects of a change (and its consequences) must be identified
■ A service change is evaluated fairly, consistently, openly and objectively

6.8.2 Activities, methods, and techniques

The change Evaluation process consists of the following activities:

1. Create an evaluation plan
2. Understand the intended effect of a change
3. Understand the unintended effect of a change
4. Identify the factors for considering the effect of a service change
5. Evaluate the predicted performance
6. Evaluate the actual performance
7. Perform risk management
8. Generate an evaluation report

Figure 6.10 shows the Change Evaluation process including inputs and outputs.

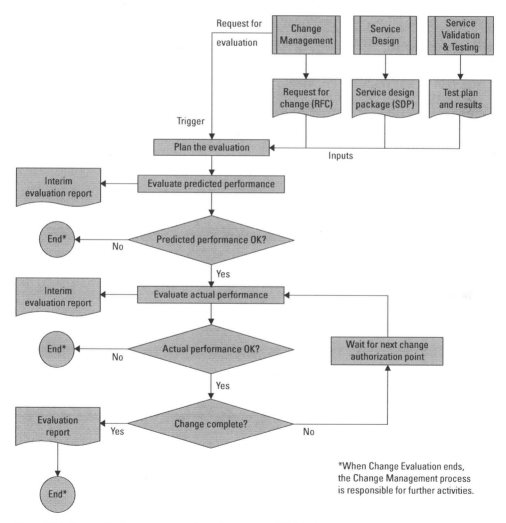

Figure 6.10 Change Evaluation process (based on source: AXELOS)

6.8.3 Information management
■ The SKMS provides most of the information required for Change Evaluation
■ All evaluation reports should be checked into, and out of, the CMS
■ Softcopy versions of the reports should be stored in the SKMS

6.8.4 Interfaces
■ **Transition Planning & Support** – To ensure that appropriate resources are available when needed
■ **Change Management** – To agree on which types of change will be subject to formal evaluation
■ **Service Design** – To provide the Service Design Package
■ **SLM** – To ensure a full understanding of the impact of any issues identified, and to obtain use of user or customer resources
■ **BRM** – To ensure a full understanding of the impact of any issues identified, and to obtain use of user or customer resources
■ **SVT** – To coordinate activities with this process to ensure that required inputs are available in sufficient time

6.8.5 Triggers
■ The receipt of a request for Change Evaluation from Change Management

6.8.6 Inputs
■ SDP, including service charter and SAC (Service Acceptation Criteria)
■ Change proposal
■ RFC, change record and detailed change documentation
■ Discussions with stakeholders
■ Test results and report

6.8.7 Outputs
■ Interim evaluation report(s) for Change Management
■ Evaluation report for Change Management

6.8.8 Critical success factors
■ Stakeholders have a good understanding of the expected performance of new and changed services
■ Change Management has good quality evaluations to help them make correct decisions

6.8.9 Metrics
■ Increased…
  • Stakeholder satisfaction with new or changed services as measured in customer surveys
  • Percentage of evaluations delivered by agreed time

- Change Management personnel satisfaction with the Change Evaluation process as measured in regular surveys.
- Reduced number of...
  - Incidents for new or changed services due to failure to deliver expected utility or warranty
  - Changes that have to be backed out due to unexpected errors or failures
  - Failed changes

6.8.10 Challenges

- Developing standard performance measures and measurement methods across projects and suppliers
- Understanding the different stakeholder perspectives
- Understanding, and being able to assess, the balance between managing and taking risks
- Measuring and demonstrating the variation in predictions during and after transition
- Taking a pragmatic and measured approach to risk
- Effectively communicating the organization's appetite and approach to risk management during risk evaluation
- Building a thorough understanding of how risks can impact successful Service Transition
- Encouraging a culture where people share information

6.8.11 Risks

- Lack of clear understanding when change evaluation should be used
- Unrealistic expectations of the time required to complete change evaluation
- Personnel with insufficient experience or organizational authority to be able to influence change authorities
- Inaccurately estimating dates for project or supplier delivery

■ 6.9   KNOWLEDGE MANAGEMENT

6.9.1 Introduction

The **goal** of Knowledge Management is to improve the quality of the (management's) decision-making process by ensuring that reliable and secure information is available during the Service Lifecycle.

The **objectives** of Knowledge Management are, among others:

- Improving the quality of the decision making process (of the management), by ensuring that accurate information is available during the Service Lifecycle
- To support the service provider in order to improve the efficiency and quality of the services

- Ensuring that the personnel of the service provider has a clear and shared understanding about how services/service delivery creates value for the customers
- Maintenance of the SKMS
- Collecting, analyzing, retrieving, sharing, using and maintaining knowledge, information and data

Scope
Knowledge Management is used throughout the entire lifecycle.

Value for the business
Knowledge Management is particularly relevant during Service Transition, since relevant and appropriate knowledge is one of the key service elements being transitioned. Specific examples of the application of knowledge management during Service Transition are:
- Training and knowledge transfer, intellectual property, compliance information and standards
- The documentation of errors, workarounds and test information

Basic concepts
Knowledge Management is often visualized using the **DIKW** structure: Data-Information-Knowledge-Wisdom. See Figure 6.11.

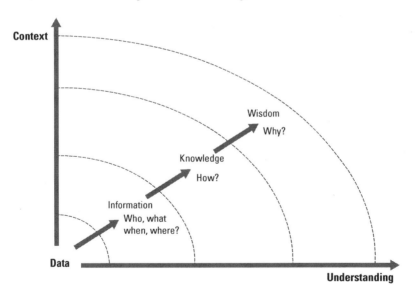

Figure 6.11 DIKW model
(source: AXELOS)

The basis of the SKMS is formed by a considerable amount of data in a central database or CMS and the CMDB: the CMDB feeds the CMS and the CMS provides input for the SKMS and so supports the decision-making process. However, the scope of the SKMS is broader: information is also stored that relates to matters such as:

- The experience and skills of personnel
- Information about peripheral matters such as the behavior of users and the performance of the organization
- Requirements and expectations of service providers and partners
- High quality information, as can be found on an intranet

6.9.2 Activities, methods, and techniques

Knowledge Management is comprised of the following activities, methods, and techniques:
1. Knowledge management strategy
2. Knowledge transfer
3. Data and information management
4. The use of the SKMS

1. Knowledge management strategy

An organization needs an overall knowledge management strategy. If such a strategy is already in place, the service management knowledge strategy can link into it. The knowledge management strategy also focuses specifically on documenting relevant knowledge, and on the data and information that support this knowledge.

2. Knowledge transfer

The transfer of knowledge is a challenging task, requiring, in the first place, an analysis to determine what the knowledge gap is between the department or person in possession of the knowledge and those in need of the knowledge. Based on the outcome of this analysis, a communication (improvement) plan is formulated to facilitate the knowledge transfer.

3. Information management

Data and information management consists of the following activities:
- Establishing data and information requirements
- Definition of information architecture
- Establishing data and information management procedures
- Evaluation and improvement

4. Use of the SKMS

Supplying services to customers in different time zones and regions and with different operating hours imposes strenuous requirements on the sharing of knowledge. For this reason the service provider must develop and maintain an SKMS system that is available to all stakeholders and suits all information requirements.

In addition to material for training and knowledge gathering it is useful to:
- Incorporate (IT and business) terminology lists and their translation into the system
- Document the operational processes and where they interface with IT

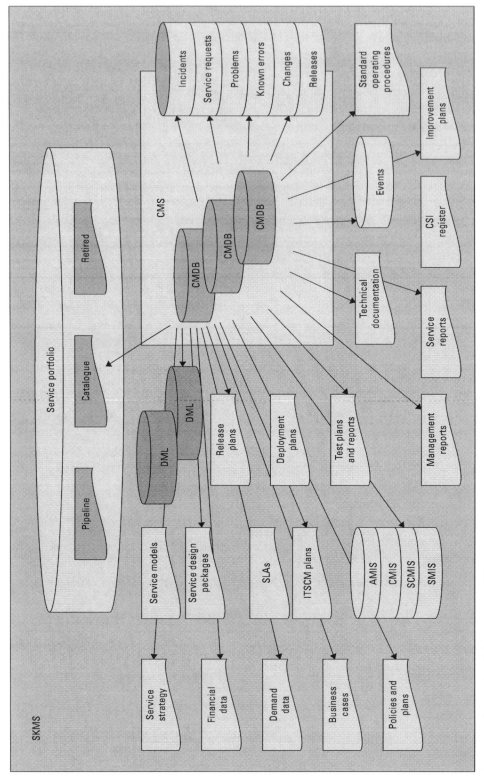

Figure 6.12 Sample SKMS (source: AXELOS)

- Include SLA and other contracts that can change as a result of a Service Transition
- Include known errors, workarounds and process diagrams

6.9.3 Information management

- The SKMS consists of a large number of tools and repositories, either running independently or within a federated model allowing for cross-referencing, thus creating additional value.
- The most important aspect of information management is to understand and document items of data, information, and knowledge that the organization actually needs.

6.9.4 Interfaces

- The SKMS can only be truly effective if all personnel, through the execution of all process activities, use it to store and manage data and information. All processes managing their data and information should use knowledge management concepts and activities to manage these.
- The selection of a knowledge management tool will impact the tool selection for all other service management processes, and vice versa.

6.9.5 Triggers

- BRM storing the minutes of a customer meeting
- Updates to the service catalogue or service portfolio
- Modification of a Service Design Package
- Creation of a new or updated capacity plan
- Receipt of an updated user manual from a supplier
- Creation of a customer report
- Updates to the CSI register

6.9.6 Inputs

- Inputs to knowledge management include all data, information, and knowledge used by the service provider, as well as relevant business data

6.9.7 Outputs

- The knowledge, maintained within the SKMS, that is required to make decisions and to manage the IT services
- Errors detected during a Service Transition will be made available to the personnel involved with Service Operation functions

6.9.8 Critical success factors

- Availability of information and knowledge that supports management decision-making
- Reduced time and effort required in supporting and maintaining services

- Successful implementation with few knowledge-related errors and early life operation of new and changed services
- Improved management of standards and policies
- Reduced dependency on personnel for knowledge

6.9.9 Metrics
- Reduced transfer of issues to other people and more resolution at lower levels
- Increased number of times that material is re-used in documentation such as procedures, test design and service desk scripts
- Increased percentage of incidents solved by use of known errors
- Increased percentage of successful service transitions
- Increased number of times that standards and policies in the SKMS have been accessed
- Increased percentage of standards and policies that have been reviewed by the agreed review date
- Increased percentage of SKMS searches that receive a rating of "*good*" by users, IT personnel and management

6.9.10 Challenges
- Justifying the effort needed to create a consistent architecture for managing data, information, and knowledge
- Helping all the stakeholders understand the added value of pursuing a holistic and ongoing approach to knowledge management

6.9.11 Risks
- Focusing on the technology instead of creating value
- Insufficient understanding of the data, information, and knowledge that are needed by the organization
- Lack of investment in planning, designing, implementing, and maintaining the SKMS, including technology and personnel
- Focusing too much on capturing knowledge to the detriment of knowledge transfer and re-use
- Storing and sharing outdated and irrelevant data, information and knowledge
- Lack of support and commitment from stakeholders

■ 6.10 ORGANIZATION

On the whole, the activities of a process are not carried out by a single department. The different activities, for example of SACM, are carried out by departments such as service production, application management, network management, and system management. Therefore, the process activities are related to the different IT departments and their respective personnel. Roles and responsibilities are also defined.

6.10.1 Generic roles

Process owner – The process owner ensures all process activities are carried out and:

■ Is responsible for the process strategy, and assists in the design
■ Provides process documentation, guidelines and procedures and their application
■ Ensures there are adequate resources

Service owner – The service owner holds responsibility, to the customer, for the initiation, transition, and maintenance of a service and:

■ Is the contact person and ensures that the service meets the requirements
■ Identifies improvement points and provides data and reports for service monitoring
■ Is accountable to IT management for the delivery of the service

6.10.2 Organizational context

The interfaces of other departments and third parties in Service Transition must be clearly defined and known. Programs, projects, service design, and service provider all contribute towards the Service Transition.

Service Transition is actively managed by a **service transition manager**. The service transition manager is responsible for the daily management and control of the service transition teams and their activities. An example of a Service Transition organization is presented in Figure 6.13.

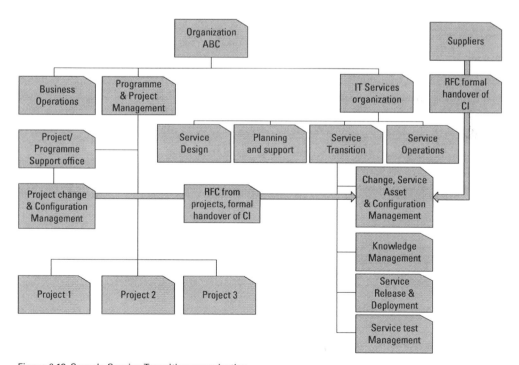

Figure 6.13 Sample Service Transition organization

(source: AXELOS)

6.10.3 Service Transition roles and responsibilities

This section describes a number of roles and responsibilities within Service Transition, although some roles also fall within other lifecycle phases. Depending on the size of the organization and the scope of the service that is changed, some of these roles can be carried out by one person.

The responsibilities of the **service asset manager** include:
- Formulating process objectives and implementing the policy, the process standards, plans and procedures
- Indicating the scope and function of the process, which items must be managed and the information that must be established
- Taking care of communication about the process and making it known
- Taking care of resources and training
- Setting up the identification and naming conventions of assets
- Taking care of the evaluation of the use of tooling
- Setting up interfaces with other processes
- Planning the completion of the asset database
- Making reports
- Assisting with audits and taking care of corrective actions

The responsibilities of the **configuration manager** include:
- Formulating process objectives and implementing the policy, the process standards, plans and procedures
- Evaluating the existing configuration management systems and implementing the new systems
- Indicating the scope and function of the process, which items must be managed and the information that must be established
- Taking care of communication about the process and making it known
- Taking care of resources and training
- Setting up the identification and naming conventions of CI
- Taking care of the evaluation of the use of tooling
- Setting up interfaces with other processes
- Evaluating existing CMS systems and implementation of new systems
- Planning the filling in of CMS in the CMDB
- Making reports
- Assisting with audits and taking corrective actions

The **change manager** has responsibilities (some of which can be delegated) including:
- Receiving, logging and prioritizing (in collaboration with the initiator) RFC, rejecting RFC based on the agreed criteria
- Preparing and chairing CAB and ECAB meetings
- Deciding who attends which meeting, receives RFC, what must be changed
- Publishing Changes Schedules (SCs)

- Maintaining change logs
- Closing RFC
- Reviewing implemented changes
- Making reports

The **CAB** is an advisory consultation body. The specific roles and responsibilities of the CAB are explained in Section 6.4.

The responsibilities of the **release packaging and build manager** include:
- Final release configuration
- Building the final release and testing it (before independent testing)
- Reporting known faults and workarounds
- Input to the final implementation sign-off

The **deployment manager** is responsible for the following including:
- The final service implementation
- Coordination of all release documentation, release notes, and communication
- Planning of the deployment, in combination with Change Management, Knowledge Management and SACM
- Providing guidance during the release process
- Giving feedback concerning the effectiveness of a release
- Recording metrics for deployment to ensure within agreed SLA

ITIL recognizes the following roles in the Service Transition phase of the Service Lifecycle, but this falls outside the scope of this book and the ITIL Foundation exams:
- Configuration analyst
- Configuration manager
- CMS manager
- Configuration management team
- Change authority
- Risk-evaluation manager
- Service knowledge manager
- Test support
- Early life support (ELS)
- Building and test environment management

6.10.4 Organizational change management

Significant change of a service also means a change of the organization. This can vary from "*the transfer of a personnel member to another department*" to large changes such as "*the manner of working in the organization*". For example: a mail order company no longer sells its products by a printed catalogue but via a website.

The following aspects are important in organizational change management:
■ The emotional change cycle
■ The role of Service Transition in organizational changes
■ Planning and implementation of organizational changes
■ Products
■ Evaluation of readiness for organizational change
■ Monitoring of progress
■ Managing organizational changes in sourcing
■ Methods and techniques for organizational changes regarding the sourcing of IT services. E.g.: the decision to outsource a part of the IT infrastructure

6.10.5 Stakeholder management

Stakeholder management is a critical success factor in Service Transition. This is why a strategy should be developed in the Service Design phase. It explains:
■ Who the stakeholders are
■ What their interest are
■ What their influence is
■ How they are included in the project or program
■ What information is shared with them

A stakeholder map is a useful tool to map the different interest of the stakeholders (see Figure 6.14).

Stakeholders	Strategic direction	Financial	Operational changes	Interface with customers	Public safety	Competitive position
Business partner	●	●		●		●
Project teams			●			
Customers		●		●	●	
Press and media						●
Trade unions			●			
Staff	●		●			
Regulatory bodies		●			●	

Figure 6.14 Sample stakeholder map

(source: AXELOS)

Further, a **stakeholder analysis** assists in finding out what the requirements and interests of the stakeholders are, and what their final influence and power will be during the transition.

Finally, the turnover of stakeholders during the Service Lifecycle must also be considered. In practice there is a continual in, though, and out stream of stakeholders, with all consequences for the knowledge regarding service delivery, internal agreements, and manners of communication.

■ 6.11   METHODS, TECHNOLOGY AND TOOLS

Technology plays an important part in the support of Service Transition. It can be divided into two types:

- **ITSM systems**:
  - Enterprise frameworks which offer integration capabilities to integrate and link in the CMDB or other tools
  - System, network and application management tools
  - Service dashboards and reporting tools

- **Specific ITSM technology and tools**:
  - Service knowledge management systems
  - Collaboration tools, content management systems and workflow tools
  - Tools for data mining, data extraction and data transformation
  - Tools for measuring and reporting
  - Test (management) tools
  - Publication tools
  - Release and deployment technology

In addition, specialized tools are available for Change Management, configuration management and release management, such as:
- Configuration management
- Tools for version control
- Document management systems
- Design tools
- Distribution and installation tools
- Construction and deployment tools

■ 6.12   IMPLEMENTATION

The implementation of Service Transition in a *"greenfield"* situation (from zero) is only feasible when establishing a new service provider. Most service providers focus on the improvement of the Service Transition (processes). For the improvement of Service Transition (processes) the following five aspects are also important:
1. Justification
2. Design

3. Introduction
4. Cultural aspects
5. Risks and advantages

Even though this book presents Service Transition as a more or less delimited lifecycle phase, this does not mean that it can be viewed on its own. Without the input from Service Design and the output to Service Operation, Service Transition has no purpose.

6.12.1 Challenges
For a successful Service Transition, several challenges need to be conquered, such as:
- Taking into account all stakeholders (and their different perspectives) and maintaining relationships that could be important within Service Transition
- The lack of harmonization and integration of processes and disciplines that influence Service Transition
- Finding the balance between a stable operational environment and being able to respond to changing business requirements in a flexible manner
- Finding the balance between pragmatism and bureaucracy
- Creating an environment in which standardization and knowledge sharing is fostered
- Creating a culture in which one is responsive to cooperation and cultural changes
- Ensuring that the quality of services corresponds to the quality of the business
- Finding the balance between "*taking risks*" and "*avoiding risks*"; this balance must correspond to that of the business
- The integration with other lifecycle phases, processes and disciplines
- A clear definition of the roles and responsibilities

6.12.2 Critical success factors
- Management support
- Business support
- Hiring and retaining well qualified personnel
- Service management training
- Appropriate tools
- Test validity
- Measuring and reporting

6.12.3 Risks
Potential risks of Service Transition are:
- De-motivation of personnel as a result of changed responsibilities and roles
- Unforeseen expenses
- Resistance to change
- Lack of knowledge sharing
- Poor integration between processes
- Lack of maturity and integration of systems and tools

7 Service Operation Phase

■ 7.1 INTRODUCTION TO SERVICE OPERATION

Well designed and implemented processes are of little value when the day-to-day fulfilment of these processes is not well organized. Nor are service improvements possible when the day-to-day performance measuring and data gathering activities are not fulfilled systematically during Service Operation.

The five closely related processes in Service Operation are (see Figure 7.0):
1. Event Management
2. Incident Management
3. Problem Management
4. Request Fulfilment
5. Access Management

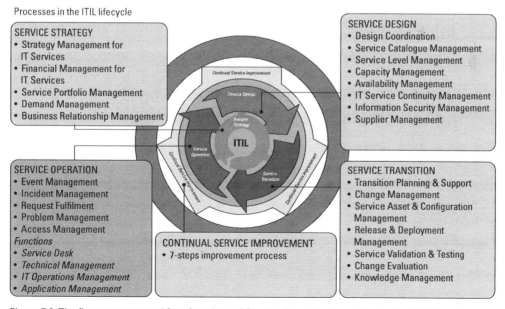

Processes in the ITIL lifecycle

SERVICE STRATEGY
- Strategy Management for IT Services
- Financial Management for IT Services
- Service Portfolio Management
- Demand Management
- Business Relationship Management

SERVICE DESIGN
- Design Coordination
- Service Catalogue Management
- Service Level Management
- Capacity Management
- Availability Management
- IT Service Continuity Management
- Information Security Management
- Supplier Management

SERVICE OPERATION
- Event Management
- Incident Management
- Request Fulfilment
- Problem Management
- Access Management
Functions
- *Service Desk*
- *Technical Management*
- *IT Operations Management*
- *Application Management*

CONTINUAL SERVICE IMPROVEMENT
- 7-steps improvement process

SERVICE TRANSITION
- Transition Planning & Support
- Change Management
- Service Asset & Configuration Management
- Release & Deployment Management
- Service Validation & Testing
- Change Evaluation
- Knowledge Management

Figure 7.0 The five processes and four functions of Service Operation in relation to the ITIL lifecycle

7.1.1 Goal and Objectives

The goals of Service Operation are to coordinate and fulfil activities and processes required to provide and manage services for business users and customers with a specified agreed level. Service Operation is also responsible for management of the technology required to provide and support the services.

The **goals** of Service Operation are:
- Maintaining the satisfaction and confidence from the business in the IT by delivering the agreed IT services in an effective and efficient manner
- Minimalizing the impact of interruption of service on daily business activities.
- Assuring that access to the agreed IT services is offered to only those who are authorized to use these services.

7.1.2 Scope

Service Operation is about fulfilling all activities required to provide and support services:
- The services
- The service management processes
- The technology
- The people (IT and non-IT)

■ 7.2   MONITORING AND CONTROL

7.2.1 Introduction

Monitoring and control of services is based on a continuous cycle of monitoring, reporting, and initiating action. This cycle is crucial to providing, supporting, and improving services.

Basic concepts

> **Monitoring:** refers to the observation of a situation to discover changes that occur over time.
> **Reporting:** refers to the analysis, production, and distribution of the output of the activity that is being monitored.
> **Control:** refers to the management of the usefulness or behavior of a device, system, or service. There are three conditions for control:
> 1. The action must ensure that the behavior conforms to a defined standard or norm
> 2. The conditions leading to the action must be defined, understood and confirmed
> 3. The action must be defined, approved, and suitable for these conditions

7.2.2 The monitoring/control loop

The best-known model for the description of control is the monitoring/control loop. Although it is a simple model it has many complex applications in ITSM. In this section we describe the basic concepts of the model. Next we will show how important these concepts are for the service management lifecycle. Figure 7.1 reflects the basic principles of control.

This cycle measures an activity and its benefits by means of a pre-defined norm or standard to determine whether the results are within the target values for performance or quality. If this is not the case, action must be taken to improve the situation or resume the normal performance.

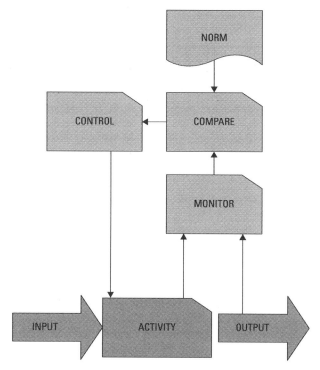

Figure 7.1 Sample monitor/control loop

(source: AXELOS)

There are two types of monitoring/control loops:
- **Open loop systems** – are designed for a specific activity, irrespective of the environmental conditions; making a backup, for instance, can be initiated at a specified moment and be completed regardless of other conditions.
- **Closed loop systems** – Monitoring of an environment and responding to changes in this environment; if, in a network, the network transactions exceed a certain number, the control system will redirect the "*traffic*" via a backup circuit in order to regulate the network transactions.

Figure 7.2 shows a sample **complex monitoring/control loop**: a process that consists of three important activities. Each activity has an input and output and in turn this output

is the input for the next activity. Every activity is controlled by its own monitoring/ control loop with the aid of a series of norms for that specific activity.
A coordinating monitoring/control loop monitors the entire process and ensures that all norms are suitable and are being complied with.

The monitoring/control loop concept can be used to manage:
- The performance of activities in a process or procedure
- The effectiveness of the process or procedure as a whole
- The performance of a device or a series of devices

Figure 7.3 shows a sample **ITSM monitoring/control loop** and shows how the control of a process or the components of that process can be used to provide a service.

There are two levels of monitoring: *internal monitoring and control* and *external monitoring and control*

Monitoring without control is irrelevant and ineffective. Monitoring must always be aimed at achieving the service and operational objectives. If, therefore, there is no clear reason for the monitoring of a system or service, there should be no monitoring.

In order for an organization to determine what it wants to monitor, therefore, it must first define the desired outcome: **monitoring and control objectives**. Ideally this process should start with the definition of Service Level Requirements.

7.2.3 Tools
There are different types of monitoring tools, whereby the situation determines which **type of monitoring** is used:
- **Active versus passive monitoring**:
  - *Active monitoring* refers to the continual "*interrogation*" of a device or system in order to determine its status.
  - *Passive monitoring* is more commonly known and refers to generating and passing on events to a device or monitoring agent.
- **Reactive versus proactive monitoring:**
  - *Reactive monitoring* is designed to request an action after a certain type of event or disruption.
  - *Proactive monitoring* is used to trace patterns of events that indicate that a system or device may break down. Proactive monitoring is generally used in more mature environments, where these patterns can be detected earlier.
- **Continuous measuring versus exception-based measuring:**
  - *Continuous measuring* is aimed at the real-time monitoring of a system to ensure that it complies with a certain performance norm.
  - *Exception-based* measuring does not measure the current performance of a service or system, but discovers and reports exceptions. An example is the generation of

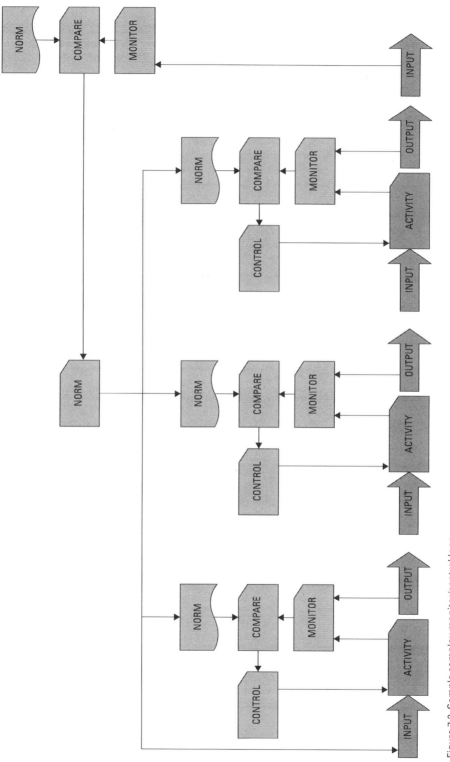

Figure 7.2 Sample complex monitor/control loop
(source: AXELOS)

an event if a transaction is not completed. It is used for less essential systems or for systems where costs are important.

■ **Performance versus output** – There is an important distinction between reporting on the performance of components, or personnel versus reporting on the output – service quality objectives – that have been achieved.

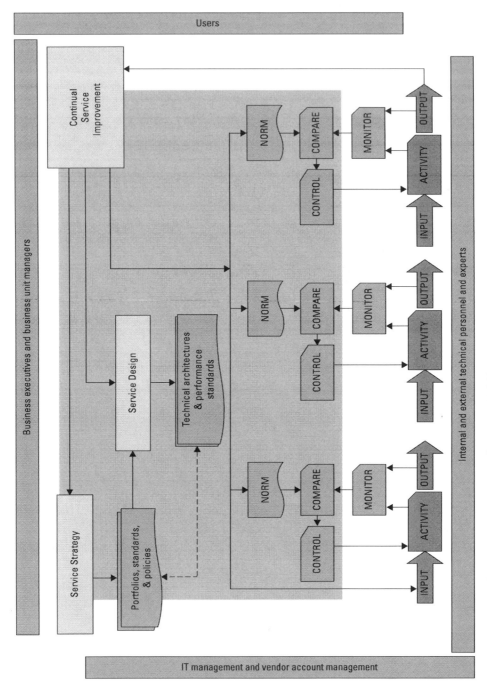

Figure 7.3 Sample ITSM monitoring/control loop (source: AXELOS)

■ 7.3   EVENT MANAGEMENT

7.3.1 Introduction

Events are typically notifications created by an IT service, CI, or monitoring tool. To ensure effective Service Operation, an organization must be aware of the status of its infrastructure and be able to detect deviations from the regular or expected operation. Good monitoring and control systems are required.

The **goal** of Event Management is the control of "*events*" throughout their entire lifecycle: to detect them, analyze them and determine the right management action.

The **objectives** of Event Management are:
- To detect all changes of state that have significance for the management of CI and IT services
- To ensuring that all events are communicated to the appropriate functions that need to be informed or take further control actions
- To provide the trigger, or entry point, for the execution of many Service Operation processes and operations management activities
- To provide the means to compare actual operating performance and behavior against design standards and SLA
- To providing a basis for service assurance, reporting and service improvement

Scope

Event Management can be applied to any aspect of service management that requires control and can be automated. For example CI, security, software license monitoring and environmental conditions (e.g.: detecting fire and smoke).

> **The difference between monitoring and event management**
> Monitoring and event management are closely related, but slightly different in nature. Event management is focused on generating and detecting meaningful notifications about the status of the IT infrastructure and services.

Value for the business

Event Management generally has indirect value. Some examples of benefit for the business:
- Event Management provides mechanisms for early detection of incidents
- Event Management makes it possible for some types of automated activity to be monitored by exception
- If Event Management is integrated into other service management processes, it may detect status changes or exceptions; this allows the right person or team to respond more quickly, thereby improving the process performance
- Event Management provides a basis for automated operations; this improves effectiveness and frees up costly human resources for more innovative work

Basic concepts

ITIL defines an event as follows:

> An **event** can be defined as any change of state that has significance for the management of a CI or IT service

There are many different event types, such as:
- Events that indicate a normal operation, such as a user logging on to use an application
- Events that indicate an exception, such as a user who is trying to log on to an application with an incorrect password or a PC scan that reveals the installation of unauthorized software
- Events that signify an unusual but not exceptional operation; it may provide an indication that the situation requires a little more supervision. For example, utilization of a server's memory reaches within five percent of its highest acceptable level

7.3.2 Activities, methods, and techniques

Figure 7.4 reflects a sample flow for Event Management. Like all sample flows provided in this book, it is a high level and generic representation and should be used as a reference point rather than an actual Event Management (process) flowchart.

The main activities of the Event Management process are summarized below.

1. Event occurs

Events occur continuously, but not all of them are detected or registered. It is therefore important that everybody involved in designing, developing, managing and supporting IT services and the IT infrastructure that they run on understands what types of event need to be detected.

2. Event notification

Many CI are configured to generate a standard set of events, based on the designer's experience of what is required to operate the CI, with the ability to generate additional types of event by "*turning on*" the relevant event generation mechanism. For other CI types, some form of "*agent*" software will have to be installed in order to initiate the monitoring.

3. Event detection

Once an event notification has been generated, it will be detected by an agent running on the same system, or transmitted directly to a management tool specifically designed to read and interpret the meaning of the event.

4. Event logged

There should be a record of the event and any subsequent actions. The event can be logged as an event record in the event management tool or it can simply be left as an entry in

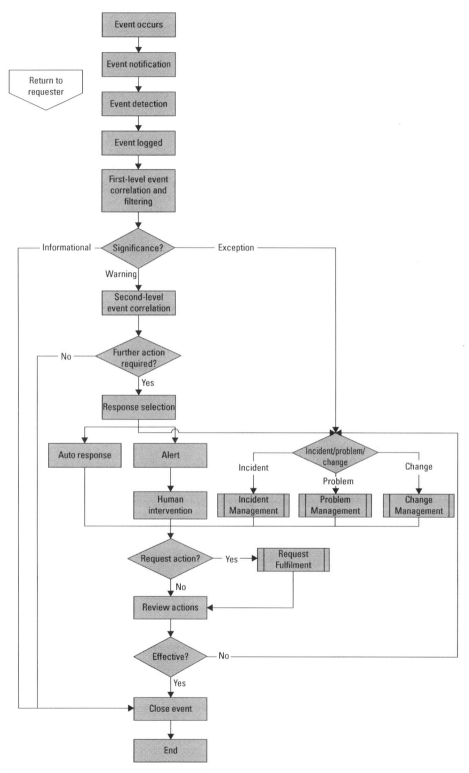

Figure 7.4 Sample Event Management flow

the system log of the device or application that generated the event. No matter what the case is, there needs to be a standing order for the appropriate operations management staff to check the logs on a regular basis and clear instructions about how to use each log.

5. First-level event correlation and filtering

The purpose of first-level event correlation and filtering is to decide whether to communicate the event to a management tool or to ignore it. If ignored, the event will usually be recorded in a log file on the device, but no further action will be taken.

6. Significance of events

Every organization will have its own categorization of the significance of an event, but it is suggested that at least these three broad categories be represented:

■ Informational – an event that does not require any action and does not represent an exception. They are typically stored in the system or service log fi les and kept for a predetermined period. Informational events are typically used to check on the status of a device or service, or to confirm the successful completion of an activity.

■ Warning – an event that is generated when a service or device has reached a threshold. Warns the right person, process, or tool in order that the situation can be brought back to control and the proper actions can be taken to prevent that an exception occurs.
Example of an alert: the actual memory capacity in use on a server is 65 percent and increasing. When the level increases to 75 percent, the response times will be too long and the OLA or SLA will not be met with.

■ Exception – means that a service or device is currently operating abnormally (as defined by the organization). Typically, this means that an OLA and SLA have been breached and the business is being impacted. Exceptions could represent:
  • A server is *"out of order"*
  • The response time of a standard transaction via the network is longer than fifteen seconds.
  • A part of the network does not react on routine requests.

7. Second-level event correlation

If an event is a warning, a decision has to be made about exactly what the significance is and what actions need to be taken to deal with it. It is here that the meaning of the event is determined.

Correlation is normally done by a *"correlation engine"*, usually part of a management tool that compares the event with a set of criteria and rules in a prescribed order. These criteria are often called business rules, although they are generally fairly technical.

8. Further action required?

If the second-level correlation activity recognizes an event, a response will be required. There are many different types of responses, each designed specifically for the task it has to initiate.

Response selection

At this point in the process, there are a number of response options available. It is important to note that the response options can be chosen in any combination.

- Auto response
- Alert and human intervention
- Incident, problem, or change?

9. Review actions

With thousands of events being generated every day, it is not possible formally to review every individual event. However, it is important to check that any significant events or exceptions have been handled appropriately, or to track trends or counts of event types etc.

10. Close event

Some events will remain open until a certain action takes place, for example an event that is linked to an open incident. However, most events are not "*opened*" or "*closed*".

Designing for Event Management

Event Management is the basis for monitoring the performance and availability of a service. This is why Availability Management and Capacity Management must specify and agree on the precise monitoring targets and mechanisms. Various instruments exist for this purpose:

- Instrumentation
- Error messages
- Event detection and alert mechanisms

7.3.3 Information management

- Technical information about the status of components of an IT infrastructure
- The ability to interrogate varied data sources and files formats and compare them to a predefined norm
- Software agents for event monitoring tools
- Correlation engines detailing rules to determine significance of events and appropriate control actions

7.3.4 Interfaces

Event Management can interface to any process that requires monitoring and control, whether real-time or not, and requires some form of intervention following an event or group of events.

Service Design

- **SLM** – For early detection of real or potential service level target breaches to ensure timely corrective action

- **Information Security Management** – Interface with business applications and/or business processes allowing potentially or real significant and disruptive security-related events to be detected and acted upon.
- **Capacity Management and Availability Management** – To define and categorize events, thresholds, and appropriate control action. Event Management for improving the performance and availability of services by responding according to design requirements

Service Transition
- **SACM** – to use events to determine the current status (within its lifecycle) of any CI in the infrastructure.
- **Knowledge Management** – to act as a rich source of information that can be processed for inclusion in the SKMS
- **Change Management** – To identify conditions that may require a response or action

Service Operation
- **Incident Management and Problem Management** – To assist in the resolution of incidents and problems and to identify the conditions that may require appropriate control action
- **Access Management** – To detect unauthorized access attempts and security breaches

7.3.5 Triggers
- Exceptions to any level of CI performance defined in the design specifications
- Exceptions to an automated procedure or process
- An exception within a business process monitored by Event Management
- The completion of an automated task or job
- A status change in a server or database CI
- Access of an application or database by a user or automated procedure or job
- A situation where a device, database, or application etc. has reached a predefined threshold of performance

7.3.6 Inputs
- Operational and service level requirements associated with events and their actions
- Thresholds for recognizing events, warnings, and alerts
- Event correlation tables, rules, event codes and automated response solutions enabling or supporting Event Management activities
- Roles and responsibilities for taking appropriate actions
- Operational procedures for identifying, logging, correlating, escalating, and communicating events

7.3.7 Outputs
- Events communicated and escalated to those responsible for further action

- Event logs describing appropriate events details, escalation, and communication activities taken to support further activities
- Events indicating an incident has occurred
- Events indicating a change has occurred
- Events indicating the potential breach to an agreement; SLA, OLA, or UC
- Events indicating status of activities within any process requiring it
- SKMS updated with event information and history

7.3.8 Critical success factors

- Detecting all changes of state that have significance for the management of CI and IT services
- Ensuring all events are communicated to the appropriate functions that need to be informed or take further control actions
- Providing the trigger, or entry point, for the execution of many Service Operation processes and operations management activities
- Provide the means to compare actual operating performance and behavior against design standards and SLA
- Providing a basis for service assurance, reporting and service improvement

7.3.9 Metrics

- Events compared with the number of incidents
- Each type of event by service, system or component
- Events that required human intervention and whether this was performed
- Incidents without a corresponding event
- Events that resulted in incidents or changes
- Events caused by existing problems or known errors
- Events indicating utility or warranty issues
- Repeated or duplicated events

7.3.10 Challenges

- To obtain funding for the necessary tools and effort needed to install and exploit the benefits of the tools
- Setting the correct level of filtering
- Deploying the necessary monitoring agents across the entire it infrastructure
- Automated monitoring activities can generate additional network traffic that might impact planned network capacity levels
- Acquiring the necessary skills can be time-consuming and costly
- Deploying event management tools without an appropriate Event Management process in place

7.3.11 Risks

- Failure to obtain adequate funding
- Ensuring the correct level of filtering

■ Failure to maintain momentum in deploying the necessary monitoring agents across the IT infrastructure

■ 7.4   INCIDENT MANAGEMENT

7.4.1 Introduction

The Incident Management process handles all incidents. These may be failures, questions, or queries that are reported by users (generally via a call to the service desk) or technical staff, or that are automatically detected and reported by tools to monitor events.

The main objective of the Incident Management process is:
■ In case of incidents, to resume the regular state of affairs as quickly as possible;
■ To minimize the negative impact on business processes
■ Assuring that the best achievable quality levels and service availability are maintained

> **"Normal Service Operation"** is defined as an operational state where services and CI are performing within their agreed service and operational levels.

The **objectives** of Incident Management are:
■ Assuring that standard methods and procedures are applied.
■ Increase visibility and communication of incidents to business and IT support personnel
■ Maintain quality of IT services as perceived by the business
■ Align Incident Management activities and priorities with those of the business
■ Maintain user satisfaction with IT services

Scope

Incident Management covers every event that disrupts or might disrupt a service. This means that it includes events reported directly by users, either via the service desk or via various tools.

Incidents can also be reported or logged by technical staff, which does not necessarily mean that every event is an incident.

While incidents and *service requests* are both reported to the service desk, they are not the same thing. *Service requests* are not service disruptions but user requests for support, delivery, information, advice, or documentation.

Value for the business
■ The possibility to track and solve incidents results in reduced downtime for the business; as a result the service is available for longer

- The possibility to align IT operations with the business priorities; the reason is that Incident Management is able to identify business priorities and distribute resources dynamically
- The possibility to establish potential improvements for services

Incident Management is clearly visible to the business, meaning that its value is easier to demonstrate than for other areas in Service Operations. For this reason, it is one of the first processes to be implemented in service management projects.

Basic concepts
ITIL defines an incident as:

> An **incident** is an unplanned interruption to an IT service or reduction in the quality of an IT service. Failure of a CI that has not yet affected service is also an incident.

The following elements should be taken into account in Incident Management:
- **Time limits** – Agree on time limits for all phases and use them as targets in OLA and UC
- **Incident models** – An incident model is a way to determine the steps that are necessary to execute a process correctly (in this case, the processing of certain incident types); it means that standard incidents will be handled correctly and within the agreed timeframes.
- **Major incidents** – A separate procedure is required for major incidents, with shorter timeframes and higher urgency; agree what a major incident is and map the entire incident priority system.

People sometimes confuse a major incident with a problem. However, an incident always remains an incident. Its impact or priority may increase, but it never becomes a problem. A problem is the underlying cause of one or more incidents and always remains a separate entity.

7.4.2 Activities, methods, and techniques
The main activities of the Incident Management process are (see figure 7.5):
1. Identification
2. Registration
3. Classification
4. Prioritization
5. Diagnosis
6. Escalation
7. Investigation and diagnosis
8. Resolution and recovery
9. Closing

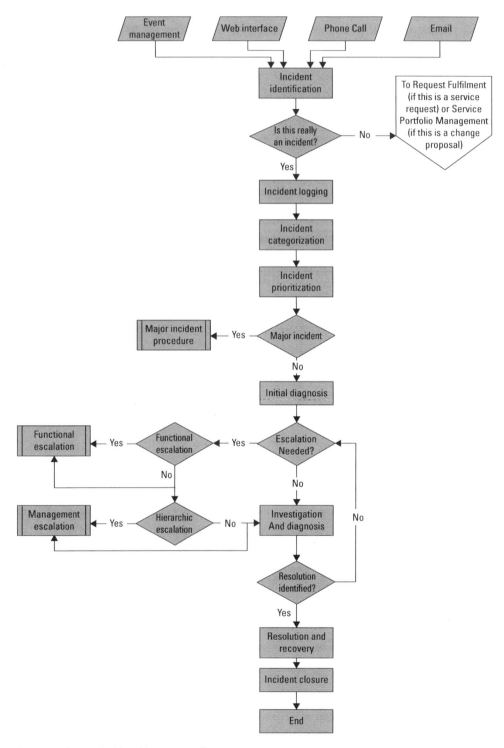

Figure 7.5 Sample Incident Management flow

(source: AXELOS)

1. Identification

It is important to quickly determine if an accident has occurred. This is called incident identification. From a business perspective, it is generally unacceptable to wait until a user experiences the impact of an incident and contacts the service desk. The organization must try to monitor all important components, so that failures or potential failures can be detected as early as possible and the Incident Management process initiated. In an ideal situation, incidents are solved before they have an impact on users.

2. Registration

All incidents must be registered in full, including date and time: **incident registration**. This applies to incidents received via the service desk as well as those that are detected automatically via an event warning system. Register all relevant information relating to the nature of the incident to ensure a complete historical record. If the incident is transferred to other support groups, they will have all of the relevant information at their disposal.

3. Classification

Based on the incident registration incidents can be classified. **Incident classification** means that incidents are classified according to the impact they have on the business (e.g. a service is not available or has a bad performance) and which configuratie items (CI) are involved (network, servers, application etc.). Incident classification is important at a later stage when incident types and frequencies are analyzed, to establish trends that can be used for problem management, provider management and other ITSM activities.

4. Prioritization

Another important aspect of registering every incident is to allocate the right **priority code**. Support agents and tools use this code to determine how they should handle the incident. The priority of an incident can usually be determined by establishing its urgency (how fast the business needs a solution) and impact. The number of users affected by an incident is often an indication of its impact.

5. Diagnosis

When a user reports an incident via the service desk, the service desk agent must try to record the greatest possible number of symptoms of the incident in terms of a first **diagnosis**.

Incident matching procedure

A procedure for matching incident classification data against that for problems and known errors allows for efficient and quick access to proven resolution actions, thus reducing the time it takes to restore service back to users. This activity also minimizes the need for escalation to other support staff.

The service desk agent also tries to establish what went wrong and how it should be corrected. Diagnostic scripts and known error information can be very useful in this context. If possible, the service desk agent solves the incident immediately and closes the incident. If this is impossible, the incident is escalated.

6. Escalation
If it is clear that the first line service desk personnel cannot solve the incident quickly enough, the incident must be escalated immediately to a second line support group (functional escalation). Eventually, the relevant IT managers must be warned (hierarchical escalation).

7. Investigation and diagnosis
When handling an incident, each support group investigates what went wrong. It also makes a diagnosis. Document all these activities in the incident record to ensure that a complete overview of all activities is available.

8. Solving and closing
When the incident has been **solved**, the support group returns the incident to the service desk, which **closes** the incident. However, it first checks that the incident has been solved and that the users are satisfied with the solution. It must also close the classification, check that the user is satisfied, update the incident documentation, determine whether the incident could recur, and decide whether action should be taken to prevent this. The incident can then be formally closed.

7.4.3 Information management
Most information used in Incident Management comes from the following sources: *Incident management tools; Incident records; Service catalogue*. Incident Management also requires access to the known error databases and to the CMS.

7.4.4 Interfaces
- **SLM** – To define the acceptable levels of service within which Incident Management works
- **Information Security Management** – Providing security-related incident information by maintaining logs, audit files, and incident records
- **Capacity Management** – Incident Management provides a trigger for performance monitoring and Capacity Management assists in developing workarounds for incidents
- **Availability Management** – To determine the availability of IT services and investigate improvements to reduce mean time to repair and increase mean time between failures
- **SACM** – To provide the data used to identify and progress incidents. Incident Management can assist with the verification activity of SACM when working to resolve an incident

- **Change Management** – To implement a workaround or resolution using change models. Incident Management identifies incidents arising from changes
- **Problem Management** – To investigate and resolve the underlying cause to prevent or reduce the impact of recurrence. To provide information on problems, known errors, and workarounds
- **Access Management** – To record as incidents any detected unauthorized access attempts and security breaches

7.4.5 Triggers

- The service desk receives an incident call (by phone or e-mail)
- A user reports an incident via a web-based incident-logging screen
- Technical staff detects – using event management tools – that an incident has occurred.
- Suppliers report that they have detected errors in the systems managed or supplied by them.

7.4.6 Inputs

- Information about CI and their status
- Information about known errors and their workarounds
- Communication and feedback about incidents and their symptoms
- Communication and feedback about RFC and releases that have been implemented or planned for implementation
- Communication of events that were triggered from Event Management
- Operational and service level objectives
- Customer feedback on success of incident resolution activities and overall quality of Incident Management activities
- Agreed criteria for prioritizing and escalating incidents

7.4.7 Outputs

- Resolved incidents and actions taken to achieve their resolution
- Updated incident management records with accurate incident detail and history
- Updated classification of incidents to be used to support proactive problem management activities
- Raising problem records for incidents where an underlying cause not been identified
- Validation that incidents have not recurred for problems that have been resolved
- Feedback on incidents related to changes and releases
- Identification of CI associated with or impacted by incidents
- Satisfaction feedback from customers who have experienced incidents
- Feedback on level and quality of Event Management activities
- Communications about incident and resolution history detail to assist with identification of overall service quality

7.4.8 Critical success factors
- Resolve incidents as quickly as possible, minimizing impacts to the business
- Maintain quality of IT services
- Maintain user satisfaction with IT services
- Align Incident Management activities and priorities with those of the business
- Increase visibility and communication of incidents to business and IT support staff

7.4.9 Metrics
- Mean times
  - To repair
  - To restore service
  - Between failures
  - Between service/system incident
- Breakdown of incidents at each stage
- Size of current incident backlog for each IT service
- Percentage of incidents
- Average cost per incident
- Number and percentage of incidents…
  - Closed at "*first point of contact*"
  - Classified as major
  - Incorrectly assigned
  - Incorrectly categorized
  - Processed by IT personnel
  - Related to changes and releases
  - Handled within agreed response
  - Resolved remotely, without the need for a visit

7.4.10 Challenges
- The ability to detect incidents as early as possible
- Convincing all IT personnel that all incidents must be logged, and encouraging the use of self-help web-based capabilities
- Availability of information about problems and known errors
- Integration into the CMS to determine relationships between CI and to refer to the history of the CI
- Integration into the SLM process

7.4.11 Risks
- Lack of available or properly trained resources, resulting in delays in handling incidents within agreed timescales
- Lack of support tools to raise alerts and prompt progress, causing a backlog in handling incidents

- Inadequate tools or lack of integration between tools, resulting in missing or poor access to data and information sources
- Poorly aligned or non-existent OLA and/or UC

■ 7.5   REQUEST FULFILMENT

7.5.1 Introduction

Request Fulfilment is the processing of service requests that all users submit to the IT department. For example, a service request can be a request for a password change or the additional installation of a software application on a certain work station. Because these requests occur on a regular basis and involve little risk, it is better that they are handled in a separate process.

The **goal** of Request Fulfilment is managing the lifecycle of all service requests.

The **objectives** of the Request Fulfilment process are:
- To offer users a channel through which they can request and receive services; to this effect an agreed approval and qualification process must exist
- To provide users and customers with information about the availability of services and the procedure for obtaining these services
- To supply the components of standard services (for instance, licenses and software media)
- To assist with general information, complaints or comments

Scope
The process for handling requests depends on the nature of the request. In most cases the process can be divided into a series of activities that need to be completed. Some organizations treat service requests as a special type of incident. However, there is an important difference between an incident and a service request. An incident is usually an unplanned event, whereas a service request tends to be something that can and must be planned.

Value for the business
The value of Request Fulfilment is the ability to offer fast and effective access to standard services that the business can use to improve the productivity or the quality of the business services and products.

Request Fulfilment reduces the amount of "*red tape*" in requesting and receiving access to existing or new services. This reduces the cost for the supply of these services.

Basic concepts

ITIL uses the term *"service request"* as a general description for the varying requests that users submit to the IT department.

A **service request** is a request from a user for information, advice, a standard change, or access to a service.

Many service requests recur on a regular basis. This is why a process flow can be devised in advance, stipulating the phases needed to handle the requests, the individuals or support groups involved, time limits and escalation paths. The service request is usually handled as a standard change.

A substantial percentage of all service requests are requests for delivering standard services, e.g.: the request for a new pc or adding MS Visio to a standard MS Office software suite. These changes can be handled as **standard change**. Standard changes are low risk, relatively common and follow a procedure or work instruction. For a standard change is a change the approach is pre-authorized by Change Management, and this approach follows an accepted and established procedure.

7.5.2 Activities, working methods and techniques

Request Fulfilment consists of the following activities, methods, and techniques:

1. **Menu selection** – by means of Request Fulfilment, users can submit a service request via access to the tool preferably via a web interface.
2. **Financial approval** – most service requests have financial implications; the cost for handling a request must first be determined. It is possible to agree fixed prices for standard requests and give instant authorization for these requests; in all other cases the cost must first be estimated, after which the user must give permission.
3. **Fulfilment** – the actual fulfilment activity depends on the nature of the service request; the service desk can handle simple requests, whereas others must be forwarded to specialized groups or suppliers.
4. **Closure** – once the service request has been completed the service desk will close off the request.

7.5.3 Information management

- Which service is being requested?
- Who requested and/or authorized the service?
- Which process will be used to fulfil the request?
- Who was it assigned to? What action was taken?
- All relevant dates and times throughout the request lifecycle
- Closure details
- Request for change
- The service portfolio and the service catalogue
- Security policies

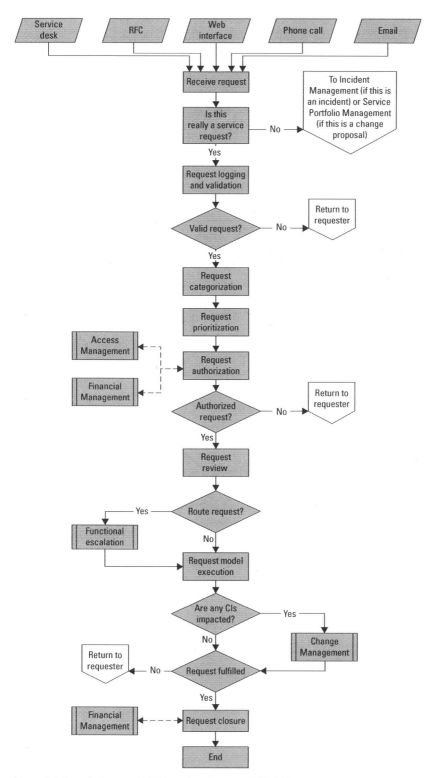

Figure 7.6 Sample Request Fulfilment flow (source: AXELOS)

7.5.4 Interfaces

- **Financial Management for IT Services** – To identify, if required, the costs for fulfilling requests
- **Service Catalogue Management** – To ensure that available requests are well communicated to users
- **RDM** – To create *"release models"* that can be predefined, built and tested but only deployed upon request by those who want the *"release"*
- **SACM** – To reflect changes that may have been made as part of fulfilment activities
- **Change Management** – To correctly log requests that are actually changes and vice versa and to progress RFC through Change Management
- **Incident Management** – To correctly log requests that are actually incidents and vice versa and to progress incidents through Incident Management. Some organizations will develop separate processes to handles incidents and requests. Other organizations will use the incident process to handle request and simply use a category called *"request"*
- **Access Management** – To ensure that those making requests are authorized to do so in accordance with the information security policy

7.5.5 Triggers

- User calling the service desk
- A user completing a form of self-help web-based input screen

7.5.6 Inputs

- Work requests
- Authorization forms
- Service requests
- RFC
- Request for information

7.5.7 Outputs

- Authorized/rejected service requests
- Request Fulfilment status reports
- Fulfilled service requests
- Incidents
- RFC/standard changes
- Asset/CI updates
- Updated request records
- Closed service requests
- Canceled service requests

7.5.8 Critical success factors

- Requests must be fulfilled in an efficient and timely manner that is aligned to agreed service level targets for each type of request

- Only authorized requests should be fulfilled
- User satisfaction must be maintained

7.5.9 Metrics
- Percentage of service requests...
  - Completed within agreed target times
  - Fulfilled that were appropriately authorized
  - At each stage of their lifecycle
  - Closed at "*first point of contact*"
  - Handled remotely, through automation, or without the need for a visit
- The average cost per type of service request
- The average elapsed time for handling each type of service request
- Level of user satisfaction with the handling of service requests
- The size of current backlog of outstanding service requests

7.5.10 Challenges
- Defining and documenting the type of requests that will be handled within the request fulfilment process
- Establishing self-help front-end capabilities that allow the users to interface successfully with the request fulfilment process
- Establishing agreed and communicated service level targets for each type of request
- Agreeing to the costs for fulfilling requests
- Agreeing which services will be standardized and who can request them
- Ensuring easy accessibility to information about which requests are available to the organization
- Identifying and documented request models
- Setting and managing user and customer satisfaction

7.5.11 Risks
- Poorly defined scope
- Poorly designed or implemented user interfaces
- Badly designed or operated back-end fulfilment processes
- Inadequate monitoring capabilities

■ 7.6   PROBLEM MANAGEMENT

7.6.1 Introduction
The **goal** of Problem Management is managing the lifecycle of all problems, starting from the moment that a problem has been identified and subsequently diagnosing the cause of the problem, retrieving all information and taking actions, when necessary, to solve the problem.

The **objectives** of Problem Management are:
- Eliminate repeating incidents by eliminating the root cause of those incidents.
- Minimize the impact of incidents that cannot be prevented.
- Prevent problems and incidents resulting from them

Scope
Problem Management comprises all the activities needed to diagnose the underlying cause of incidents and to find a solution for these problems. It must also ensure that the solution is implemented via the correct control procedures – in other words, through the use of Change Management and Release Management.

Value for the business
Problem Management works together with Incident Management and Change Management to ensure improvements in the availability and quality of the IT service provision. When incidents are resolved the solution is registered. At a given moment this information is used to accelerate the incident handling and identify permanent solutions. This reduces the number of incidents and the handling time, resulting in shorter disruption times and fewer disruptions to the business critical systems. When within the Problem Management process the root cause of the occurring incidents has been found, than it may possible to get a final solution for this problem. When there a need for a change, it needs to be approved by the Change Management process.

Basic concepts
Many problems are unique and need to be handled separately. However, it is possible that some incidents may occur more than once as a result of underlying problems.

ITIL defines a problem as follows:

> A **problem** is the cause of one or more incidents.

ITIL defines a known error as:

> A **known error** is a problem that has a documented root cause and a workaround.

ITIL defines a workaround as:

> **Workaround:** reducing or eliminating the impact of an incident or problem for which a full resolution is not yet available.

Known Error Database (KEDB)
The **KEDB** is a database in which all known errors are recorded, including the available workarounds. This enables a fast diagnosis. Additional to the development of a KEDB, development of a **problem model** to be able to deal with future problems may be useful.

This standard model will help to establish:
- Which steps need to be made
- The responsibilities of the persons involved
- The required time planning

In addition to creating a KEDB for faster diagnoses, the creation of a **problem model** for the handling of future problems may be useful. Such a standard model supports with the steps that need to be taken, the responsibilities of people involved and the necessary timescales.

7.6.2 Activities, methods, and techniques

Problem Management consists of two important processes: *reactive and proactive problem management*. **Reactive problem management** deals with solving problems that are identified as a result of incidents that have taken place. **Proactive problem management** is aimed at identifying and solving problems and known errors before incidents related to these take place.

Reactive problem management

Reactive problem management consists of the following activities (See figure 7.7):
1. Identification
2. Registration
3. Classification
4. Prioritization
5. Investigation and diagnosis
6. Decide on workarounds
7. Identification of known errors
8. Resolution
9. Conclusion
10. Review

1. Identification

Identification of problems is carried out using the following methods:
- The service desk suspects or identifies an unknown cause of one or more incidents. This results in a problem registration.
- Analysis of an incident by the technical support group reveals that there is an underlying problem.
- There is automatic tracing of an infrastructural or application error, whereby event or alert tools automatically create an incident registration that highlights the need for a problem registration.
- The supplier reports a problem that needs to be resolved.
- Analysis of incidents takes place as part of corrective problem management.

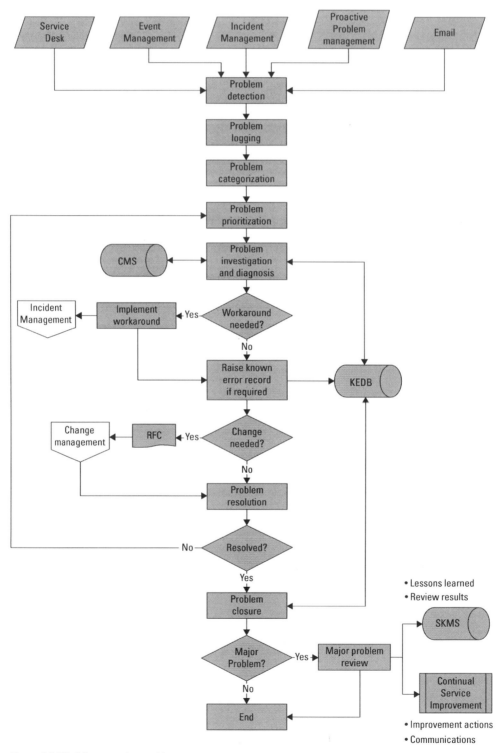

Figure 7.7 Workflow reactive problem management

(source: AXELOS)

2. Registration

Irrespective of the identification method, all details of the problem must be registered (**problem registration**), so that a comprehensive historic report is created. The information must be date- and time-stamped, so that proper control and escalation are possible.

3. Classification

Problems must be classified in the same way as incidents, so that the true nature of the problem can be established quickly and easily. **Problem classification** provides useful management information.

4. Prioritization

As is the case for incidents, problems must also be given a **priority** in the same manner and for the same reasons. In this context also take into account the frequency and impact of the related incidents and the seriousness of the problems.

5. Investigation and diagnosis

In order to find the underlying cause of the problem and make a **diagnosis**, an **investigation** must be performed. The speed and nature of this investigation depend on the impact, seriousness, and urgency of the problem. Use the proper level of resources and expertise to find a solution.

Table 7.1 Sample problem analyses, diagnosis and solution techniques

Chronological analysis	Affinity mapping
Pain value analysis	Hypothesis testing
Kepner and Tregoe	Technical observation post
Brainstorming	Ishikawa diagrams
5-Whys	Pareto analysis
Fault isolation	

6. Decision on workarounds

In some cases a temporary solution, a **workaround**, is possible for incidents that were caused by a problem. It is important, however, that the problem reporting remains open and that the details about the workaround are included in the problem reporting.

7. Identification of known errors

As soon as the diagnosis has been made, and especially if a workaround has been found, the **identified known errors** must be listed in a known error report and placed in the known error database. If other incidents and problems occur they can be identified and the service can be resumed more quickly.

8. Solution

As soon as a **solution** has been found it should, ideally, be applied to resolve the problem. In reality, there are preventative measures to make sure that the solution does not cause further problems. If a change in functionality is needed a *Request for Change* is required that must follow the steps of the Change Management process.

9. Close-off

If the change has been completed and successfully evaluated and the solution has been applied, the problem report can formally be **closed off**, as can the related incident reports that are still outstanding. Remember to check whether the report contains a full description of all the events.

10. Evaluation

After every **major problem** a **review** must be performed to learn lessons for the future. It is very rare that new applications, systems, or software releases do not contain **errors**. In most cases a priority system is used during testing that removes the most serious errors, but it is possible that minor errors are not corrected.

Proactive problem management

Proactive problem management is a more or less continuous series activities with the purpose to improve the overall availability of IT services and the overall end user satisfaction with IT services.

Examples of proactive problem management activities are:
1. Conducting periodic scheduled reviews of incident records to find patterns and trends
2. Conducting reviews of major incidents
3. Conducting reviews in operational log books and   doing reviews on operational loggings and servicing data
4. Doing periodical reviews on logging data from Event Management
5. Conducting brainstorm sessions to identify trends that may lead to future incidents
6. Using check lists to collect data proactively regarding operational or service-related quality issues that may help to detect underlying causes

Identified problems that are output of these activities, are the input for the CSI register and are used to document and manage options for improvement.

7.6.3 Information management
- Configuration management system
- Known error database
- Incident registrations

7.6.4 Interfaces

Service Strategy

- **Financial Management for IT Services** – To assist in assessing the impact of proposed resolutions or workarounds, as well as *"pain value analysis"*. Problem Management provides information about the cost of resolving and preventing problems

Service Design

- **Availability Management** – To reduce downtime and increase uptime using availability management methods and techniques, and helping in assessing proactive measures.
- **Capacity Management** – To improve performance issues, to assist problem investigation using Capacity Management methods and techniques, and helping in assessing proactive measures.
- **ITSCM** – To act as an entry point into IT SCM to address an unresolved significant problem before it impacts the business.
- **SLM** – To contribute in improving the service levels. SLM provides prioritization parameters.

Service Transition

- **Change Management** – To ensure that all resolutions or workarounds that require a change to a CI are submitted using an RFC.
- **SACM** – To identify faulty CI and also to determine the impact of problems and resolutions.
- **RDM** – To assist in ensuring that new known errors in the development KEDB are transferred into the known error database.
- **Knowledge Management** – The problem and know error databases are part of the SKMS.

Continual Service Improvement

- **Seven-step improvement process** – To provide a basis for identifying opportunities for service improvement

7.6.5 Triggers

Reactive problem management
- One or more incidents
- Release testing
- Notifications from suppliers
- Proactive problem management
- Identification of patterns and trends
- A review of…
  - Operational logs
  - Operational communications
  - Event logs

7.6.6 Inputs
- Incident records
- Incident reports and histories
- Information about CI and their status
- Communication and feedback about incidents, RFC, releases, and events
- Operational and service level targets
- Customer feedback
- Agreed problem prioritization and escalation criteria
- Risk management reports

7.6.7 Outputs
- Resolved problems and actions taken to achieve their resolution
- New or updated Problem Management records
- Requests for changes
- Workarounds for incidents
- New or updated known error records
- Problem management reports
- Major problem review action items and reports

7.6.8 Critical success factors
- Minimize the impact to the business of incidents that cannot be prevented
- Maintain quality of IT services through elimination of recurring incidents
- Provide overall quality and professionalism of problem handling activities to maintain business confidence in IT capabilities

7.6.9 Metrics
- The number of known errors properly added to the KEDB
- Number and percentage of
  - Incidents closed by *"first point of contact"*
  - Major problem reviews completed successfully and on time
  - Problems incorrectly assigned
  - Problems incorrectly categorized
  - Outstanding problems and the associated trends
  - Problems resolved/not resolved within service level targets
- Average incident resolution time for incidents linked to problem records
- Average cost per problem

7.6.10 Challenges
- Establishing an effective Incident Management process and related tools
- Improving the analytical and investigative skills and capabilities of Problem Management personnel
- Ensuring that Problem Management personnel are able to use all resources available (CMS and SKMS) to investigate and resolve problems

- Ensuring ongoing training of technical staff in the business implications of the services they support, as well as the technical aspects of their job
- The ability to…
  - Link incident records to problem records
  - Integrate Problem Management activities with the CMS
  - Have a good working relationship between all four functions: Service Desk, IT Operations, Technical Management and Application Management as well as with suppliers

7.6.11 Risks

- Lack of available or properly trained resources, resulting in delays in handling incidents within agreed timescales
- Lack of support tools to raise alerts and prompt progress, causing a backlog in handling incidents
- Inadequate tools or lack of integration between tools, resulting in missing or poor access to data and information sources
- Poorly aligned or non-existent OLA and/or UC
- Lack of analytical and investigative skills for Problem Management personnel

7.7 ACCESS MANAGEMENT

7.7.1 Introduction

The **goal** of Access Management is to grant authorized users to right to use a service, or to a group of services. Some organizations also call it "*rights management*" or "*identity management*".

The **objectives** of the Access Management process are:

- Implementing the policies and guidelines of the Information Security Management process
- Enable that confidentiality, integrity of the business data and the intellectual property are well managed
- Ensure that rights are assigned in a correct manner

Scope

Access Management ensures that users have access to a service, but it does not guarantee that access is always available at the agreed times. This is handled by Availability Management.

Value for the business

- Controlled access to services enables the organization to maintain confidentiality of its information more effectively
- Staff has the right access level to do their jobs properly

- The risk of errors during data entry or the use of a vital service by an unqualified user is lower
- There is the option to withdraw access rights more easily when access may be necessary for compliance (e.g.: SOX, HIPAA and COBIT)

Basic concepts
- **Access** – refers to the level and scope of the functionality of a service or data that a user is allowed to use
- **Identity** – refers to the information about the people who the organization distinguishes as individuals; establishes their status in the organization
- **Rights** (also called privileges) – refers to the actual settings for a user; which service (group) they are allowed to use; typical rights include reading, writing, executing, editing and deleting
- **Services or service groups** – most users have access to multiple services
- **Directory services** – refers to a specific type of tool used to manage access and rights

7.7.2 Activities, methods, and techniques
Access Management consists of the following activities (See figure 7.8):
1. **Verification** – Access Management must verify every access request for an IT service from two perspectives:
   - Is the user requesting access truly the person they say they are?
   - Does the user have a legitimate reason to use the service?
2. **Granting rights** – Access Management does not decide who gets access to what IT services; it only executes the policy and rules defined by Service Strategy and Service Design.
3. **Monitoring identity status** – User roles may vary over time, with an impact on their service needs; examples of what may change a role are: job changes, promotion, dismissal, retirement, or death.
4. **Registering and monitoring access** – Access Management does not only respond to requests; it must also ensure that the rights it has granted are used correctly.
5. **Revoking or limiting rights** – In addition to granting rights to use a service, Access Management is also responsible for withdrawing those rights; but it cannot make the actual decision.

7.7.3 Information management
- Identity is usually established using some of the following pieces of information:
  - Name
  - Address
  - Contact details
  - Physical documentation
  - Unique identifier
  - Biometric information
  - Expiration date

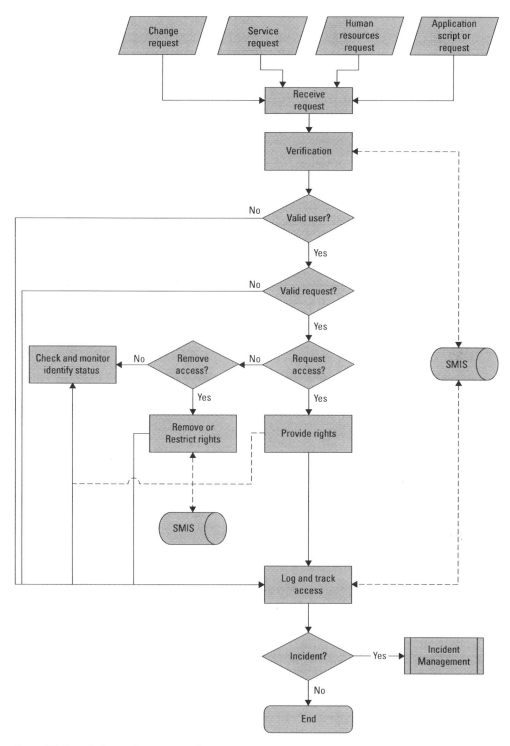

Figure 7.8 Sample Access Management flow

(source: AXELOS)

- A user identity is provided to anyone with a legitimate requirement to access IT services or organizational information:
  - Employees; IT and non-IT
  - Contractors
  - Vendor personnel
  - Customers
  - Users, groups, roles and service groups
- While each user has an individual identity, and each IT service can be seen as an entity in its own right, it is often helpful to group them together so that they can be managed more easily. Sometimes the terms *"user profile"*, *"user template"*, or *"user role"* are used to describe this type of grouping.

7.7.4 Interfaces

- **Demand Management** – To identify the necessary resource levels to handle expected volumes of requests for access
- **Strategy Management for IT Services** – To determine if Access Management activities could be more efficient if they were handled locally rather than centrally
- **Information Security Management** – To provide the security and data protection policies and tools needed to execute access management. Human resource management to assist in verifying user identity and the services they are entitled to use
- **Service Catalogue Management** – To provide methods and means by which users can access the services they are entitled to use
- **ITSCM** – To manage access to services in the event of a major business disruption
- **SLM** – To maintain the agreements (SLA, OLA, UC) for access to each service
- **Change Management** – To control the actual requests for access because any request for access is usually processed as either a standard change or a service request
- **SACM** – To identify data storage and interrogate CI to determine current access details
- **Request Fulfilment** – To provide methods and means by which users can request access to the services they are entitled to use

7.7.5 Triggers

- An RFC
- A service request
- A request from human resources management
- A request from a manager
- A request from a user

7.7.6 Inputs

- Information security policies
- Operational and service level requirements and targets for Access Management activities
- Authorized requests to grant or terminate access rights

7.7.7 Outputs

■ Provision of access to IT services in line with information security policies
■ Access Management records and reports
■ Timely communications concerning inappropriate access or abuse of services

7.7.8 Critical success factors

■ Ensuring that the confidentiality, integrity and availability of services are protected in accordance with the information security policy
■ Providing timely communications about improper access or abuse of services on a timely basis
■ Providing appropriate access to services on a timely basis that meets business needs

7.7.9 Metrics

■ Number and percentage of…
  • Incidents regarding inappropriate attempts to access a service
  • Incidents requiring a reset of access rights
  • Incidents caused by incorrect access settings
  • Requests for access that were provided within established SLA and OLA
■ Number of audit findings regarding users who have changed roles or left the company
■ Average duration of access-related incidents

7.7.10 Challenges

■ Monitoring and reporting on access activity, access-related incidents and problems
■ Verifying…
  • The identity of a user
  • The identity of the approving person or body
  • A user qualifies for access to a specific service
■ Linking multiple access rights to an individual user
■ Determining the status of users at any time
■ Managing changes to access requirements for a user
■ Restricting access rights to unauthorized users
■ Building and maintaining a database of all users and the rights that they have been granted

7.7.11 Risks

■ Lack of appropriate supporting technologies to manage and control access to services
■ Controlling access from "*back door*" sources such as application interfaces and changes to firewall rules for special needs
■ Managing and controlling access to services by external third-party suppliers
■ Lack of management support for Access Management activities and controls
■ Ensuring that necessary levels of access to services and the necessary management controls are provided without hindering the business

■ 7.8   IMPLEMENTATION

7.8.1 Achieving balance in Service Operation

Procedures and activities take place in a continually changing environment. This can give rise to a conflict between maintaining the current situation and reacting to changes in the business and technical environment. Consequently, one of the key roles of Service Operation is handling these conflicts. It must try to achieve a balance between conflicting priorities (see Figure 7.9).

The internal IT view versus the external business view
The view that IT is part of IT services (the external business view) is the opposite of the idea that IT is a series of technological components (the internal IT view). This causes the key conflict in all phases of the ITSM lifecycle.

The external IT view is about the way users and customers experience services. The internal IT view is about how the IT organization manages IT components and systems to provide services.

Stability versus responsiveness
On the one hand, Service Operation must ensure that the IT infrastructure is stable and available. At the same time, Service Operation must recognize that business and IT requirements change.

Some changes take place gradually and can be planned. They do not jeopardize stability. The platform functionality, performance, and architecture will change over a number of years.

However, other changes can happen very quickly, sometimes under extreme pressure. For example, a business department wins a contract that suddenly requires additional IT services and more capacity.

To achieve an IT organization in which stability and response are in balance:
- ■ Invest in adaptable technologies and processes, for example, virtual server and application technology.
- ■ Build a strong SLM process that is active from the Service Design phase to the Continual Service Improvement phase of the ITSM Lifecycle.
- ■ Encourage integration between SLM and the other Service Design processes, so that business requirements match the operational IT activities and components of the IT infrastructure.
- ■ Initiate changes in the ITSM Lifecycle as soon as possible; they can be taken into account in the functional and management requirements.

- Involve IT as soon as possible in the change process in case of business changes; this helps ensure scalability, consistency, and IT services that include the business changes.
- Have the Service Operation teams provide input for the design and the refining of architecture and IT services.
- Implement and use SLM to prevent the business and IT managers and personnel from negotiating agreements informally.

Service quality versus service costs
Service Operation must provide IT services to customers and the users continually, and to the agreed level. At the same time, they have to keep the costs and use of resources at an optimal level. Many organizations are strongly pressured to enhance the service quality, while they have to reduce costs.

Achieving an optimal balance between costs and quality is a key task of service management. Many organizations leave this to the Service Operations team, who lack the authority, but the Service Strategy and Service Design phase are more appropriate for this. Service level requirements and a clear understanding of the goals and dangers of service business can help ensure that the service is provided with the right costs.

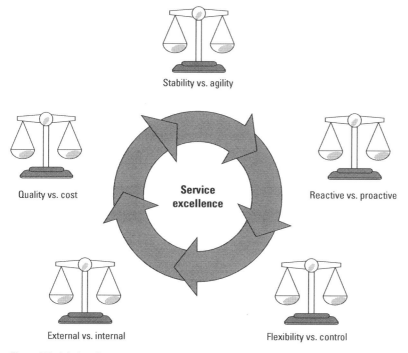

Figure 7.9 A balancing act

(source: AXELOS)

Being reactive versus being proactive

A reactive organization does nothing until an external stimulus forces it to act. For instance, it only develops a new application when a new business requirement arrives. A proactive organization always looks for new opportunities to improve the current situation. Usually, proactive behavior is viewed positively, because it enables the organization to keep a competitive advantage in a changing environment. However, an over-proactive attitude can be very costly, and can create distracted personnel. For an optimal result, reactive and proactive behavior must be well-balanced.

7.8.2 Challenges

For the implementation of Service Operation in such a way that it can achieve its goal, there are a lot of challenges.

Internal and external relations

One of the most important challenges facing Service Operation managers is the balance between the many internal and external relationships. There is an increasing use of networks, partnerships, and shared services models. A Service Operation manager must invest in relation management knowledge and skills in order to handle the complexity of these challenges. Service Operation managers also have to deal with virtual teams. Traditional, hierarchical management structures are unable to handle the complexity and diversity of most organizations. Knowledge management and mapping authority structures becomes increasingly important as organizations expand and diversify. Service Strategy will expand on this further.

Justifying funding

Often it is difficult to justify expenditure for Service Operation because funds spent are often considered to be "*infrastructure*" costs. In reality, many investments in ITSM, especially for Service Operation, can save money and show a positive ROI as well as improving service quality.

Risks caused by changes

Service Operation staff must implement changes without negative impact on the stability of the IT services offered.

Change triggers

There are many things that can trigger change in the Service Operation environment, including:

- New (or to be upgraded) hardware or software
- Legislation
- Obsolete components
- Business imperatives
- Process enhancements

- Changes in management or personnel
- Change in service levels
- New services

Change assessment
Involve Service Operation as early as possible in assessment of all changes. This way, operational issues will be handled properly.

Assessing and managing risk in Service Operation
In a number of cases, it is necessary that risk evaluation is conducted swiftly, in order to take appropriate action. This is especially necessary for potential changes or known errors, but also in case of failures, projects, environmental risks, vendors, security risks, and new customers who need support.

Lack of engagement with development and project staff
Service Design has the tendency to focus on one service while Service Operation aims at delivering and supporting all services. Service Design will often be conducted in projects while Service Operation focuses on continual management processes and activities that recur. The two phases of the lifecycle possess different metrics that encourage Service Design to conclude the project on time, as specified and within the arranged budget. However, it is hard to predict how the service will look, and that will be the costs after roll-out and some initial time in service. If the service does not work as expected, IT Operations Management will be responsible.

Historically, there is a separation between Service Operation staff and staff involved in the development of new applications or in the execution of projects that deliver new functionality in an operational environment.

This image is damaging, because contemplating Service Operation issues is best done at the beginning of new developments or projects, when there is still time to include these factors in the planning stages.

Improving Service Operation
Service Operation can be improved in two ways:
- Long-term incremental improvement – This is based on the review of the Performances and output of all Service Operation processes, functions and outputs over time; examples include putting new tools into use or changes in the design process.
- Short-term on-going improvement of existing situations within the Service Operation processes, functions and technology – These are small changes that are implemented to change the fundamental significance of a process or technology; examples are tuning, training or personnel transfer.

■ 7.9   SERVICE OPERATION ORGANIZATION

7.9.1 Introduction
There are several ways to organize Service Operation functions, and each organization will come to its own decisions based on its size, geography, culture, and business environment.

Organization by technical specialization
This organization type creates departments according to the technology, the skills, and activities necessary to manage that technology. IT operations follow the structure of the technical management and application management departments. As a consequence IT operations are geared to the operational agendas of the technical management and application management departments, and all groups have to be defined during the Service Design phase.

Organization by activity
This type of organization structure focuses on the fact that similar activities are performed on all technologies within an organization. This means that people who perform similar activities, regardless of the technology, are grouped together, although teams may occur within each department that is involved with a specific technology, application, etc.

Organizing to manage processes
It is not a good idea to structure the entire organization according to processes. Processes are used to eliminate the *"silo effect"* of departments, not to create silos.

In process-based organizations, people are organized in groups or departments that perform or manage a specific process. However, this type of organization structure should only be used if IT Operations Management is responsible for more than IT operations. In some organizations IT operations is also responsible for defining the SLA and negotiating the UC.

Process-based departments are only effective if they are capable of coordinating process execution throughout the entire organization. This means that process-based departments can only be considered if IT Operations Management can play the role of process owner for specific processes.

Organizing IT operation by geography
IT operations can be physically spread out, and in some cases each location must be organized according to its own context. This structure is usually used in the following circumstances, when:
■ Data centers are geographically distributed
■ Different regions or countries possess different technologies or offer a different range of services

- There are different business models or organizational structures in the different regions; in other words, the business is decentralized according to geography and the each business unit is fairly autonomous
- Legislation differs between country and region
- Different standards apply, per country or region
- There are cultural or language differences between the personnel who are managing IT

Hybrid organization structures

It is unlikely that IT Operations Management will be structured using only one type of organizational structure. Most organizations use a technical specialization combined with some extra activity or process-based departments:

- **Combined functions** – The IT operations, technical management, and application management departments are included in one structure; this sometimes occurs when all groups are co-located in one data center; in these situations, the data center manager assumes responsibility for technical, application, and IT production management.
- **Combined technical and application management structure** – Some businesses organize their Technical Management and Application Management functions according to systems; this means that every department contains application specialists and IT infrastructure technical specialists who manage services based on a series of systems.

7.9.2 Critical success factors

Management support

Support from higher and middle management is necessary for all ITSM activities and processes, especially in Service Operation. It is crucial for obtaining sufficient financing and resources. Senior management must also offer visible support during the launch of new Service Operation initiatives.

Business support

It is also important that Service Operation is supported by the business units. This works better if the Service Operation personnel involve the business in all their activities, and are open about successes and failures.

Regular communication with the business is crucial to building a good relationship and to ensuring support; Service Operation will be better placed to understand the aspirations and concerns of the business. Additionally, the business can provide feedback on the efforts of Service Operation to satisfy the business needs.

Hiring and retaining staff

The correct number of staff with the correct skills is critical for successful Service Operation. Consider the following challenges:

- Projects for new services often clearly specify what the new skills must be, but may underestimate how many staff are needed and how skills can be retained.

■ There may be a lack of staff with solid knowledge of service management; having good technicians is important, but there must also be a certain number of people who have knowledge of both technological and service problems.
■ Because personnel with both technological and service knowledge are fairly rare, they are often specially trained; it is important to retain them by offering a clear career path and solid compensation.
■ Personnel are often assigned new tasks too quickly, while they are still extremely busy with their current workloads. Successful service management projects may require a short term investment in temporary workers.

Service management training
Good training and awareness can provide great advantages. In addition to increasing expertise, they can generate enthusiasm in people. Service Operation staff must be aware of the consequences of their actions for the organization. A *"service management culture"* must be created. Service management will only be successful if the people are focused on overall service management objectives.

Appropriate tools
Many service management processes and activities cannot be effectively executed without proper support tools. Senior management must ensure that financing for such tools is included in annual budgets, and must support acquisition, implementation, and maintenance.

Test validity
The quality of IT services provided by Service Operation depends on the quality of systems and components that are delivered in the operational environment.

The quality level will improve considerably if solid and complete testing of new components and releases is performed in a timely manner. Also, the documentation should be independently tested for completeness and quality.

Measuring and reporting
Clear agreements are necessary regarding the way in which things are measured and reported; all staff will have clear targets to aim for, and IT and business managers will be able to evaluate quickly and simply whether progress is being made and which areas deserve extra attention.

7.9.3 Risks

Consider the following risks:
■ **Service loss** – The greatest risk run by Service Operation is the loss of essential IT services, with adverse impact on staff, customers, and finances. In extreme cases, loss may occur to life and health, when IT services are used for essential health and security purposes.

■ **Risks to successful Service Operation**:
- Insufficient financing and resources
- Loss of momentum
- Loss of important staff
- Resistance to change
- Lack of management support
- If the design fails the requirements, successful implementation will never deliver the required results; this will require new design
- In some organizations, service management is viewed with suspicion by both IT and the business; the advantages of service management must be clear for all stakeholders; this problem can be solved by clear SLM and careful communication during Service Design

.

8 Continual Service Improvement Phase

IT must continually align and re-align IT services to the changing business needs by identifying and implementing improvements to IT services that support the business. ITIL places this within the lifecycle phase of **Continual Service Improvement**.

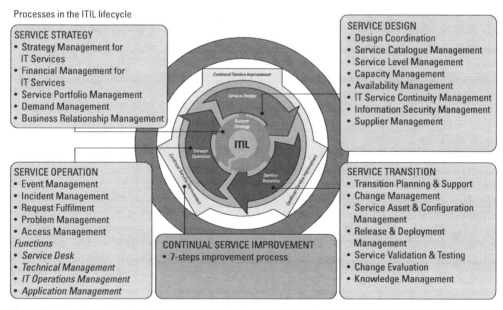

Figure 8.0 Continual Service Improvement in relation to the ITIL lifecycle

In English there is a difference between *continual* and *continuous*:
- *Continuous* means that the organization is involved in an activity without interruption; the efforts are constantly at the same level; for example, continuous operation
- *Continual* means a succession of closely placed activities; in this way a sequence of improvement efforts is created: continual improvement

An IT service is created by a number of activities. The quality of these activities and the process that links these activities determine the quality of the eventual service. CSI focuses on the activities and processes to improve the quality of services. To this end, it uses the *Plan-Do-Check-Act* Cycle of Deming (PDCA). This cycle prescribes a consolidation phase for each improvement, to embed the new procedures in the organization. This implies a repeating pattern of improvement efforts with varying levels of intensity, instead of a single continuing improvement effort that is always on the same level. This is the reason why, in ITIL, the "**C**" of CSI stands for *continual* and not *continuous*.

Measuring and analyzing is crucial to CSI; by measuring it is possible to identify which services are profitable and which services can do better. The **CSI improvement process** has a seven step plan. Creating a **Service Improvement Plan** (SIP) is an SLM activity within the CSI scope. First of all, we will consider the justification of CSI and a number of basic concepts.

8.1.1 Goal and objectives
The **goal** of CSI is for continual improvement of the effectiveness and efficiency of IT services, allowing them to meet the business requirements better. This entails both achieving and surpassing the objectives (**effectiveness**), and obtaining these objectives at the lowest cost possible (**efficiency**). To increase effectiveness you can, for instance, reduce the number of errors in a process. To make a process more efficient you can eliminate unnecessary activities or automate manual operations.

By measuring and analyzing the process results in all Service Lifecycle phases you can determine which results are structurally worse than others. These offer the highest improvement probability.

CSI mainly measures and monitors the following matters:
- **Process compliance** – Does business follow the latest or revised service management processes and do they use the new "*tools*"?
- **Quality** – Will the various process activities achieve their goals?
- **Performance** – How efficient is the process? Which time periods have passed?
- **Business value of a process** – Does the process bring any results? Is it effective? What is the customer's opinion about the process?

The main **objectives** of CSI are:
- To recommend improvements in all phases of the lifecycle
- To measure and analyze service level achievements by comparing them to the requirements in the Service Level Agreement (SLA)
- To introduce activities that will increase the quality, efficiency, effectiveness and customer satisfaction of the services and the ITSM processes

- To operate more cost effective IT services without sacrificing customer satisfaction
- To use suitable quality management methods for improvement activities

8.1.2 Scope

The scope of CSI contains four important components:

- Justifiable (in terms of costs and results) gradual and continuous improvement of the quality of service delivery
- Continual tuning of the IT services to the current and future needs of the business
- Continual tuning of cost effectiveness
- Identifying all options for improvement in all phases of the lifecycle and within all processes
- Identifying the options for tuning the organization, the ability to deliver all resources, to work with partners, improving the competences of the personnel and the training required and the quality of communications

■ 8.2   BASIC CONCEPTS

8.2.1 The CSI register

The CSI register contains important information for the overall service provider. It is an integral part of the SKMS.

The CSI register provides both structure and visibility to CSI by ensuring that all improvement initiatives are recorded and benefits realized. The benefits are measured to demonstrate the achievement of the desired outcomes. Proposed benefits should be quantified in terms of key performance indicator (KPI) metrics. This will assist the prioritizing of initiatives delivering the most significant and cost-effective incremental benefit to the business.

8.2.2 CSI and organizational change

In order to make continual improvement a permanent part of the organizational culture, a change in mentality is often needed. This is one of the most difficult aspects of CSI and, in reality, many CSI programs fail because they do not (or cannot) achieve this cultural change. John P. Kotter, *Professor of Leadership* at Harvard Business School, examined over a hundred companies and discovered eight crucial steps needed to successfully change an organization:

1. Create a sense of urgency
2. Form a leading coalition
3. Create a vision
4. Communicate the vision
5. Empower others to act on the vision
6. Plan for and create quick wins

7. Consolidate improvements and create more change
8. Institutionalize the changes

8.2.3 The PDCA Cycle

A *"big bang"* approach does not usually result in a successful improvement program. That is why the American statistician Dr. W. Edwards Deming developed a systematic improvement approach in the 1980s: the ***Plan-Do-Check-Act* Cycle** (**PDCA**):

Next is a consolidation phase to embed the changes into the organization. The Cycle is also known as the **Deming Cycle** (Figure 8.1).

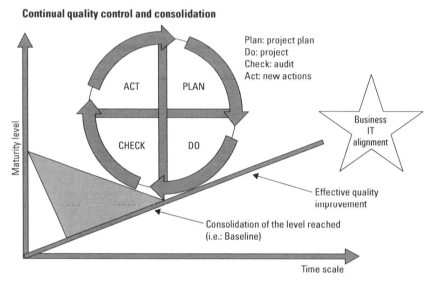

Figure 8.1 The Plan-Do-Check-Act Cycle

(source: AXELOS)

CSI uses the PDCA Cycle in two areas:
- Implementation of CSI
- Continual improvement of services and processes

Now, we discuss the Cycle for the *implementation of CSI* (Figure 8.2):

Plan CSI:
- Determine the scope
- Determine the requirements CSI must meet
- Set goals, for instance using gap analysis
- Define action points
- Determine which checks need to be executed during the check phase
- Determine the interfaces between CSI and the rest of the lifecycle
- Determine which process activities need to be introduced

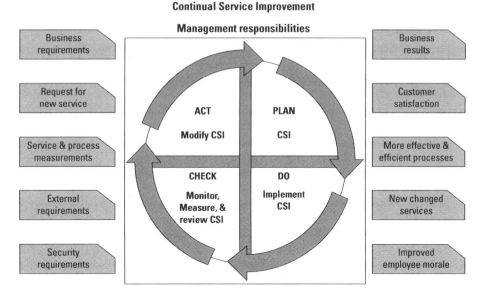

Figure 8.2 The PDCA Cycle for the improvement of services

- Set (management) roles and responsibilities
- Find out which tools are needed to support and document processes
- Select the methods and techniques to measure and document the quality and effectiveness of the services and processes

Implement CSI (*Do*):
- Determine the budget
- Document roles and responsibilities
- Determine the CSI policy, plans and procedures, maintain these, communicate about them and train your staff
- Supply monitoring, analysis and reporting tools
- Integrate CSI with Service Strategy, Service Design, Service Transition and Service Operation

Monitor, measure, and evaluate CSI (*Check*):
- Report on the accomplishments with regard to the plans
- Evaluate the documentation
- Perform process assessments and audits
- Formulate proposals for process improvement

Adjust CSI (*Act*):
- Introduce the improvements
- Adjust the policy, procedures, roles, and responsibilities

8.2.4 Metrics, KPI and CSF

An IT service manager needs to know whether their organization as a whole meets its goals and which processes contribute to this. **Metrics** measure the results of a process or activity by determining whether a certain variable meets its set target. For instance, a metric measures whether the required numbers of incidents are resolved within one hour.

Metrics are mainly interpreted on a strategic and tactical level. They must describe all processes within an organization. Three types are needed for CSI:
- **Technology metrics** – Measuring the performance and availability of components and applications.
- **Process metrics** – Measuring the performance of the service management processes (time to market, quantities, waiting time, etc.).
- **Service metrics** – The results of the end-to-end service to users, for which performance requirements are specified in the service level agreement (SLA).

A metric originates from the goal set by an organization. If the business views IT as a *cost center* then it will probably want to decrease the costs. If, however, it sees IT as the enabler of the company, then the goal will probably be to develop flexible services that will decrease the *time-to-market*. The measuring system should not focus solely on only one of the three aspects of money, time, and quality; otherwise the remaining two aspects will receive insufficient attention.

For the business mission, a **critical success factor (CSF)** is defined as: these are elements essential to achieving the mission. The **key performance indicators (KPI)** following on from these CSF determine the quality, performance, value, and process compliance. They can either be *qualitative* (such as customer satisfaction), or *quantitative* (such as costs of a printer incident).

At the start of the improvement program two to three KPI per CSF will already supply a great deal of information that will need to be processed. The KPI can be extended or adjusted later according to new developments – for instance, if the organization has achieved its goals or when new service management processes are introduced.

Data, information, knowledge, and wisdom (DIKW)

Metrics supply quantitative **data**; for instance, that the service desk registers 12,000 incidents each month. CSI transforms this data into qualitative **information**, a received and understood message which stems from processed and grouped data; such as the fact that 18 percent of the incidents reported are related to the organization's email facility. By combining information with experience, context, interpretation and reflection it becomes **knowledge**; for example, since we know that the organization is a web store, we can determine the impact of the incidents concerning the email facility.

What it comes down to in CSI is **wisdom**: being able to make the correct assessments and the correct decisions by using the data, information, and knowledge in the best possible way. For example, because we know the impact of the email incidents on the customer, we can decide to focus on this service because we want to improve our customer service. The CSI improvement process focuses on the acquirement of wisdom (see Section 8.4 "CSI 7-step improvement process" and step 6 in the CSI improvement process about service reporting).

8.2.5 Governance

Governance drives organizations and controls them. *Corporate governance* provides a good, honest, transparent, and responsible management of an organization. *Business governance* results in good company performances. Together they are known as *enterprise governance*.

IT governance is also part of *enterprise governance*. It shapes the processes and structure of an IT organization and ensures that it achieves its goals. Complying with the new rules, such as the American *Sarbanes-Oxley Act* from 2002 (corporate governance), and constantly performing better at a lower cost (business governance) are both part of IT governance.

These two developments are the main motive for CSI: IT service providers must offer their services from a strategic rather than a tactical perspective. IT departments that only focus on technology will soon become less appealing to their business.

An ITSM standard such as ITIL helps to control an organization by forging it into a coherent system of roles, responsibilities, processes, policy, and *controls*.

8.2.6 CSI policies and procedures

The CSI policies capture agreements concerning the measuring, reporting, the service levels, the CSF, the KPI, and the evaluations. These must be known to the whole organization. Most organizations assess the process results each month. It is wise to evaluate new services more often.

An IT organization should implement the following CSI policies:
- All improvement initiatives must go through the Change Management process
- All functional groups are responsible for CSI activities
- CSI roles and responsibilities are recorded and announced

■ 8.3 CSI ACTIVITIES

8.3.1 Introduction
To improve the services of the IT organization CSI measures the yield of these services. The main CSI activities are:

Check:
- Check the results of the processes
- Examine customer satisfaction
- Assess process maturity
- Check whether the personnel follow the internal guidelines
- Analyze the measurement data and compare these to the goals set in the SLA

Report:
- Propose improvements for all phases in the lifecycle
- Consider the relevance of existing goals

Improve:
- Introduce activities that increase the quality, efficiency, effectiveness, and customer satisfaction of the services
- Use appropriate quality management methods for improvement activities

8.3.2 CSI approach
The effect of the improvement is greatly determined by the direction in which the improvement takes place.

> "Would you tell me, please, which way I ought to go from here?" asked Alice.
>
> "That depends a good deal on where you want to get to," said the Cat.
>
> "I don't much care where –" said Alice.
>
> "Then it doesn't matter which way you go", said the Cat.
>
> "– so long as I get somewhere," Alice added as an explanation.
>
> "Oh, you're sure to do that," said the Cat, "if you only walk long enough."
>
> Source: Lewis Carroll, *Alice's Adventures in Wonderland*, 1865

Without a vision about the direction of the improvement, an improvement has only a limited value. Because of this, determine a vision including its goals before you start with an improvement process.

The organization must continually assess its current improvement course (CSI goals) on relevance, completeness, and feasibility. The **CSI approach** in Figure 8.3 can provide some support.

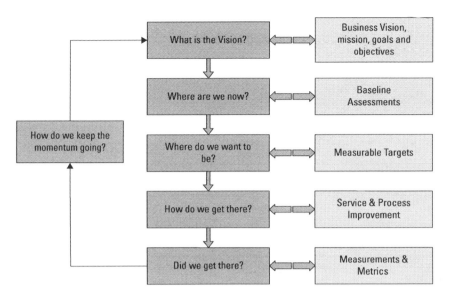

Figure 8.3 CSI approach

This continual cycle consists of six phases:
1. Determine the vision
2. Record the current situation
3. Determine measurable targets
4. Plan
5. Check
6. Assure (maintaining the momentum)

Announce this plan to the whole organization in order to create a consciousness, understanding, enthusiasm, and support. Create a dialogue with the organization and regularly communicate and report on the actual achievements.

8.3.3 Service measurement
Measuring enables an organization to analyze and determine the true cause and effect of either positive or negative situations.

IT services have become an integral means for conducting business. This holds true for businesses of all types and sizes, in any industry, whether private sector or public sector. Without IT services most organizations would not be able to deliver the products and services in today's marketplace.

Design and develop a service measurement framework.
Setting up a framework is as much an art as a science. Service measurement is not an end in itself but should enable and support improving both services and accountability.

The primary output of a service measurement framework is to provide the ability for making operational, tactical, or strategic decisions. This can only be accomplished if the organization selects a combination of measures that provides an accurate, balanced, and unbiased perspective capable of handling change.

Different levels of measurement and reporting
Creating a service measurement framework will require the ability to build upon different metrics and measurements. When developing a service management framework it is important to understand which are the most suitable types of report to create, their target audience and intended usage.

Service management process measurement
There are four major levels to report on. The first (bottom) level contains the activity metrics for a process. The second level contains the KPI associated with each process. The third level represents the high-level goal of the process. Finally, the fourth (top) level represents the balanced scorecard for IT or for the organization.

Creating a measurement framework grid
It is recommended to define the high-level goals and identify the KPI that will support those goals.

8.3.4 Service reporting
Service reporting is the process that is responsible for the generation and supply of reports about the results achieved and the developments in service levels. A reporting approach that focuses equally on the future and the past provides the service provider with the means to market its services and accomplishments directly aligned to the experiences of the business, either positive or negative.

Numerous policies and rules can exist as long as it is clear for each report which policies and rules have been applied. However, all policies and rules form part of the single reporting framework.
- Targeted audience(s) and the related business views on what the service delivered is
- Agreement on what to measure and report
- Agreed definitions of all terms and boundaries
- Basis of all calculations
- Reporting schedules
- Access to reports and medium to be used
- Meetings scheduled to review and discuss reports

Right content for the right audience
Reports should be presented via the medium of choice such as paper-based copies, online soft copies, web-enabled dynamic HTML, current snapshot whiteboards, or even

real-time portal/dashboards. The targeted audience must receive relevant, unambiguous, and, clear information in a style and language of their choice.

■ 8.4   CSI 7-STEP IMPROVEMENT PROCESS

8.4.1 Introduction
The **CSI improvement process** or **7-step improvement process** describes how to measure and report on services as well as initiating improvement efforts. Improvement takes place according to the PDCA Cycle (Deming's cycle). The most significant output of this phase, other than reports, is the **service improvement plan (SIP)**. Section 8.5 will explain how an organization can set up such a plan.

It is important to note that all improvement initiatives require a business impact analysis, and a cost-benefit analysis, and they must follow the Change Management process. Whenever possible the benefits anticipated by the improvement effort must be quantified in monetary terms. This is called the return on investment (ROI). However, not all benefits are tangible; some have to do with perception, and preferences, which are two elements of how the customer defines value. This is known as the Value On Investment (VOI).

8.4.2 Activities, methods, and techniques
CSI is already incorporated in every process, thus everyone is involved in CSI. CSI simply uses the outputs of the other processes, analyzes them, and proposes improvement ideas. In some cases it might be possible to recommend *not* improving something because the workaround is good enough for the customer or because that solution might be prohibitive in terms of cost, time, and effort. It may also be possible for the service to be scheduled for retirement in the near future.

If someone working in SLM discovers that something could improve, they will turn to CSI. Using CSI methods and techniques, this individual can think up activities to accomplish these improvements. Still using CSI, this person will create a SIP for execution purposes. This will transform "*improvement*" into an actual process with input, activities, output, roles, and reports.

CSI will measure and process these measurements in a continual improvement process (Figure 8.4). This will take place in **seven steps from measurement to improvement**:

1. Identify the strategy for improvement
2. Define what you will measure
3. Gather data (measure)
4. Process data
5. Analyze data

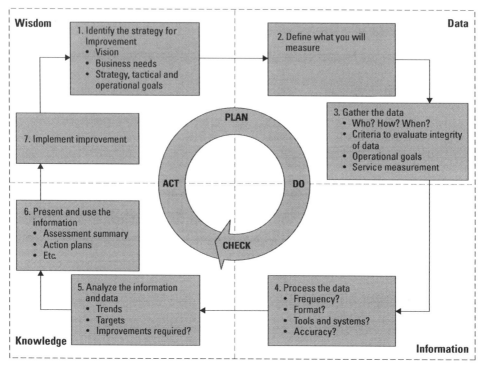

Figure 8.4 The CSI Improvement Process

(source: AXELOS)

6. Present and use information
7. Implement corrective action

The cycle is preceded and closed by **identification of vision and goals** *(identify)*. This is where the vision, strategy, tactical and operational goals are charted. This step returns in Phase I of the CSI approach: determine the vision. Steps 1 and 2 should be the direct result of the strategic, tactical, and operational goals of the organization. They are iterative: in every step you should question whether you are measuring what you should be measuring and whether the measured values are reliable and useful. Answer these questions together with the business in order to be sure that you will be able to provide it with useful information in Step 6.

If no **baseline** has yet been determined, that measurement must take place first. The first measuring results will be the baseline. Every level should be charted in this process: strategic goals and objectives, tactical process maturity and operational **metrics** and KPI. In this way, a knowledge spiral develops: the information from Step 6 in the operational level is input for Step 3 (gather data) of the tactical level, and information from the tactical level will provide data to the strategic level (Figure 8.5).

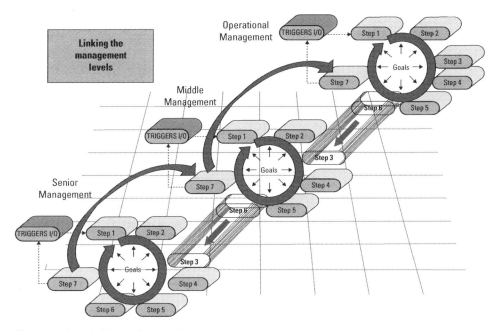

Figure 8.5 Sample Knowledge spiral

If there is little data available, you must first determine a basic measurement system. Start collecting consistent data, for example by having IT staff record data in the same way. You can also measure the process maturity of current processes to discover those processes that deviate most from *best practice*. However, this will only show a lack of data; you will not be collecting any new information in this way.

Never allow "*measuring*" to become a goal unto itself. Before a manager decides what they will be measuring and for how long, they should consider why they should measure and how they will put the results to use. This depends on the goal of the manager. The four most common reasons to measure are (Table 8.1):

Table 8.1 The four most common reasons to measure

Validate	To test prior decisions
Direct	Set direction to activities in order to reach goals
Justify	Support for the necessity of a certain action
Intervene	Determine a point at which corrective actions or changes in the process are required

In addition, it is important to also determine what we are measuring. We measure to ensure that people *comply* with the services and processes based on a defined and adopted standard. We measure to ensure the services and processes *perform* as planned. We measure to ensure the services and processes are delivered at the right level of

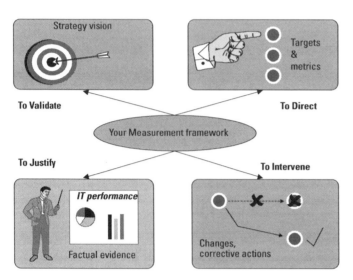

Figure 8.6 Why do we measure?

defined *quality*. Finally, we measure to ensure the services and processes actually make a difference: that is, they deliver *value*.

It is always important to keep sight of these reasons, including when we measure something. Concerning reports, a manager should ask:

■ *"Do we (still) need this"*?
■ *"What am I really measuring"*?
■ *"How will I retrieve the information"*?

The above questions are always important and should be regularly asked against all reports. The responsibility for this lies with the owner of every dashboard; they must create useful reports and make sure that the (customer) organization actually uses them.

Step 1 – Identify the strategy for improvement

In an ideal situation the **service owners** determine what they should measure. For this reason, they will chart the activities that are needed for the service management processes, or to provide services. They then plan which metrics will show whether the services actually provide what was agreed with the business, and the way in which they can measure whether processes are proceeding smoothly.

The final list should reflect the following:
1. The four Ps of strategy: perspective, position, plans, and patterns
2. The visions, missions, goals and objectives of the business and of the IT organization

This should result in a number of CSFs, as well as *Service Level Targets*. The job descriptions of IT staff should also be related to this.

You should have discussions with the business and the service providers for this purpose, and use the service portfolio, the service catalogue, and the *service level requirements* (SLR) as starting points. Prioritize the CSI activities based on the business priorities. In this, also remember internal and external service providers: what portion of theirs services should you be measuring (and possibly including) in your service reporting in determining whether you are capable or not of providing your service?

Inputs into Step 1:
- Business plans and strategy
- Vision, mission, goals, and objectives of the organization as a whole, and of the various units
- Legislative requirements
- Governance requirements
- Budgeting and accounting requirements
- Balanced scorecard
- Service level requirements and targets
- Service portfolio and service catalogue
- Service review meetings
- Customer satisfaction surveys
- CSI initiatives already logged in the CSI register
- Service models
- Service Design Package
- Benchmark and baseline data
- Risk assessments and risk mitigation plans

The **outputs** from Step 1 are:
- A service improvement strategy
- A prioritized list of improvement
- An updated CSI register

Step 2 – Define what you will measure
In this step you need to define:
1. What you should measure, based on your improvement strategy
2. Define what you can actually measure, based on your resources and capabilities
3. Carry out a gap analysis between items 1 and 2 above
4. Negotiate, bargain, discuss with the business if and when you cannot measure what you should be measuring
5. Finalize the actual measurement plan

Step 2 is iterative during the rest of the CSI activities. Depending on the goals and objectives to support service improvement activities, an organization may have to purchase and install new technology to support the gathering and processing of the data and/or hire staff with the required skills sets.

Effective service measures must concentrate on a few vital, meaningful indicators that are economical, quantitative, and usable for the desired results (business outcomes).

Inventory what you are already measuring, the reports you are producing, their frequency, and their target audience. Determine what is being measured and why. If no one uses it, why measure it in the first place?

Inputs into Step 2: The inputs into Step 1 plus
- A service improvement strategy
- A prioritized list of improvement
- An updated CSI register
- End-to-end service definition
- Process flows
- Procedures
- Work instructions
- Technical and user manuals for existing tools
- Existing reports

Outputs from Step 2:
- List of what can be measured, including CSF, KPI and metrics
- List of required adjustments to resources
- List of required adjustments to capabilities
- List of required new resources

Step 3 – Gather data (measuring)
It seems obvious that gathering data requires having monitoring tools in place. Monitoring could be executed using technology such as application, system, and component monitoring tools such as used in the Event Management process (documented in Service Operation) or via a manual process such as free-form text in various event records (sometimes referred to as *tickets*) for incidents, problems, changes, and releases – to name but a very few. The security policy will influence the data gathering, especially from the perspectives of confidentiality, integrity, and availability.

Quality is a key objective of monitoring for CSI. Monitoring will therefore focus on the effectiveness and efficiency of a service, process, tool, organization, or CI.

CSI is interested in all types of events such as business as usual, warnings and alerts. Therefore people involved in CSI need to have the right level of access to the appropriate data sources.

It is also important in this activity to look at the data that was collected and ask whether it makes any sense. If it turns out that data collected cannot be used or is unreliable, at least put it to use in analyzing which data will be needed. For this purpose, repeat steps one and two.

It is important to remember that there are three types of metrics that an organization will need to collect to support CSI and other process activities (Table 8.2).

Table 8.2 Three types of metrics

Technology metrics	These are often associated with component and application-based metrics such as performance, availability etc.
Process metrics	These are captured in the form of CSF, KPI and activity metrics for the service management processes. These metrics can help determine the overall health of a process. KPI can help answer key questions on quality, performance, value, and compliance in following the process. CSI would use these metrics as input in identifying improvement opportunities for each process.
Service metrics	These are the results of the end-to-end service. Technology metrics are normally used to help compute the service metrics.

When a new service is being designed or an existing one changed, this is a perfect opportunity to ensure that what CSI needs to monitor is designed into the service requirements (see Chapter 5 on ITIL Service Design).

The design of a new service or adjustment to an existing service is the perfect occasion to include the monitoring requirements in the service requirements.

Business requirements for monitoring will change over time. This is why Service Operation and CSI must design a process that will help business and IT reach an agreement about what should be monitored and why.

Personnel are collecting data **manually** all the time, therefore they must agree to the following:
- Who is responsible for monitoring and collecting the data?
- What data will be collected?
- Where will the data be collected and stored?
- When and how often will data be collected?
- Why is the data required?
- How will the data be collected?
- Which criteria guarantee the integrity of the data; its correctness, its reliability, and the trustworthiness of the source?

Data gathering consists of the following **activities**:
- Based on the SIP, goals, objectives and business requirements, specify which process activities you must monitor:
  - Specify monitoring requirements

- Define requirements for data collection
- Record results
- Apply for approval from the internal IT department
- Determine how and how often you want to collect data
- Determine which tools are required, develop or buy these, or customize existing tools
- Test and install the tool
- Write monitoring procedures and work instructions
- Create a monitoring plan and discuss it; ask for approval from internal and external IT service providers
- Realize availability and capacity planning
- Start monitoring and gathering data
- Organize the data in a logical fashion in a report
- Evaluate data in order to be sure that it is correct and useful

Inputs into Step 3:
- List stating what you should measure
- List stating what you can measure
- List stating what you will be measuring
- Existing SLA
- New business requirements
- Existing monitoring and data capture capability
- Prior trend analyses
- Gap analysis report
- Customer satisfaction studies
- Plans and policies from other processes
- The CSI register and existing service improvement plans (SIPs)
- Previous trend analysis reports
- Customer satisfaction surveys.

Outputs from Step 3:
- Updated availability and capacity plans
- Monitoring procedures
- Identified tools to use
- Monitoring plan
- Input on IT capability
- Collection of data
- Agreement on the integrity of the data.

Step 4 – Process data
Here you will process the raw data from Step 3 into the required format for the target audience. Follow the path from metric via KPI to CSF, right back to the vision if necessary (Figure 8.7).

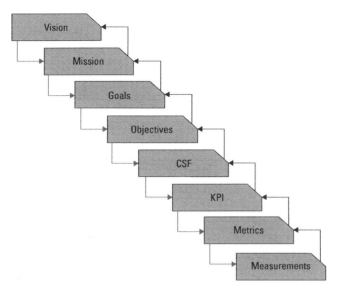

Figure 8.7 From vision to measurements and back

(source: AXELOS)

Unfortunately many people believe that once the data has been processed by the tool it can be presented and used. This is not the case. The data must be analyzed first. This is the next activity in CSI.

Report-generating technologies have the ability to transform raw data and information into a format that is much easier to analyze. The reporting tools also have the ability to provide end-to-end measuring of a service. This requires the proper tool configuration, the identification, and maintenance of configurations and relationships making up the service.

Key questions that need to be addressed in the processing activity are:
- What is the frequency of processing the data?
- What format is required for the output?
- What tools and systems can be used for processing the data?
- How do we evaluate the accuracy of the processed data?

There are two aspects to processing data. One is automated and the other is manual. While both are important and contribute greatly to the measuring process, accuracy is a major differentiator between the two types. Ongoing communication about the benefits of performing administrative tasks is of the utmost importance.

Data processing consists of the following **activities**:
- Define the requirements of the processed data based on strategy, goals, and SLA
- Determine how data is being processed; for new services or processes, it is preferable to select shorter intervals; is this by hour, day, week, or month?

- Determine the data grouping based on the method of analysis and target group; formulate the requirements for tools; develop or buy them; test and install them
- Develop procedures to process data, and train people in the procedures
- Create a monitoring plan and discuss it; ask for approval from internal and external IT service providers
- Update availability and capacity planning
- Start data processing
- Group the data in a logical fashion
- Evaluate data accuracy

Inputs into Step 4:
- Data gathered through monitoring
- Reporting requirements
- SLA, OLA, and underpinning contract (UC)
- Service catalogue
- List with metrics, KPI, CSF, objectives, and goals
- Reporting frequency
- Reporting templates

Output from Step 4:
- Current availability and capacity planning
- Reports
- Processed, logically grouped data ready for analysis

Step 5 – Analyze data

Without analysis, data is *"only"* information. It does not provide understanding of areas for improvement. Analysis evaluates whether IT services support the goals and objectives determined.

Data analysis transforms the information into knowledge of the events that are affecting the organization. More skill and experience is required to perform data analysis than data gathering and processing. Verification against goals and objectives is expected during this activity. This verification validates that objectives are being supported and value is being added. It is not sufficient to simply produce graphs of various types but to document the observations and conclusions.

What do you actually analyze?
- Positive and negative trends
- Are the agreed targets with the customer, within IT and, with the suppliers met?
- Cause and effect
- Intended vs. actual performance

However, key questions still need to be asked, such as:

- Is this good?
- Is this bad?
- Is this expected?

Without analysis the data is merely information. With analysis come improvement opportunities. Throughout CSI, assessment should identify whether targets were achieved and, if so, whether new targets (and therefore new KPI) need to be defined. If targets were achieved but the perception has not improved, then new targets may need to be set and new measures put in place to ensure that these new targets are being met.

Because of prior discussions about improvement options, IT will make the first move in the dialogue with the business that follows analysis. A good analysis of the information is also to the advantage of the business. This will allow a more accurate determination of whether improvement is required based on strategic, tactical, and operational goals. At this point, information becomes *knowledge*, according to the DIKW model.

Inputs into Step 5:

- Results of the monitored data
- Existing KPI and targets
- Perceptions from customer satisfaction surveys, etc.

Step 6 – Present and use information (service reporting)

The sixth step is to take our knowledge, which is represented in the reports, monitors, action plans, reviews, evaluations and opportunities, and present it to the target audience in a clear, digestible, and timely way. This stage involves presenting the information in a format that is understandable, at the right level, provides value, notes exceptions to service, identifies benefits that were revealed during the time period, and allows those receiving the information to make strategic, tactical and operational decisions. In other words, present the information in the manner that makes it most useful for the target audience.

Most organizations create reports and present information to some extent or another; however, it is often not done well. Many organizations simply take the gathered raw data (often straight from the tool) and report it to everyone, without necessarily processing or analyzing the data. The report should emphasize and ideally highlight areas where the recipient needs to take action.

The other issue often associated with presenting and using information it that it is overdone. Managers at all levels are bombarded with too many emails, too many meetings, and too many reports. The reality is that the managers often don't need this information or, at the very least, not in that format. It is often unclear what role the manager has in making decisions and providing guidance on improvement programs.

Here are some of the common problems associated with the presenting and reporting activity:
- Everyone gets the same report
- The format is not what people want
- Lack of an executive summary
- Reports are not linked to any baseline, or scorecard
- Too much supporting data is provided
- Reports are presented in terms that are not understandable

Inputs into step 6:
- Collated information
- Format details and templates
- Stakeholder contact details

Step 7 – Implement corrective action

An organization will not be able to implement all of the determined improvement options immediately. For this reason, options should be assigned a **priority** based on the organizational goals and external regulations determined in the Service Strategy.

It is recommended to use the knowledge gained and combine it with previous experience to make informed decisions about optimizing, improving, and correcting services. Managers need to identify issues and present solutions.

This stage may include any number of activities such as approval of improvement activities, prioritization, and submitting a business case, integration with Change Management, integration with other lifecycle stages, and guidance on how to manage an ongoing improvement project successfully, and on checking whether the improvement actually achieved its objective.

CSI identifies many opportunities for improvement, but organizations cannot afford to implement all of them. As discussed earlier, an organization needs to prioritize improvement activities for its goals, objectives, return on investment (ROI), types of service breaches etc., and document them in the CSI register. Improvement initiatives can also be externally driven by regulatory requirements, changes in competition, or even political decisions.

There are various levels of management in an organization; when implementing improvements it is important to understand which level to focus their activities on. Managers need to show overall performance and improvement. Directors need to show that quality and performance targets are being met, while risk is being minimized. Overall, senior management need to know what is going on so they can make informed choices and exercise judgment. Each level has its own perspective. Understanding these perspectives is where maximum value of information is leveraged.

Inputs into step 7:

- Knowledge gained from presenting and using the information
- Agreed implementation plans (from Step 6)
- A CSI register for those initiatives that have been initiated from other sources

Generic process information

The following information is specific to the 7-step process but not necessarily to any particular activity within the process.

8.4.3 Information management

As indicated in the activities above, the information required to understand what needs to be improved, by how much, and when comes from many sources. It is important in order to get a full and clear picture to gather and analyze all information.

- The service catalogue
- Service level requirements
- Monitored and reported service level targets
- Service knowledge management system
- Configuration management system
- Process metrics
- Customer satisfactory surveys
- Complaints and compliments
- All data, information, knowledge produced by the process itself

8.4.4 Interfaces

Like all processes, the 7 step improvement process has relationships with all other processes. Each step of the CSI lifecycle will be involved in every one of the other lifecycle stages:

- **Service Strategy** – To monitor the progress of, and analyze the results of, strategies, standards, policies, and architectural decisions that have been made and implemented
- **Service Design** – To monitor and gather data and information associated with creating and modifying services and service management processes. To measure the effectiveness and ability to measure CSF and KPI defined while gathering business requirements
- **Service Transition** – To develop and test the monitoring procedures and criteria to be used during and after implementation
- **Service Operation** – To actively gather, process, analyze, and present data and information regarding the services in the live environment

8.4.5 Triggers

Many triggers of the process are already documented and discussed within the steps discussed earlier.

8.4.6 Inputs

Here are some of the inputs required by the 7-step improvement process. Many inputs to the process are documented within the steps discussed earlier but examples of key inputs include:

- Service catalogue
- SLR
- The service review meeting
- Vision and mission statements
- Corporate, divisional, and departmental goals and objectives
- Legislative requirements
- Governance requirements
- Budget cycle
- Customer satisfaction surveys
- The overall IT strategy
- Market expectations
- New technology drivers
- Flexible commercial models

8.4.7 Outputs

Many outputs of the process are already documented and discussed within the steps discussed earlier.

8.4.8 Critical success factors

The critical success factors used to judge the success of the 7-step improvement process are actually those of the other lifecycle stages and processes to which they are applied. As a result the examples given here come from other areas.

- All improvement opportunities identified
- The cost of providing services is reduced
- The desired business outcomes from IT services are achieved

8.4.9 Metrics

The key performance indicators used to judge the success of the 7-step improvement process are actually those of the other lifecycle stages and processes to which they are applied. As a result the examples given here come from other areas.

- Percentage improvement in defects
- Percentage decrease in overall cost of service provision
- Percentage increase in customer satisfaction with the service desk

8.4.10 Challenges

Here are some of the potential challenges faced by the 7-step improvement process:

- Getting the required resources to implement and run the process
- Gathering the right level of data and having the tools to manipulate it
- To get the IT organization to approach CSI in a consistent and structured way

- Get commitment from executives, managers, and it personnel
- Obtaining sufficient information from the business regarding improvement requirements and cost reductions
- Persuading suppliers to include improvement in their contractual agreements

8.4.11 Risks
Here are some of the potential risks faced by the 7-step improvement process
- Initiatives being taken on randomly and/or in an ad hoc manner
- No formalized approach to CSI
- Insufficient monitoring and analysis in prioritizing areas with the greatest need of improvement
- The attitude of *"We have always done it this way"*, *"It has always been good enough"*
- Inability to *"sell"* the benefits of a formal approach to improvement
- Lack of, or loss of, ownership/champion
- No clear understanding of business needs and objectives

■ 8.5 ORGANIZATION

Process activities are not limited to one part of the organization. Because of this, the process manager must map the defined process roles and activities to existing staff. Clear definitions of the responsibility and accountability are required, for instance in a **RACI matrix** (*Responsible, Accountable, Consulted, Informed*).

8.5.1 Roles and responsibilities
CSI comprises permanent production roles such as the **service manager**, the **service owner**, the **process owner,** the analysts, as well as temporary project roles such as project managers and project team members.

Table 8.3 provides an overview of the accompanying key activities and roles. Not all roles are full-time. Make a global division and adjust this later on if needed.

Table 8.3 Key activities and the roles to be allocated

Key activity	Key role
Gather data from the measurement of service results and service management processes and compare these to the starting point (baseline), goals, SL A and benchmarks; analyses trends	– Service manager – Service owner – IT process owner
Set targets for efficiency improvement and cost effectiveness throughout the entire Service Lifecycle	– Service manager
Set targets for service improvements and use of resources	– Service manager – Service owner – Business process owner

Key activity	Key role
Consider new business and security requirements	– Service manager – Business process owner
Create a SIP and implement improvements	– Service manager – Service owner – Process owner
Enable personnel to propose improvements	– Service manager
Measure, report and communicate about improvement initiatives	– Service manager
Revise policy, processes, procedures and plans if needed	– Service manager
Ensure that all approved actions are completed and that they achieve the desired result	– Service manager – Business manager – IT process owner – Business process owner

Table 8.4 provides an overview of the roles, activities, and skills needed for the different steps in the CSI improvement process.

For the ITIL Foundation exam, knowledge is required on the roles printed in bold in Table 8.4. We will discuss these further, except for the role of **service level manager**. Section 5.13 in Chapter 5 on Service Design describes this role. The section *"Other roles"*, at the end of this Section 8.5, mentions other roles present in CSI.

Table 8.4 Roles for the CSI improvement process

Step	Roles	Activity types	Skills
1. What should you measure? – What can you measure?	Decision makers, such as the **service manager, service owner, service level manager, CSI manager, process owner**	– High management level – High variation – Action oriented – Communicative – Focus on future	– Management skills – Communicate – Create and use concepts – Handle complex and uncertain situations – Education and experience
2. What will you measure?	Internal and external service providers who know the possibilities, such as the **service manager, service owner, process owner** and the process manager	– Intellectual – Investigative – Medium to high variation – Goal oriented – Specialized in business management	– Analyze – Model – Inventive attitude – Education – Program
3. Gather data (measure)	Personnel who supply services in the Service Transition and Service Operation lifecycle phases, such as the service desk personnel on a daily basis	– Standardized – Routine (low variation) – Automated – Clerical level – Procedural	– Accuracy – Precision – Applied training – Technical experience

Step	Roles	Activity types	Skills
4. Process data	See step 3	– Specialized – Structures – Automated – Medium variation – Procedural	– Numerical skills – Methodical – Accurate – Applied training – Programming – Experience with tools
5. Analyze data	Internal and external service providers who know the possibilities, such as the **service owner**, **process owner** and the business and IT analysts	– See step 2	– See step 2
6. Present and use the information (reporting)	Internal and external service providers who know the possibilities and the main decision makers, such as the **CSI manager**, service manager, **service owner, service level manager, process owner**	– See step 1	– See step 1
7. Implement corrective actions	See step 6	– See step 2	– See step 2

Service manager

The **service manager** manages the development, implementation, evaluation, and ongoing management of new and existing products and services. The service manager is responsible for:

- Achieving company strategy and goals
- Benchmarking
- Financial management
- Customer management
- Vendor management
- Full lifecycle management
- Inventory management

The service manager must know a great deal about market analysis, be able to anticipate new market needs, formulate complex programs, guide personnel, and sell services.

CSI manager

Without a clear and unambiguous responsibility, improvement will not occur. As a result this new role is essential for a successful improvement program. The **CSI manager** is responsible for CSI in the organization. The CSI manager manages the measuring, analysis, investigating and reporting of trends and initiates service improvement activities. In addition, they also make sure that sufficient CSI supporting resources are available. They are responsible for:

- Development of the CSI domain
- Awareness and communication of CSI throughout the organization
- Allocating CSI roles
- Identifying and prioritizing improvement opportunities to senior management together with the service owner
- Identifying monitoring requirements together with the service level manager
- Ensuring that the proper monitoring tools are installed
- Creating SIPs together with the service level manager
- Capturing baseline data to measure improvement against it
- Defining and reporting upon CSF, KPI and activity metrics
- Using supporting frameworks and models
- Making knowledge management an integral part of the daily routine
- Evaluating analyzed data

The CSI manager must be able to lead projects throughout the organization, build good relationships with the business and IT management, have a flair for improvement opportunities throughout the company, and be able to counsel staff.

Service owner

It is crucial to appoint one person responsible for each service: this is the **service owner**. They are the central point of contact for a specific service. It does not matter where the underlying technological components, process or functions are located. The main responsibilities are:
- Owning and representing the service
- Understanding which components make up the service
- Measuring the performance and availability
- Attending CAB meetings if these changes are relevant to the service they represent
- Working with the CSI manager to identify and prioritize improvements
- Participating in internal and external service reviews
- Maintaining the service entry in the service catalogue
- Participating in the negotiation of SLA and OLA

Process owner

Having an owner is just as crucial to a process as a service owner is to a service. The **process owner** ensures that the organization follows a process. They must be a senior manager with enough credibility, influence, and authority in the organization's departments that are part of the process. The process owner performs the essential role of process champion, design lead, advocate, coach, and protector. See also Section 5.13.

Other important CSI roles
- **Service knowledge manager** – Designs and maintains a knowledge management strategy and implements this

- **Reporting analyst** – Evaluates and analyzes data, and identifies trends; often cooperates with SLM roles (see Chapter 5 on Service Design); must have good communication skills because reporting is an essential element of communication
- **Communication responsibility** – Designs a communication strategy for CSI

■ 8.6 METHODS, TECHNIQUES AND TOOLS

There are various methods and techniques to check whether planned improvements actually produce measurable improvements. One method or technique is not usually enough: you need to find the best mix for your organization. Check whether the chosen methods and techniques are suitable to measure the results of your processes, document them thoroughly, and instruct staff who will be using the method or technique.

8.6.1 Implementation review

To determine whether the improvements produce the desired effects, you have to ask whether the original problem situation has actually improved, and how the organization has planned and implemented the improvement. The following questions help with this:
- Have we correctly assessed the present situation and have we properly formulated the problem?
- Have we taken the correct decisions with respect to our strategy?
- Have we adopted the strategy in the right way?
- Have we formulated the right CSI goals?
- Have the goals been reached?
- Do we now provide better IT services?
- What are the lessons learned and where are we now?

8.6.2 Assessments

An assessment compares the performance of an operational process against a performance standard. This can be an agreement in an SLA, a maturity standard, or a benchmark of companies in the same industry. By conducting assessments, IT organizations show their commitment to improvement in maturity.

Assessments are very well suited to answer the question "*where are we now*?", and to determine the extent of the gap with "*where we want to be*?" A well-designed maturity assessment framework evaluates the viability of all aspects of the process environment including the people, process, and technology as well as factors effecting overall process effectiveness in the business. Keep in mind that the desired performance or maturity level of a process depends on the impact that the process has on the customer's business processes.

First determine the relationship between business processes, IT services, IT systems, and components. CSI can separately assess the effectiveness and efficiency results for each component. This helps in identifying areas for improvement.

It is crucial to clearly define what is being assessed. Base this on the goals and the expected future use of assessment and assessment reports. An assessment can take place on three levels: *Process only; People, process and technology; Full assessment.*

All these factors are compared to the maturity attributes of the selected maturity model.

Assessments are useful in the: *Planning phase (plan); Implementation phase (do); Measurement phase (check).*

Advantages of assessments:
- They can measure certain parts of a process independently of the rest and determine the impact of that specific component on the rest of the process
- They can be repeated

Disadvantages of assessments:
- They only offer a snapshot in time and do not give insight into the cultural dynamics of an organization
- They can become a goal in themselves instead of a means to an end
- They are labor intensive
- The results are still dependent on subjective assessors and therefore not entirely objective, even if the measurements are objective

This applies to both internal and external assessments. Table 8.5 gives an overview of the advantages and disadvantages of both forms.

Benchmarks
A benchmark is a particular type of assessment: organizations compare (parts of) their processes with the performance of the same types of processes that are commonly recognized as "*best practice*". This can be done in four ways:
- **Internal** – Against an earlier starting point (baseline)
- **Internal** – Against another system or department
- **External** – Against industry standards
- **External** – Directly with similar organizations; this is only useful, however, if there are enough similar organizations in terms of environment, sector and geographical placement

To determine this you can set up an organizational profile, which consists of four key components: *Company information profile; Current assets; Current best practices; Complexity.*

Table 8.5 Internal vs. external assessment

Internal assessment	
Advantages	**Disadvantages**
• No expensive consultants • Self-assessment sets are available for free • Promotes internal co-operation and communication • Promotes internal level of knowledge • Good starting point for CSI • Internal knowledge of existing environment	• Less objective • Disappointing acceptance of findings • Internal politics can get involved • Limited knowledge of skills • Labor intensive
External assessment	
Advantages	**Disadvantages**
• Objectivity • Expert ITIL knowledge • Wide experience with several IT organizations • Analytical skills • Credibility • Minimal impact on the provision of services	• High costs • Risk as to acceptance • Limited knowledge of existing environments • Insufficient preparation limits effectiveness

In all cases a benchmark provides the following results:
■ Represents performance
■ Shows the gaps
■ Shows the risks of not closing these gaps
■ Helps set priorities
■ Helps in communicating the information well

In this way organizations discover whether their processes are cost-effective, whether they meet customer needs, and how effective they are in comparison to other organizations. They become aware of the need to improve and the ways they can do so, for example in the areas of economies of scale, efficiency, and effectiveness. Management can then act on this. In the ideal case benchmarking forms part of a continual cycle of improvement and is repeated regularly.

A study into the performance of one's own organization and other departments or organizations takes time. Setting up a benchmark database and visiting other organizations also involves costs.

Benchmarking is done in cooperation with:
■ The business
■ Users or consumers
■ Internal service providers
■ External service providers
■ Users in the "*public domain*"
■ Benchmark your partners (other organizations who are involved in the comparison)

First look to see if there are any problem areas. Use the steps from the CSI improvement process, supported by (some of) the following techniques:

- Informal discussions with the business, personnel, or suppliers
- Focus groups
- Market research
- Quantitative research
- Surveys
- Questionnaires
- Re-engineering analysis
- Process mapping
- Quality control variation reports
- Financial ratio analysis

Two special forms of benchmarking are:

- Process maturity comparison
- Total cost of ownership (TCO)

Balanced Scorecard (BSC)

Kaplan and Norton developed the **Balanced Scorecard (BSC)** in the 1990s. Define a balanced scorecard for each business unit. Begin carefully: select two to four goals. Then you can extend this as a *"waterfall"* to the underlying components, such as the service desk. After successful implementation keep measuring regularly.

Gap analysis

This analysis naturally flows on from assessments and benchmarks. Having determined where the organization is now, the gap analysis will determine the size of the gap with where the organization wants to be. In this way light is shed on new opportunities for improvement. The *service gap model* in Figure 8.8 shows possible gaps or discrepancies.

Gap analyses can be the result of a benchmarking on service or process maturity investigations. They can be done on a strategic, tactical, or operational level. It gives an overview of the amount of resources and money that an organization has to spend to reach specific goals.

SWOT analysis

A **SWOT analysis** looks at the *Strengths, Weaknesses, Opportunities, and Threats* of an organization (component) or project. The organization then answers the following questions:

- How can we profit from strong points?
- How can we remove weak points?
- How can we use opportunities optimally?
- How can we manage and eliminate threats?

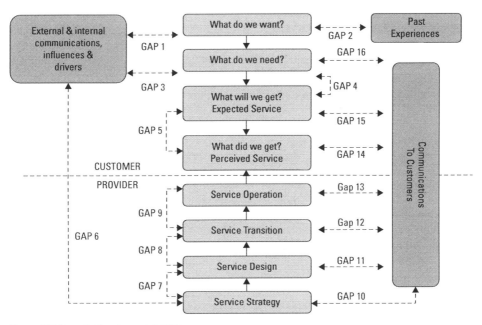

Figure 8.8 Sample Service gap model

Set your end goal before you perform a SWOT analysis. Look at which strong points help achieve a goal, which weaknesses prevent you from doing this, what external conditions promote the goal, and what external conditions prevent it.

To arrive at a SWOT of the whole organization, you can first make a SWOT for each organization component or function and then integrate into a company SWOT. See Table 8.6 for sample aspects of SWOTs.

Table 8.6 Examples of aspects from SWOT analyses

Possible strengths	Possible weaknesses
• Core competences • Financial means • Recognized as a market leader • Proven management	• No clear strategic direction • Outdated facilities • Low profits • Little insight into performance
Possible opportunities	**Possible threats**
• Creation of new customer groups • Application of skills and knowledge for new products	• Foreign competition with lower prices • Lower market growth • Expensive legislation and regulation

Rummler-Brache swim-lane diagram

Geary Rummler and Alan Brache introduced the idea of representing the relationships between processes and organizations or departments with "*swim lanes*" in a Rummler-Brache **swim-lane diagram**. This maps the flow of a process: from the customer through the department to the technology (Figure 8.9). The horizontal rows divide the separate organizations or departments from each other. Activities and decisions are connected through arrows to indicate the flow.

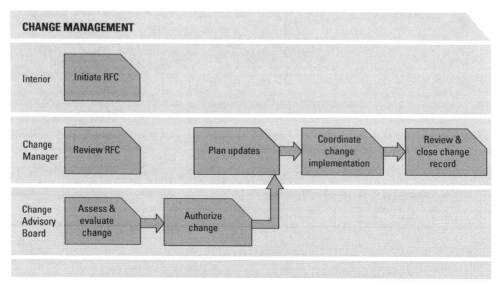

Figure 8.9 Rummler-Brache swim-lane diagram

The row in which these components are placed indicates which organizational component is responsible for the activity or decision.

Because this instrument places the whole process within a recognizable structure of organizations, it is very useful as a communication tool with the management.

8.6.3 Tools
CSI needs different types of software to support, test, monitor, and report on the ITSM processes. As part of the assessment of *"where do we want to be?"* the requirements for enhancing tools will be addressed and documented. The need and sophistication of the tools required depend on the business need for IT services and to some extent the size of the organization.

In any case, tools must monitor and analyze the most important components of a service, in a manner that supports the CSI Improvement Process. They can also centralize, automate, and integrate the key processes. This then produces new data for trend analysis.

Tools to be used for CSI are for example:
- ITSM suites
- Event management
- System and network management
- Automated incident and problem solving

- Knowledge management
- Service request and fulfilment (service catalogue and workflow)
- Performance management
- Application and service performance monitoring
- Statistical analysis tools
- Software version control/software configuration management
- Software test management
- Security management
- Project and portfolio management
- Financial management
- Business intelligence/reporting

■ 8.7 IMPLEMENTATION

Before you implement CSI you must make sure that:
- The critical roles of CSI manager, service owner, and reporting analyst have been filled
- Monitoring and reporting on technology metrics is in place
- Internal review meetings are scheduled
- External review meeting scheduled to follow internal review meetings

Communication forms an important part of any service improvement project. A communications plan is required which will need to deal with the responses and feedback from the target audience.

Define a communication plan that always states the messenger, the message, the target audience, the timing, the frequency of communication, the method of communication, and the feedback mechanism.

CSI can be implemented through various approaches: *Service approach; Lifecycle approach; Functional approach.*

8.7.1 Business case
The business case must make it clear whether it is useful to start with CSI. It must indicate what exactly will change in the intended future situation with respect to the starting situation. From a set **baseline** an organization can estimate what the present situation provides and costs, and how much the improvement of the situation will provide and

cost. Formulate this in the language that the business understands. In any case answer the following questions:

Where are we?	Determine the actual service levels.
What do we want?	Determine what the vision, mission, goals of the business are.
What do we need?	Determine which services are essential for realizing the mission and, based on this, specify priorities.
What can we afford?	Determine the budget for IT service with input from SLM and financial management and determine which actions can be done in practice.
What will we get?	Determine the desired results, together with the business
What did we get?	Arrange that Service Operation monitors the service levels and brings report.
Does it still meet our wants/ needs?	Determine possible improvements, together with the business.

For a business case, it is important to have an overview of the **costs** and benefits of CSI. Extra information about the measurement and estimation of costs and benefits can be found in Sections 8.4 and 8.5.

Costs

When deciding on an improvement initiative, always keep an eye on the costs of development, operations, and on-going maintenance. Examples of this are:

- Labor costs
- Training costs
- Tools to process measurement data
- Assessments or benchmark studies
- Management time to follow progress
- Communication campaigns to create awareness and to change the culture

Benefits

Results of a service improvement plan can be divided into:

- **Improvements** – Measurable improvements with respect to the starting situation
- **Benefits** – Profit that is the result of improvements (usually in financial terms)
- **Return on Investment (ROI)** – The difference between the costs and benefits of the improvement
- **Value on Investment (VOI)** – ROI, plus the extra value that cannot be expressed in money or that only becomes clear in the long term. It is difficult to quantify extra value such as higher customer satisfaction. If there are enough "*hard numbers*", it still does not add much; a narrative appendix as to this qualitative value is more useful

Define both direct and indirect benefits and consider each group of **stakeholders** for each organizational level. Define the benefits such that they are measurable. Put the business first. Benefit for the business can mean:

- Shorter time to market
- Customer bonding
- Lower maintenance costs for the inventory
- Larger market share

CSI can provide the following benefits:

To the business:

- More reliable support for business processes through Incident, Problem, and Change Management
- Higher productivity through increased quality and availability of IT services
- The business knows what they can expect of the IT department and what the IT department expects of them
- Procedures to ensure the continuity of IT service are oriented to the needs of the business
- Better management information about business processes and IT services
- The IT department has more knowledge of the business processes, so that it can respond better to the desires of the business
- Quality projects, releases, and changes run according to plan and provide the agreed quality at the agreed costs
- Minimal number of unused opportunities
- Better relationship between the business and IT
- Higher customer satisfaction

Financial:

- Efficient IT services
- Cost effective IT infrastructure and services
- Cost reduction, for example though lower costs for the implementation of changes and less excess processes and equipment
- Changes have less (financial) impact on the business
- Services meet the requirements but do not over perform
- Better division of resources, such that expenditures for the continuity of IT services are in proportion with the importance of the business processes that they support
- Cost structure is tuned to business needs
- Minimal costs and risks with checks that legislation is followed

Innovative:

- More proactive development of technology and services through better information on the areas in which changes can lead to profits
- The IT department reacts better to changes in demands from the business or the market and to new trends
- A business which trusts their IT service providers dares to "*think big*"

Internal benefits for the IT organization:
- More competent IT department, less chance of errors
- Integration of people and processes
- More communication and teamwork (also with the business)
- More productive and more motivated staff
- Defined roles and responsibilities
- More effective processes, better use of resources
- IT repeats and increases profit points through increased process maturity
- Better metrics and management reports through structured approach to measurement and knowledge gathering
- Better picture of and more trust in present and future IT improvement opportunities
- Services and systems achieve feasible goals within a realistic schedule
- Better direction of service providers
- Better relationship with the business
- Cost alignment with business needs

8.7.2 Critical success factors (CSF)
A **Critical Success Factor** (CSF) is a necessary condition for a good result of a service or process. Critical success factors for CSI are:
- Appoint a CSI manager (see also "*Organization*")
- Adoption of CSI by the whole organization
- Constant visible management participation in CSI activities, for example by creating a vision and communicating about it
- Clear criteria for the prioritization of improvement projects
- Adoption of the service cycle approach
- Sufficient funding
- Resource allocation – people are dedicated to the improvement effort, not just as an add-on to their already long list of tasks to perform
- Technology to support improvement activities
- Embrace service management processes and do not adapt it to meet personal needs and agendas

8.7.3 Challenges and risks
Introduction of CSI comes with the following challenges and risks:
- Lack of management commitment
- Poor relationship and communication between IT and the business
- Too little knowledge of the IT impact on the business and its important processes
- Too little knowledge of the business's priorities
- Lack of information, monitoring, and measurement
- Not using the information from reports
- Insufficient resources, budget, and time
- Immature service management processes
- Too little or no knowledge management (see also "*Organization*")

- Trying to change everything at once
- Resistance against (cultural) changes
- Not enough business or IT objectives, strategies and policy
- Poor supplier management
- Not testing
- Tooling is too complex or insufficient
- Differences in the technology used

8.7.4 Interfaces

CSI uses many data from the entire lifecycle of a service. The information that results from this, together with the demands of the business, the technical specifications, the opportunities of IT, the budget, trends and legislation, gives insight into the opportunities for the improvement of an organization.

Service Level Management (SLM)

SLM is the most important process for CSI: it discusses with the business what the IT organization needs to measure and what the results should be. That is why this section begins with information on what SLM and CSI have in common. For more information about the SLM process see Chapter 5 about Service Design.

After each phase of the lifecycle, test whether the improvement initiative has met its goals. This can be done using the **Post Implementation Review (PIR)** from the Change Management process. Because steps 1 and 2 of the CSI improvement process lie primarily with SLM and CSI, an overview of the common ground between CSI and the other ITIL processes and the different Service Lifecycle phases is given starting from step 3 only. Service Operation also provides information about what *can* be measured before step 2.

In the light of CSI, the objective of SLM is to maintain and improve the quality of IT services. SLM does this by making a constant cycle of agreements, monitoring, and reporting about IT service levels.

In the CSI improvement process, SLM plays a role with:
- Identifying the strategy for improvement:
- Defining what you will measure
- Data gathering (measuring)
- Data processing
- Data analysis
- Presenting the information: (reporting)
- Implementing corrective actions: (service improvement plan)

In this way SLM determines what the organization measures and monitors; together with the business, it reports on the performance and signals new business demands.

Using this information CSI identifies and prioritizes improvement opportunities. This is the most important input for the SIP (Service Improvement Plan).

It is recommended that an annual budget is set for SIPs. SLM and CSI can then take quick action, which leads to a proactive attitude.

If an organization outsources its Service Delivery processes, it must also negotiate regarding CSI and include this in the SLA. Otherwise the acting party will no longer be motivated to deliver more than is agreed upon in the contract.

Monitor and gather data measurement (step 3)
In the Service Lifecycle, *Service Strategy* monitors the effect of the strategies, the standards, and the policies upon the design decisions.

Service Design monitors and collects information related to the design and modification of services and service management processes. This phase also tests whether the CSF and KPI agreed upon with the business are measurable and effective. They also determine what should be measured and set schedules and milestones for this.

Service Transition monitors and measures data about the actual usage of services and service management processes. It develops the monitoring procedures and sets measurement criteria for after implementation.

Service Operation measures the performance of the services and components in the production environment. Once again this forms input for the CSI improvement process: what can be measured and what do these data say?

Apart from SLM, Availability Management also plays an important role in step 3. This process:
- Creates metrics in consultation with the business to measure availability
- Determines which tools are needed to make these measurements
- Monitors and measures the performance of the infrastructure and frees up enough resources for this
- Provides data to CSI
- Updates availability plans

Capacity Management also undertakes these actions; it does this in order to measure whether the IT organization can provide the requested services. This can be done from three perspectives: *Business capacity management*; *Service capacity management*; *Component capacity management*

Incident Management defines monitoring requirements to track events and incidents, preferably automated, before they cause problems. It also monitors the reaction, repair, and resolution time and the number of escalations. For example, the service desk monitors the number of reports, the average response time, and the percentage of callers who hang up prematurely.

Information Security Management monitors and measures the security and records security incidents and problems.

And, finally, Financial Management monitors and measures the costs and keeps an eye on the budget. It also contributes to the reports as to the costs and ROI of improvement initiatives.

Process data (step 4)

Service Operation processes the data in logical groups. Within these groups Availability Management and Capacity Management process the data at the component level regarding availability and capacity. They work together with SLM to give these data an "*end-to-end*" perspective and use the agreed upon reporting form to do this.

Incident Management and Service Desk check and process data about incidents and service requests, and the KPI related to this. Information Security Management checks and processes data about security incidents and provides reports on them.

Analyze data (step 5)

Service Strategy analyzes trends, looks at whether the strategies, policies, and standards introduced achieve their goal, and looks at whether there are opportunities for improvement. *Service Design* analyzes the results of design and project activities, and researches trends and opportunities for improvement. It also looks at whether the CSF and KPI set in step 2 are still adequate. *Service Operation* also analyzes results, trends, and opportunities for improvement.

The most important Service Operation process for CSI is Problem Management. This process finds the underlying causes of problems, and these form important opportunities for improvement.

Availability Management analyzes performance and trends about components and service data. It compares data with earlier months, quarters, and years. It also looks at whether the correct information is being measured and whether SIPs are needed. It uses the following techniques:
- Component Failure Impact Analysis (CFIA) – see Figure 8.10
- Fault Tree Analysis (FTA) – see Figure 8.11
- Service Failure Analysis (SFA)
- Technical Observation (TO)
- Expanded Incident Lifecycle

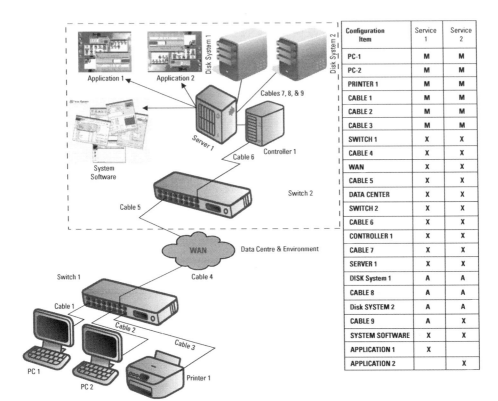

Configuration Item	Service 1	Service 2
PC-1	M	M
PC-2	M	M
PRINTER 1	M	M
CABLE 1	M	M
CABLE 2	M	M
CABLE 3	M	M
SWITCH 1	X	X
CABLE 4	X	X
WAN	X	X
CABLE 5	X	X
DATA CENTER	X	X
SWITCH 2	X	X
CABLE 6	X	X
CONTROLLER 1	X	X
CABLE 7	X	X
SERVER 1	X	X
DISK System 1	A	A
CABLE 8	A	A
Disk SYSTEM 2	A	A
CABLE 9	A	X
SYSTEM SOFTWARE	X	X
APPLICATION 1	X	
APPLICATION 2		X

Figure 8.10 Sample CHA matrix

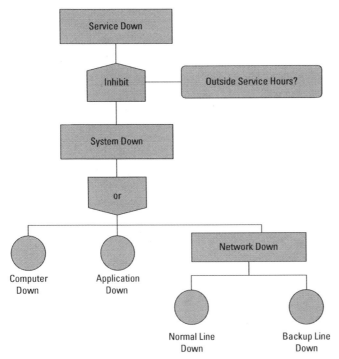

Figure 8.11 Sample Fault Tree Analysis

Capacity Management analyzes when which customer uses what services, how they use them, and how this influences the performance of one or more systems or components. This again provides improvement opportunities to CSI.

Whereas Problem Management is oriented toward resolving problems that have already occurred in the past, Capacity Management tries to prevent problems proactively, by making extra storage capacity ready on time, for example. Often this is done by reproducing the situation in a model, and then asking a number of *"what if"* questions.

Incident Management and the Service Desk can compare the collected data with earlier results and the agreed service levels. They can also propose SIPs or corrective actions.

Information Security Management uses all the other processes to find the origin of security incidents and problems. It looks for trends and possible improvements in the area of monitoring and looks at whether security strategies produce the intended results.

Every improvement initiative must consult ITSCM to make sure that the IT services are not put at risk. **Risk management** plays a central role in this. It analyzes what effects an improvement can have, while in turn CSI analyzes the results of risk management activities, to discover opportunities for improvement. See also Service Design regarding risk management.

Present and use (step 6)
Service Strategy presents results, trends, and recommendations for the improvement of adopted strategies, policies, and standards. *Service Design* does this for design improvements and project activities and *Service Transition* and *Service Operation* for service and service management processes.

Availability Management, Capacity Management, Incident Management, Service Desk, Problem Management, and Information Security Management help with creating reports and prioritizing corrective actions.

The Knowledge Management process is very important in CSI when presenting and using the information. This is the only way CSI can get a good overview of the knowledge of the organization and the opportunities for improvement. It is also important in order to ensure continual improvement and to ensure that all the knowledge and experience gathered is shared and stored. For more information about Knowledge Management see also Section 6.9 in the chapter about *"Service Transition"*.

Implement corrective actions (step 7)
Availability Management, Capacity Management, Incident Management, Service Desk, Problem Management and Information Security Management perform incremental or corrective actions where approval from the business is not required.

Capacity Management can also proceed by introducing **Demand Management** measures to influence the behavior of the end-user:

- Calculation of costs
- Making policy for the proper use of the services
- Communicating expectations
- Education about proper use
- Negotiating maintenance times
- Setting use restrictions, such as limiting the amount of storage space

As with all other changes in the lifecycle, CSI changes must go through the change, release, and deployment process. CSI must therefore submit a Request for Change (RFC) with Change Management and conduct a PIR after implementation. Also consider the updating of the CMDB by means of configuration management. After this, ITSCM must keep the continuity plan up-to-date.

8.7.5 Finally

The introduction of CSI is not simple. It requires conscious striving toward continual improvement as part of the culture and behavior of the organization, and a proactive attitude. In a world where the technology changes very quickly, such a proactive attitude is a big challenge; after all we are constantly controlled by the changes. In a situation of increasing outsourcing and professional development of ITSM, service quality is progressively becoming a distinguishing factor. To get "*in control*" and to achieve the desired quality it is preferable to work proactively. CSI is essential to this.

Annex A REFERENCES

Amit, Raphael & Paul J. H. Schoemaker (1993). Strategic Assets and Organizational Rent, in: Strategic Management Journal, Vol. 14, No. 1. (Jan., 1993), pp. 33-46

Bernard, P. (2012). *The IT Service Part 1 - The Essentials.* Van Haren Publishing

Bernard, P. (2012). *The IT Service Part 2 - The Handbook.* Van Haren Publishing

Bon, J. van (Managing Editor) (2006). *Foundations of ITIL V3.* Van Haren Publishing

Brooks, Peter (2012). *Metrics for Service Management,* Van Haren Publishing

Cambridge Advanced Learner's Dictionary, http://dictionary.cambridge.org/

Grembergen W. van, S. de Haes, E. Guldentops (2003). *Structures, Processes and relational mechanisms for Information Technology Governance: Theories and practices, Strategies for Information Technology Governance,* book edited by W. Van Grembergen, Idea Group Publishing.

Kaplan, R., & D. Norton (1992, January-February). The Balanced Scorecard – measures that drive performance. *Harvard Business Review,* Vol. 70, No. 1, p. 71-79

Kaplan, R., & D. Norton (1993, September-October). Putting the Balanced Scorecard to work. *Harvard Business Review,* Vol. 71, No. 5, p. 134-142

Kotter, J.P. (1996). *Leading Change.* Harvard Business School Press

Mintzberg, H. (1994). *The Rise and Fall of Strategic Planning: reconceiving roles for planning, plans, planners.* The Free Press

Nolan, R. (1973). Managing the computer resource: a stage hypothesis. *Communications of the ACM,* Vol. 16, Issue 7, July, p. 399 – 405

OGC (2009). *Managing Successful Projects with PRINCE2® 2009 Edition.* TSO

OGC (2011). *ITIL - Continual Service Improvement.* TSO

OGC (2011). *ITIL - Service Design.* TSO

OGC (2011). *ITIL - Service Operation.* TSO

OGC (2011). *ITIL - Service Strategy.* TSO

OGC (2011). *ITIL - Service Transition.* TSO.

O'Loughlin, Mark (2011). *The Service Catalog.* Van Haren Publishing

Rovers, Mart (2011). *ISO/IEC 20000:2011 – A Pocket Guide.* Van Haren Publishing

Schilt, Jan & Paul Wilkinson (2008). *ABC of ICT.* Van Haren Publishing

Annex B Differences between ITIL V3 and ITIL 2011 Edition

■ B.1 ITIL SERVICE STRATEGY UPDATES

This short section provides a summary of the updates between the 2007 edition and the 2011 edition for the ITIL core book *Service Strategy* published by TSO.

The concepts within the Service Strategy publication have been clarified, without changing the overall message. The updated publication includes more practical guidance and more examples where relevant.

The newly defined process of Strategy Management for IT Services is responsible for developing and maintaining business and IT strategies, and there are now separate descriptions of business strategy and IT strategy. Financial Management has been expanded, and BRM and Demand Management are now covered as processes.

Table B.1 Summary of updates: ITIL Service Strategy

Area of update	Description
Service Strategy processes	The processes have now been clearly named and defined: Strategy Management for IT Services; Service Portfolio Management; Financial Management for IT Services; Demand Management; and BRM. Each process has been described using a standard template.
Business strategy and IT strategy	Business strategy and IT strategy are two different things, and ITIL Service Strategy now describes these separately and explains the relationship between the two: business strategy defines IT strategy, and IT strategy supports business strategy.
Strategy assessment, generation and execution	More detailed guidance has been included on how an organization should go about assessing, generating, and executing its IT strategy, giving practical examples of how to proceed.
Value creation	Greater clarification is provided around how services add and realize value. New text has been included to describe how value is created, and how to differentiate between value added and value realized. A new table provides examples of utility and warranty.

Area of update	Description
Customers	It is now clearer how customers differ from users and consumers; how internal and external customers are differentiated; how business units and other IT departments as customers differ; and how IT performs its role as an external service provider.
Customer and service assets	Definitions of customer asset and service asset have been clarified, with an explanation around why these concepts are important and how they are used – including aligning service assets with customer outcomes.
Strategy Management for IT Services	The newly defined process of Strategy Management for IT Services is responsible for developing and maintaining business and IT strategies.
Financial Management for IT Services	The Financial Management for IT Services process has been expanded to include some of the key elements included in the earlier ITIL publications which had been excluded in the 2007 edition of Service Strategy – such as accounting, budgeting and charging.
BRM	BRM is now covered as a process as well as a role. The differentiation between BRM for a Type I, II, and III service provider is better explained and clarified.
Governance	There is now more detail on governance, including a fuller definition of what governance means, the difference between governance and management, a governance framework, and how service management relates to governance.
Cloud computing	Some coverage has been added on how ITSM is impacted by the prevalence of cloud computing, and a new appendix has been added specifically covering Service Strategy and the cloud: characteristics, types, types of service, and components of cloud architecture.
Types of service management implementation	Coverage has been added regarding the types of service management implementation: even keel, trouble, growth, and radical change.
Organization	Some discussion on functions has been added and a logical organization structure for service management has been included, with supporting diagrams.

■ B.2   ITIL SERVICE DESIGN UPDATES

This short section provides a summary of the updates between the 2007 edition and the 2011 edition for the ITIL core book *Service Design* published by TSO.

Throughout the updated ITIL Service Design publication, there has been particular focus on alignment with ITIL Service Strategy.

A number of concepts and principles have been clarified, most significantly the flow and management of activity throughout the overall Service Design stage with the addition of the "*Design Coordination*" process. Other significant clarifications include the five aspects of Service Design, the design of the service portfolio, and the terminology related to views of the service catalogue.

Table B.2 Summary of updates: ITIL Service Design

Area of update	Description
Five aspects of Service Design	There is now consistency and clarity of references to the five aspects of Service Design.
Transition of a service from pipeline to catalogue to retired	The descriptions in the 2007 editions of Service Strategy and Service Design were unclear. In the 2011 edition, they have been updated to provide clarity on the definite transition points and the places for policy setting. A new status has been added to make policy setting easier.
Design Coordination process	The Design Coordination process has been added to clarify the flow of activity in the Service Design lifecycle stage.
Service catalogue terminology	The service catalogue language has been revised with regard to the customer's view of the service catalogue, versus the technical or IT view.

■ B.3 ITIL SERVICE TRANSITION UPDATE

This short section provides a summary of the updates between the 2007 edition and the 2011 edition for the ITIL core book *Service Transition* published by TSO.

The structure, content, and relationships of the CMS and SKMS have been clarified to help the reader to understand these key concepts.

There is new content explaining how a change proposal should be used. The evaluation process has been renamed *"change evaluation"* and the purpose and scope have been modified to help clarify when and how this process should be used.

The SACM process has additional content relating to asset management, and there are improvements in the flow and integration of a number of processes, including Change Management, Release & Deployment Management, and Change Evaluation.

Table B.3 Summary of changes: ITIL Service Transition

Area of update	Description
Change Management	Top-level flowchart and section headings have been modified so that they are consistent with each other.
Change process model	The name *"change model"* is now used consistently. Previously the description used the term *"change process model"* but many places in Service Transition and the other publications used *"change model"*.
Change proposal	More detail has been added to help clarify how and when a change proposal should be used.
Configuration record, CI, CMS, SKMS	Many people were confused by the descriptions of a configuration record, CI, CMS and SKMS in the 2007 edition of Service Transition and wanted a clear and unambiguous explanation of these concepts.

Area of update	Description
Evaluation	The process name has been changed to "*Change Evaluation*" and the purpose and scope have been clarified to show that this process is used for evaluating changes only.
RDM	Some sections have been reordered and a high-level process diagram has been provided showing how it all fits together.
SACM	Text has been added to explain the service asset management aspects better.

■ B.4   ITIL SERVICE OPERATION UPDATES

This short section provides a summary of the updates between the 2007 edition and the 2011 edition for the ITIL core book *Service Operation* published by TSO.

Process flows have been updated or added for all processes including Request Fulfilment, Access Management, and Event Management.

Key principles – including guidance around service requests and request models, and proactive problem management – have been clarified. The publication has been updated to explain how basic events flow into filters and rule engines to produce meaningful event information. The relationship between application management activities versus application development activities is also clarified.

Other improvements include an expanded section on problem analysis techniques, a procedure flow for incident matching, and further guidance for escalating incidents to Problem Management. In addition, the guidance for managing physical facilities has been expanded.

Table B.4 Summary of updates: ITIL Service Operation

Area of update	Description
Service request	The concept of a service request has been significantly enhanced to provide a clearer definition, with examples and diagrams to illustrate how service requests link with the services they support. The relationship of service requests to request models and standard changes is also highlighted.
Request model	This concept has been expanded to clarify how each service request should be linked to a request model that documents the steps and tasks, and the roles and responsibilities needed to fulfil requests.
Event filtering and correlation	Additional clarification has been provided to illustrate how basic events flow into filters and rule engines to produce meaningful information.
Normal Service Operation	A clearer definition for this has now been included and added to the glossary.
Incident matching	A procedure has been added to provide examples of how incidents should initially be matched against known error records before escalation. A detailed procedure flow for matching incidents and escalating to Problem Management has been added.

Area of update	Description
Request Fulfilment process flow	A new process flow now illustrates a suggested set of activities and steps for the request fulfilment process. This process flow also includes decision points for escalating requests to Service Transition as change proposals or Incident Management as incidents.
Problem analysis techniques	This section has been expanded to include more techniques for finding root causes. In addition, each technique now indicates the kinds of situations and incidents where it may be advantageous to use the particular technique described.
Problem investigation and analysis	A concept has been added to recreate problems when they are being investigated.
Mainframe and server management	The concept that the activities and procedures for managing mainframes are no different from servers has been added. How these activities might be carried out may differ, but the outcomes and kinds of management task are essentially the same.
Proactive problem management	The concept and description of activities for proactive problem management have been added to the Problem Management process.
Application management vs. application development	The differences between application management and application development are now clarified. A diagram has been added to show the key activities that take place during each stage of the application management lifecycle to demonstrate how application management differs from application development.
Facilities management	This appendix has been greatly enhanced with additional information for managing physical facilities.

■ B.5   ITIL CONTINUAL SERVICE IMPROVEMENT UPDATE

This short section provides a summary of the updates between the 2007 edition and the 2011 edition for the ITIL core book *Continual Service Improvement* published by TSO.

The seven-step improvement process and its relationship with the Plan-Do-Check-Act cycle (Deming Cycle) and Knowledge Management have been clarified. The Continual Service Improvement (CSI) model has been re-named the CSI approach, and the concept of a CSI register has been introduced as a place to record details of all improvement initiatives within an organization.

Minor changes have been made throughout the publication to clarify the meaning and to improve readability. Particular emphasis has been placed on documenting the interfaces between CSI and other lifecycle stages.

Table B.5 Summary of updates: ITIL Continual Service Improvement

Area of update	Description
Introduction of the CSI register	The CSI register is where all improvement opportunities are recorded. Each opportunity should be categorized as a small, medium, or large undertaking. An indication of the amount of time it would take to complete the initiative should also be provided, along with the associated benefits. Together, this information will help produce a clear prioritized list of improvement initiatives. A full description of the CSI register is given in Chapter 3, and an example is provided in Appendix C.
Service measurement and service reporting	The treatment of service measurement and service reporting has been clarified. Because all processes have an element of measurement and reporting embedded within them, service measurement and service reporting are not considered to be processes. Therefore, these topics are covered in Chapters 3 and 5, rather than Chapter 4.
Seven-step improvement process	It is now clear that the seven-step process only contains seven steps. Some step names and activities have been amended, but the overall purpose of the process remains unchanged. The interface with the Deming Cycle and with Knowledge Management has been clarified.
The CSI approach	The CSI model has been re-named the CSI approach, because it is an approach to continual improvement and not a model.

ITIL Glossary

The ITIL glossary has been aligned with the core publications, and reflects the updates made in those publications. There are around 55 new terms which have been added to the ITIL glossary, and approximately 30 terms have been deleted. Other terms have been updated – some more significantly than others – to reflect the content of the core publications.

The updated ITIL glossary can be found in English and other languages here:
http://www.itil-officialsite.com/InternationalActivities/ITILGlossaries.aspx

All translated glossaries are in line with the English version.

Where a term is relevant to a particular phase in the Lifecycle of an IT service, or to one of the Core ITIL publications, this is indicated at the beginning of the definition. This glossary is based on the "**ITIL_2011_English_glossary_v1.0**" published in July 2011.

In order to simplify the text, all acronyms are "*singular*"; there is no "*s*" at the end to differentiate between singular or plural.

Again, in order to make the text more legible, excessive capitalization has been removed and only the proper names, the product names, and the acronyms are capitalized.

Index

73850970R00194

Made in the USA
Middletown, DE
18 May 2018